International and Development Education

The *International and Development Education Series* focuses on the complementary areas of comparative, international, and development education. Books emphasize a number of topics ranging from key international education issues, trends, and reforms to examinations of national education systems, social theories, and development education initiatives. Local, national, regional, and global volumes (single authored and edited collections) constitute the breadth of the series and offer potential contributors a great deal of latitude based on interests and cutting edge research. The series is supported by a strong network of international scholars and development professionals who serve on the International and Development Education Advisory Board and participate in the selection and review process for manuscript development.

SERIES EDITORS
John N. Hawkins
Professor Emeritus, University of California, Los Angeles
Senior Consultant, IFE 2020 East West Center

W. James Jacob
Assistant Professor, University of Pittsburgh
Director, Institute for International Studies in Education

PRODUCTION EDITOR
Heejin Park
Project Associate, Institute for International Studies in Education

INTERNATIONAL EDITORIAL ADVISORY BOARD
Clementina Acedo, *UNESCO's International Bureau of Education, Switzerland*
Philip G. Altbach, *Boston University, USA*
Carlos E. Blanco, *Universidad Central de Venezuela*
Sheng Yao Cheng, *National Chung Cheng University, Taiwan*
Ruth Hayhoe, *University of Toronto, Canada*
Wanhua Ma, *Peking University, China*
Ka-Ho Mok, *University of Hong Kong, China*
Christine Musselin, *Sciences Po, France*
Yusuf K. Nsubuga, *Ministry of Education and Sports, Uganda*
Namgi Park, *Gwangju National University of Education, Republic of Korea*
Val D. Rust, *University of California, Los Angeles, USA*
Suparno, *State University of Malang, Indonesia*
John C. Weidman, *University of Pittsburgh, USA*
Husam Zaman, *Taibah University, Saudi Arabia*

Institute for International Studies in Education
School of Education, University of Pittsburgh
5714 Wesley W. Posvar Hall, Pittsburgh, PA 15260 USA

Center for International and Development Education
Graduate School of Education & Information Studies, University of California, Los Angeles
Box 951521, Moore Hall, Los Angeles, CA 90095 USA

Titles:

Higher Education in Asia/Pacific: Quality and the Public Good
Edited by Terance W. Bigalke and Deane E. Neubauer

Affirmative Action in China and the U.S.: A Dialogue on Inequality and Minority Education
Edited by Minglang Zhou and Ann Maxwell Hill

Critical Approaches to Comparative Education: Vertical Case Studies from Africa, Europe, the Middle East, and the Americas
Edited by Frances Vavrus and Lesley Bartlett

Curriculum Studies in South Africa: Intellectual Histories & Present Circumstances
Edited by William F. Pinar

Higher Education, Policy, and the Global Competition Phenomenon
Edited by Laura M. Portnoi, Val D. Rust, and Sylvia S. Bagley

The Search for New Governance of Higher Education in Asia
Edited by Ka-Ho Mok

International Students and Global Mobility in Higher Education: National Trends and New Directions
Edited by Rajika Bhandari and Peggy Blumenthal

Curriculum Studies in Brazil: Intellectual Histories, Present Circumstances
Edited by William F. Pinar

Access, Equity, and Capacity in Asia Pacific Higher Education
Edited by Deane Neubauer and Yoshiro Tanaka

Policy Debates in Comparative, International, and Development Education
Edited by John N. Hawkins and W. James Jacob

Increasing Effectiveness of the Community College Financial Model: A Global Perspective for the Global Economy
Edited by Stewart E. Sutin, Daniel Derrico, Rosalind Latiner Raby, and Edward J. Valeau

Curriculum Studies in Mexico: Intellectual Histories, Present Circumstances
William F. Pinar

The Internationalization of East Asian Higher Education: Globalization's Impact
Edited by John D. Palmer, Amy Roberts, Young Ha Cho, and Gregory S. Ching

Taiwan Education at the Crossroad: When Globalization Meets Localization
Chuing Prudence Chou and Gregory S. Ching

Forthcoming title:
Mobility and Migration in Asian Pacific Higher Education
Deane E. Neubauer and Kazuo Kuroda

The Internationalization of East Asian Higher Education

Globalization's Impact

Edited by
John D. Palmer, Amy Roberts, Young Ha Cho, and Gregory S. Ching

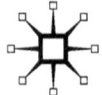

THE INTERNATIONALIZATION OF EAST ASIAN HIGHER EDUCATION
Copyright © John D. Palmer, Amy Roberts, Young Ha Cho, and Gregory S. Ching, 2011.

All rights reserved.

First published in 2011 by
PALGRAVE MACMILLAN®
in the United States—a division of St. Martin's Press LLC,
175 Fifth Avenue, New York, NY 10010.

Where this book is distributed in the UK, Europe and the rest of the world, this is by Palgrave Macmillan, a division of Macmillan Publishers Limited, registered in England, company number 785998, of Houndmills, Basingstoke, Hampshire RG21 6XS.

Palgrave Macmillan is the global academic imprint of the above companies and has companies and representatives throughout the world.

Palgrave® and Macmillan® are registered trademarks in the United States, the United Kingdom, Europe and other countries.

ISBN: 978–0–230–10932–2

Library of Congress Cataloging-in-Publication Data

    The internationalization of East Asian higher education : globalization's impact / edited by John D. Palmer...[et al.].
      p. cm.—(International & development education)
    Includes bibliographical references and index.
    ISBN 978–0–230–10932–2 (hardback)
      1. Education, Higher—East Asia. 2. Education and globalization—East Asia. 3. Transnational education—East Asia. 4. Education, Higher—International cooperation. I. Palmer, John D. (John David)

LA1144.7.I58 2011
378.5—dc23   2011019997

A catalogue record of the book is available from the British Library.

Design by Newgen Imaging Systems (P) Ltd., Chennai, India.

First edition: November 2011

Contents

List of Figure and Tables vii

Acknowledgments ix

List of Acronyms and Abbreviations xi

Introduction   Ideologies of the Globalization and Internationalization of Higher Education: An East Asian Context   1
Amy Roberts and John D. Palmer

1 Internationalization of Higher Education as a Major Strategy for Developing Regional Education Hubs: A Comparison of Hong Kong and Singapore   11
David Kinkeung Chan

2 Concepts, Contributions, and Challenges of the Contemporary University Community in Taiwan   41
Amy Roberts and Gregory S. Ching

3 A Pearl on the Silk Road? Internationalizing a Regional Chinese University   63
Anthony R. Welch and Rui Yang

4 Minority Students' Access to Higher Education in an Era of Globalization: A Case of Ethnic Koreans in China   91
Heejin Park and W. James Jacob

5 Does Internationalization Really Mean Americanization? A Closer Look at Major South Korean Universities' Internationalization Policies   119
John D. Palmer and Young Ha Cho

6 What It Takes to Internationalize Higher Education in Korea and Japan: English-Mediated Courses and International Students   147
   Jae-Eun Jon and Eun-Young Kim

7 Higher Education Global Rankings System in East Asia   173
   Peter Gregory Ghazarian

8 Internationalization of Higher Education in East Asia: Issues, Implications, and Inquiries   197
   Mary Shepard Wong and Shuang Frances Wu

List of Contributors   215

Index   219

Figure and Tables

Figure

8.1	Typology of Change	209

Tables

3.1	Changing Proportions of Xinjiang Population by Principal Ethnic Minorities, 1948–2004	69
3.2	Countries of Origin of XU International Students, 2000	76
3.3	Highest and Lowest Scores at Entrance Examination, Minority Students of Class 2, 1992, Electronics Department	82
3.4	Basic Mathematics Test Results, Enrolling Minority Students, by Departments, 1998	83
6.1	International Student Mobility in Japan and Korea	152
6.2	Number of International Students in Japan by Country of Origin, 2007	152
6.3	Number of International Students in Korea by Country of Origin, 2008	152
7.1	Indicators and Weights for the ARWU and *THE*	179
7.2	R-Squares for Indicators and ARWU Total Score	191

Acknowledgments

The editors would first like to thank all the contributors to the volume. Throughout the process, all the authors and editors proved to be "comparative and international" scholars as they were traveling and researching around the world, which made it quite difficult to meet certain deadlines and address the editors' comments. We therefore appreciate their dedication to this volume.

A special thank you from the editors goes to Heidi Ross, professor and director of the East Asian Studies Center and professor of Educational Leadership and Policy Studies at Indiana University. Ross served as our symposium discussant at both the Comparative and International Education Society (CIES) and American Educational Research Association Annual Meetings in 2010. In both cases, she provided valuable feedback, which we implemented in our final work.

Along these same lines, we would like to recognize CIES Higher Education Special Interest Group (HESIG) for first accepting our symposium proposal, and then assisting, and eventually accepting our edited book proposal. We are particularly thankful to W. James Jacob and John N. Hawkins in addressing our multiple questions, as well as supporting our work throughout the entire process.

Individually, Palmer appreciates Colgate University's financial and academic support in conducting research in South Korea through the Freeman Grant, Arnie Sio Diversity Chair, and the dean of Faculty Office. While there are so many individuals associated with these three systems that it is impossible to name them all; however, he would like to personally acknowledge Dean Lyle Roelofs, Chair Nina Moore, and Chair Padma Kaimal. Through Colgate's assistance, he has been able to establish a firm foundation for educational research in South Korea.

Roberts is indebted to the Fulbright Foundation, the Taiwan Fulbright Office, and the National Cheng-Chi University College of Education for support of a Fulbright award to lecture and conduct research contributing to this volume.

Cho wishes to acknowledge the assistance of Kyung Hee University and all the universities' Offices of International Affairs that assisted in the research project. In addition, the Republic of Korea Ministry of Education, Science and Technology and the Korean Educational Development Institute were instrumental in supporting him in investigating the national policies associated with internationalization of higher education.

Ching would like to thank the Taiwan Ministry of Education for awarding him the Taiwan Scholarship during his doctoral studies, and the National Cheng-Chi University for the financial support in accomplishing his research studies contributing to this volume.

Acronyms and Abbreviations

ACE	American Council of Education
AERA	American Educational Research Association
AHCI	Arts and Humanities Citation Index
ARWU	Academic Ranking of World Universities
C-EDB	Chinese Education Bureau
CAE	Contents Area Expert
CASE	Consumer Association of Singapore
CCP	Chinese Communist Party
CIES	Comparative and International Education Society
CNPC	China National Petroleum Company
CSCSE	Chinese Service Center for Scholarly Exchange
EGM	Emerging Global Model
GATS	General Agreement on Trade in Services
GDP	Gross Domestic Product
GKS	Global Korea Scholarship
GPA	Grade point average
GSIS	Graduate School of International Studies
HEFCE	Higher Education Funding Council of England
HEI	Higher education institution
HKCAAVQ	Hong Kong Council for Accreditation of Academic and Vocational Qualifications
HKIEd	Hong Kong Institute of Education
HKSAR	Hong Kong Special Administrative Region
HKTDC	Hong Kong Trade and Development Council
IRB	Institutional Review Board
ISI	Institute for Scientific Information
IT	Information Technology
KAIST	Korean Advanced Institute of Science and Technology
KBE	Knowledge based economy
KEDI	Korean Educational Development Institute
MEST	Ministry of Education, Science and Technology

MEXT	Ministry of Education, Culture, Sports, Science and Technology
MOE	Ministry of Education
MOE & HRD	Ministry of Education and Human Resource Development
MTI	Ministry of Trade and Industry
NASULGC	National Association of State Universities and Land-Grant Colleges
NCCU	National Cheng-Chi University
NSU	Novosibirsk State University
NTU	Nanyang Technological University
NUS	National University of Singapore
OBU	Oklahoma Baptist University
OECD	Organisation for Economic Co-operation and Development
PEI	Private education institution
PISA	Programme for International Student Assessment
PolyU	Polytechnic University of Hong Kong
PRC	People's Republic of China
S-EDB	Singapore Economic Development Board
SCI	Science Citation Index
SCO	Shanghai Cooperation Organisation
SD	Standard deviation
SSCI	Social Science Citation Index
SMU	Singapore Management University
SNU	Seoul National University
SPSS	Statistics Package for Social Science
SQC-PEO	Singapore Quality Class for Private Education Organization
STB	Singapore Tourism Board
THE	*Times Higher Education*
UGC	University Grants Committee
UNESCO	United Nations Education, Scientific, and Cultural Organization
USSR	Union of Soviet Socialist Republics
WCU	World Class University
WTO	World Trade Organization
XU	Xinjiang University
XUAR	Xinjiang Uyghur Autonomous Region

Introduction
Ideologies of the Globalization and Internationalization of Higher Education: An East Asian Context

Amy Roberts and John D. Palmer

> The University is becoming a different kind of institution, one that is no longer linked to the destiny of the nation-state by virtue of its role as a producer, protector, and inculcator of an idea of national culture. (Jay 2002, 1)

The quote above encapsulates the contemporary university as an entity engulfed by the pressing challenges and trends of twenty-first century globalization and internationalization. Traditionally, universities have acted on the flow of ideas and have influenced international trends (Altbach 2003). Yet, in the contemporary era, universities striving for global competitiveness share a panorama of distinct mechanisms and processes that intersect with administrative policies, the position of students, and the labor of academics (Mok and Lee 2001). In response, university systems the world over are redefining curricula, shifting traditional paradigms of scholarship, and aligning English as the formal language of academia (Altbach 2003). As such, the contemporary globalized university system embodies a complex, contradictory, and expansive discourse shaped by the stance of leading super-research institutions (Jones 1998; Dale 1999; Mundy 1999), as well as by themes of education and global trade within the General Agreement on Trade in Services (GATS) and the World Trade Organization (WTO) (van der Wende 2001).

This discourse attracts a diverse array of international comparative researchers who critically advance accepted modes of operation and frameworks of analysis (Watson 1996). Their intent is to inform, study, and mediate competing arguments of globalization and internationalization within educational settings around the world. In part, these researchers argue that the impacts of contemporary globalization pervade the emergence of the super-research institution as a leading influence on policy for education systems worldwide. In contrast, others identify the impact of global economic processes as the leading influence on university systems. Some researchers focus exclusively on the rise of neoliberalism as a hegemonic policy discourse, while others emphasize the influence of global cultural forms, media, and technologies of communication on the membership, identity, and engagement within and across university communities. The positioning of globalization as a process of transformation used by government and university-level policy makers to inspire global competition also represents a leading thread of discourse for some international comparative researchers.

The volume editors are committed to providing "an approach with a multidimensional view of the many processes of globalization that develop in complex and uneven ways" (Martell 2007, 182). This is noteworthy, given that few empirically grounded studies offer competing arguments beyond the examination of Western industrial societies (Green 1997). The editors first vetted this phenomenon at international conferences to investigate the volume theme and title, *The Internationalization of East Asian Higher Education: Globalization's Impact*. In response, this volume originated as a set of symposiums organized at the 2009 and 2010 annual meetings of the Comparative and International Education Society (CIES) and American Education Research Association (AERA) to examine competing arguments of globalization and internationalization within an East Asian context.

The chapter authors represent a group of international researchers committed to examination of contemporary effects of globalization and internationalization on the institution of higher education in the East Asian realm. That said, the volume represents a diversity of voices (e.g., government officials, university administration, graduate students, and professors) articulated by discussions on the philosophies, purposes, and current issues related to internationalization and globalization in East Asia. The authors expand the investigation of East Asian values and contexts in comparison and separate from Western-dominant thoughts of globalization and internationalization of higher education. Through discussion of their respective research, the authors reveal how the "Westernized" model is not altogether suitable in an evolving globalized world, thereby considering how East Asian institutions are moving toward globalization theory and internationalization practice that is context specific as well as aligned with national-level global engagement.

The methodological challenges of the volume resonate with new forms of international relationships in terms of comparative and international research; the importance of collaborative research and partnerships between *insiders* and *outsiders*; research that is sensitive to local, social constructions of reality; and strategies that facilitate the strengthening of research capacity (Crossley 2001). Chapter authors rely on methodologies such as case studies, demographic profiles, evaluations, and comparative analysis to critically examine the multiple layers and dimensions of the globalization and internationalization of East Asian higher education. In brief, each chapter represents a unique discourse composed of different theoretical and political currents that nevertheless, have commonalities. The authors' epistemological assumptions and strategies differ; yet, collectively the chapters offer a panoramic and in-depth glimpse of empirically driven research derived from qualitative, quantitative, and mixed methods to address the impact of globalization and thus the internationalization of East Asian universities.

In Chapter 1, David Chan opens up the volume with a description of the two major higher educational "hubs" in East Asia—Singapore and Hong Kong—in his chapter entitled "Internationalization of Higher Education as a Major Strategy for Developing Regional Education Hubs: A Comparison of Hong Kong and Singapore." Chan concludes that, because of their history as former British colonies and the widespread usage of English, these two cities are ahead of other nations/cities in becoming the East Asian regional hubs or, in his words, "the Boston of the East." Chan establishes in each location the importance of the government's role in developing, maintaining, and directing higher education internationalization policies. In particular, he investigates aspects of "marketing strategies" and "quality assurance" as he believes that, in order to become educational leaders, regionally and globally, these cities must guarantee and market a strong product.

The comparative aspect of Chan's chapter provides valuable insight into the major similarities and differences in Singapore's and Hong Kong's higher education internationalization policies. He deciphers the difference between these two cities as Singapore is vying for local, global, and long-term recognition as an educational leader, while Hong Kong appears to be claiming the role as educational leader of the great China region. He then concludes with critical insight into both regions and, in so doing, provides implications for the two cities as well as what other East Asian nations have to consider in developing internationalization higher education policies.

In Chapter 2, "Concepts, Contributions, and Challenges of the Contemporary University Community in Taiwan," authors and coeditors Amy Roberts and Gregory Ching highlight key areas of consideration for university professors and administrators engaged with processes of globalization and internationalization at the National Cheng-Chi University (NCCU) in Taipei, Taiwan. Implications showcase the education paradox of the twenty-first century in terms of questioning the genuine improved quality in education, and academic well-being within institutions embracing the influences of globalization and internationalization. The contemporary era offers extraordinary interest and possibilities of higher education side by side with the pressure to shift traditional perspectives and methods of instruction. The NCCU is adaptable to the changing world of higher education as evidenced by the infusion of English-medium courses within a wide variety of programs, shifting pedagogical teaching styles, increasing diversity sparked by rising numbers of international students, and new benchmarks for scholarship. While the shifts in participants' teaching were nearly seamless, the pressure to publish in international journals represented complex issues and dilemmas.

At first glance, the status of the NCCU as a world-class institution appears trendy—imitative rather than creative. That said, the chief vehicle for developing and sustaining the NCCU as a world-class institution is not the policy, established publication records in leading international journals, or number of cooperative agreements signed, but rather, the engagement of faculty within both local and global dimensions. Participants illustrated the importance of the ability of academics to change in order to meet the needs of contemporary higher education. Key themes generated from the participants suggested that when change is embraced and paradigms shift, professorial teaching is transformed. Participants' views, strategies, and practices represented a blending of contradictory positions and discourses that were not uniform yet showcased an innovative and united ideology. In light of this, participants were situated as cultural conduits through which both global and local practices flowed. They represented a national core of academics committed to both the global arena and the national intellectual capital. To nurture core faculty in terms of recognizing and authenticating their teaching practice diverts attention from the accepted discourse of the world-class university, yet offers stability, as well as cultural and intellectual rootedness to the NCCU as an aspiring world-class institution.

In Chapter 3, "A Pearl on the Silk Road? Internationalizing a Regional Chinese University," esteemed scholars in the region, Anthony R. Welch and Rui Yang, investigate Xinjiang University (XU), which is located in a particular region of China that provides a unique view of the internationalization of higher education. Indeed, XU falls outside of the major developing areas of eastern China's seaboard and, at the same time, is one of the regions where ethnic minorities are the majority of the population.

The authors first provide an in-depth historical perspective of the development of XU, in particular of the former Union of Soviet Socialist Republics' (USSR's) and Mao Tse Tung's influence in the region, as a way to illustrate the long-standing internationalization policies of XU. Then, using empirical data from both questionnaires and interviews, the authors critically analyze several key issues related to internationalization at this regional university. In particular, similar to other university and national leaders' concerns, XU continued to see some of its top students and scholars leave for both the more illustrious Chinese universities in the major cities and overseas. The authors connected the internationalization efforts, especially international communications, of XU with the rise in the brain drain of the region. The authors' interpretation of the contradictions between XU's strengths, as it relates to the development and education of the ethnic minority population, and its transregional aspirations allows for fresh policy perspectives of the internationalization efforts of other less established universities in East Asia.

In Chapter 4, "Minority Students' Access to Higher Education in an Era of Globalization: A Case of Ethnic Koreans in China," Heejin Park and W. James Jacob provide a comprehensive understanding of the educational issues and challenges faced by Korean nationals in China. Ultimately, the study aimed to assist the Chinese government to develop educational policies that better support their minority constituents. External and internal factors were examined with a special emphasis on the impact of internationalization phenomena, taking the case of Korean nationals. Interviews were recorded, transcribed, and translated into English.

Among the 56 officially recognized minority groups in China, some minority nationalities have regional autonomy according to the Constitution of the Peoples' Republic of China (Ma 2007). Universities in these autonomous regions have played a significant role for minorities and Chinese society as a whole. Minority students' choice of higher education institutions however, are influenced by various social, economic, and political factors. Specifically, Korean minorities have their autonomous prefecture in the northeast region of China, and they have their own higher education institution, Yanbian University, which is the first university specialized for ethnic minority studies.

Koreans' zeal for education enable them to become one of the most successful minorities in educational achievement at every education level. However, recent research argues that they have encountered a number of educational problems due to China's rapid transition toward a market economy. Considering the significance that higher education has for most Korean families, it is important to understand Chinese higher educational policies that support these minority students, in particular, the responses of the government to globalization.

In Chapter 5, "Does Internationalization Really Mean Americanization?: A Closer Look at Major South Korean Universities' Internationalization

Policies," authors and coeditors John D. Palmer and Young Ha Cho examine the impact of globalization on South Korean universities in terms of campus climate, the role of students, and society in general. Relying upon globalization theory—specifically on newly created thoughts of *grobalization* and *glocalization* (Martell 2007)—the authors reveal how power and privilege are embedded within internationalization efforts as well as how globalization impacts the Korean culture (Altbach and Teichler 2001; Altbach and Knight 2007).

The authors' intent is to provide new ways of viewing globalization from multiple and complex perspectives. Given the inclusion of a diversity of people involved in globalizing Korean universities, the authors suggest that nearly all South Korean institutions are attempting to become leaders in the evolving globalized world. In particular, they note the initiative of South Korean universities to carve out a special role in the globalized world by educating students from industrializing countries. Findings suggest that students from industrializing countries look to Korean universities for opportunities to become leaders in the globalized world. Some of the universities viewed this aspect as internationalizing Korea, as well as playing a role in supporting industrializing countries' inclusion in the globalized world.

In Chapter 6, "What it Takes to Internationalize Higher Education in Korea and Japan: English-Mediated Courses and International Students," authors Jae-Eun Jon and Eun-Young Kim investigate the effects of globalization on universities in Korea and Japan. The authors reveal how leading universities in Korea and Japan attempt to represent themselves as world-class research universities through internationalization strategies that resemble those in the West, such as recruiting international students and increasing the number of classes taught in English.

The perspective of *glonacal agency heuristic*, which considers global, national, and local levels together in studying comparative higher education (Marginson and Rhoades 2002), and the concept of *peripheries and centers* in the higher education system (Altbach 2006) guided the study. Interviews were conducted with Korean faculty and students regarding their opinions on the internationalization of their institutions and the practice of teaching courses in English. Government documents, scholarly papers, and newspaper articles were used together as resources for understanding the internationalization of higher education. Results illustrate that using English as a medium of teaching may be effective in attracting international students and advertising institutions as internationalized top research universities. However, the data suggest that there are issues of the quality of courses and pressure and resistance from both faculty and students in teaching and learning in the English-language courses. Moreover, recruiting *foreign* students, mainly from Asia, led to issues of academic quality and tension with domestic students. The authors argue that internationalization strategies for Westernization without consideration for the specific context should be avoided, but that internationalization for the particular context is needed.

In Chapter 7, "Higher Education Global Rankings Systems in East Asia," Peter Ghazarian presents an in-depth critical analysis of the international ranking systems—Academic Ranking of World Universities (ARWU) and the *Times Higher Education* (*THE*)—and their impact upon East Asian higher education's internalization policies. Throughout, the author remains quite critical of the methods these ranking systems employ. Indeed, Ghazarian illustrates how these ranking systems favor firmly established and highly esteemed universities, especially those in the United States and United Kingdom.

The author argues that the major flaw in these rankings may come from the impact they have on how the public views the university. In that, students looking to study abroad, and in this case in East Asia, may uphold the rankings as one of the main criteria in their decision making. For example, Ghazarian postulates that students may select a university based upon its ranking, without closely looking at some of the finer points such as how well the university accommodates international students' cultural needs. More specifically, if a student is not interested in nature and science, which is a main indicator on the ranking system, this student may find that the university is not well equipped in the social sciences and humanities.

Nevertheless, the rankings set high standards for newly established universities as well as universities looking to "improve" their ranking. Here, the author contends that the rankings could provide a "level playing field" for second-tier universities to now equally compete with the top-tier universities. This analysis is helpful in understanding governments' and individual universities' internationalization policies. Certainly, the ranking systems are driving these policies as nations and universities vie to improve their ranking, which in the end allows researchers and educational policy makers to better understand the context of East Asian higher education development.

In Chapter 8, Mary Shepard Wong and Shuang Frances Wu draw the volume to a close with a synthesis of Chapters 1 through 7 in "Internationalization of Higher Education in East Asia: Issues, Implications, and Inquiries." They note that, collectively, the chapters cast a wide perspective on the reaction of East Asian higher education processes of globalization and internationalization. That said, the volume does not devalue the importance of investigating the reach of globalization within all central societal dimensions; rather, the chapters are dedicated to the arena of higher education in order to offer an in-depth analysis, which, in turn, has implications for society and the region as a whole. All in all, context underpins the essence of the research presented in this volume to examine new directions in the understanding of the effects of globalization and internationalization within individual and regional university environments. An undercurrent of the chapters therefore is that globally minded scholars and practitioners have an obligation to address issues, dilemmas, and problems that impact and connect with the academic community. Through their studies of the globalization and internationalization of East Asian universities within diverse and contested environments the chapter authors expose interactive processes, tensions, and contradictions as connected to global dilemmas in localized settings. The chapters offer a critical interpretation, to the extent that the authors do not accept particular forms of globalization as a given. Rather, globalization has become an ideological discourse impacting change. In response, chapter authors agree that change is inevitable, yet it can occur in different, equitable, and just forms. In sum, the contributors of this volume acknowledge contemporary trends of globalization and internationalization as well as alternative implications for shaping and altering available choices for educational policies and practices beyond prescriptive interpretation.

REFERENCES

Altbach, Philip G. 2003. "Why the United States Will Not Be a Market for Foreign Higher Education Products: A Case Against GATS." *International Higher Education* 31 (Spring): 5-7. Available online at: http://www.bc.edu/research/cihe.html.

Altbach, Philip G. 2006. "The Dilemmas of Ranking." *International Higher Education* 42 (Winter): 2-3.

Altbach, Philip G., and Jane Knight. 2007. "The Internationalization of Higher Education: Motivations and Realities." *Journal of Studies in International Education* 11 (3&4): 290-305.

Altbach Philip G., and Ulrich Teichler. 2001. "Internationalization and Exchanges in a Globalized University." *Journal of Studies in International Education* 5 (1): 5-25.

Crossley, Michael. 2001. "Cross-Cultural Issues, Small States and Research: Capacity Building in Belize." *International Journal of Educational Development* 21 (3): 217-230.

Dale, Roger. 1999. "Specifying Globalization Effects on National Policy: A Focus on the Mechanisms." *Journal of Educational Policy* 14 (1): 1-17.

Green, Andy. 1997. *Education, Globalization and the Nation-State*. London: Macmillan Press.
Jay, Paul. 2002. "Globalization and the Teaching of Writing." Paper presented at the Modern Language Association Meeting, New York, December 2002.
Jones, Ronald W. 1998. "Globalization and Internationalism: Democratic Prospects for World Education." *Comparative Education* 34 (2): 143-155.
Ma, Rong. 2007. "Bilingual Education for China's Ethnic Minorities." *Chinese Education and Society* 40 (2): 9-25.
Marginson, Simon, and Gary Rhoades. 2002. "Beyond National States, Markets, and Systems of Higher Education: A Glonacal Agency." *Heuristic Higher Education* 43 (3): 281-309.
Martell, Luke. 2007. "The Third Wave in Globalization Theory." *International Studies Review* 9 (2): 173-196.
Mok, Ka Ho, and Haeyoung Lee. 2001. "Globalization and Changing Governance: Higher Education Reforms in Hong Kong, Taiwan and Mainland China." Paper presented at the Australian Association for Research in Education Annual Conference, University of Notre Dame Australia Fremantle, Australia, December 2001.
Mundy, Karen. 1999. "Educational Multi-Lateralism in a Changing World Order: UNESCO and the Limits of the Possible." *International Journal of Educational Development* 19 (1): 27-52.
Watson, Keith. 1996. "Banking on Key Reforms for Educational Development: A Critique of the World Bank Review." *Mediterranean Journal of Educational Studies* 1 (11): 43-61.
van der Wende, Marijk. 2001. "Internationalization Policies: About New Trends and Contrasting Paradigms." *Higher Education Policy* 14 (3): 249-259.

Chapter 1

Internationalization of Higher Education as a Major Strategy for Developing Regional Education Hubs: A Comparison of Hong Kong and Singapore

David Kinkeung Chan

Educational Restructuring and Policy Changes in East Asia

Despite diverse views on the impact of globalization on state governance, increasing globalization has caused many nation-states to rethink their governance strategies in order to cope with the rapid social and economic changes. Obviously, educational policy, management, and governance are not immune from the growing pressure to improve service delivery, with better governance and overall performance. Aiming at adapting to the rapidly changing socioeconomic and political environments, universities have changed their governance paradigm from one of "managerialism" and "monetarism" (Gouri et al. 1991; World Bank 1995), to a paradigm combining freedom of choice with market mechanisms (Apple 2000).

Through revitalizing the role of the family and individuals within the private sector, the market and other nonstate sectors are becoming more popular educational service providers in East Asia (Mok 2005).

This happens within the context of globalization in which recent education reforms in East Asia are mostly finance-driven and characterized by decentralization, privatization, and better performance (Mok and Chan 2001; Mok 2003a, 2003b, 2005; Mok and Welch 2003; Chan and Lo 2008). Such changes accelerate when more governments explore additional resources from civil society (Coleman 1990; Meyer and Boyd 2001).

In short, the diversification of educational service and funding providers, coupled with the revitalization of civil society's involvement in education, opens up new avenues for nation-states to reinvent the ways in which education is governed. Not surprisingly, nonstate sectors have more control and influence over education policy and educational development. This new kind of "co-management" relationship between state and nonstate sectors has altered the public-private partnership in the delivery of social services in general, and that of educational services in particular.

As a result of the Uruguay Round negotiations, the General Agreement on Trade in Services (GATS) became a treaty in January 1995 in which all member nations of the World Trade Organization are signatories. On that basis, the advent of transnational education is a phenomenon that is part of the globalization of trade in goods and services (McBurnie and Ziguras 2001) and its emergence is fueled by the inclusion of higher education as an industry under this framework (Knight 2002). The fundamental reason for the internationalization of higher education is mainly economic in nature (Knight 2004), and it all comes down to "the competitive rush for international students and their money" (De Vita and Case 2003, 384).

In this regard, higher education is now seen as an important knowledge industry and a prime instrument for upgrading national economic competitiveness. Thus, the provision for higher education has become a battleground in the international education marketplace (Yonezawa 1999; Gamage and Suwarnabroma 2006). In order to capture a piece of this pie, various Asian nations are now trying to transform their own national higher education institutions into international ones, in an attempt to actively compete with other global players (Chan and Mok 2001; Mok and Chan 2001; Lo and Tai 2003; Mok and Tan 2004; Oba 2004; Chan 2007a, 2007b; Chan and Lo 2007, 2008).

This chapter starts with the premise that both Hong Kong and Singapore want to become regional education hubs with "world-class universities," although their strategies to achieve this are rather different (Huang 2006; Chan and Lo 2007; Chan and Ng 2008a, 2008b), in terms of employing the internationalization agenda for their development of higher education. Recent educational reforms in Hong Kong and Singapore clearly demonstrate that the two higher education sectors in these cities have moved from a relatively centralized model (Mok and Tan 2004) to a more corporate and managerial one (Chan 2009). Competition has become the norm among universities in the two cities, while "quality" and "accountability" are the themes accompanying their new managerial and entrepreneurial cultures.

Bearing in mind that the two cities are striving to be regional education hubs, the chapter attempts to focus on four major areas: (1) vision of government, (2) cross-border education, (3) marketing strategies, and (4) strengthening the steering capacity through a quality assurance system. In examining and evaluating the recent education reforms in these two Asian cities, I argue that they are using a similar process of internationalization but in a rather diverse way, which reflect their fundamental differences in terms of mind-set and underlying philosophy.

The Internationalization of Higher Education in East Asia

In the past, higher education in East Asia was mainly local. In that, prestigious universities were satisfied with their dominant positions from either a local or a regional perspective. The lack of competition caused an elitist and often isolated atmosphere in East Asian academic circles (see Postiglione 2007; Yonezawa 2007). Nevertheless, globalization has broken down national borders and has blurred many differences across nations and cultures (Urry 1998), which has further led to a systemization of world knowledge, upon which ideas, people, and resources have been fused in different and dynamic ways (Denman 2002). In response to this global trend, local academia needs to establish linkages with international academic communities. This trend toward the "internationalization" of higher education should be seen as part of the strategies for building "world-class universities."

This explains why world university league tables are taken as symbolic indicators of the standard of universities in the globalized education marketplace. Indeed, many of these ranking exercises are taken seriously by many governments and universities in East Asia, and their influence is expanding rapidly in the academic field of the region (Mok 2007).

Climbing up the world university league tables and becoming "world-class" is seen as an important step toward the internationalization of higher education. As Jane Knight and Hans de Wit point out, the internationalization of higher education is "the process of integrating an international dimension into the teaching, research and service functions of an institution of higher education" with the international dimension to be introduced into higher education as "a perspective, activity or program which introduces or integrates an international/intercultural/global outlook into the major functions of a university or college" (1995, 15).

Knight (2006a, 18) further indicates that this process involves both campus-based activities and cross-border initiatives with a wide diversity of activities, including

> international cooperation and development projects; institutional agreements and networks; the international/intercultural dimension of the teaching/learning process, curriculum and research; campus-based extra-curricular clubs and activities; mobility of academics through exchange, field work, sabbaticals and consultancy work; recruitment of international students; student exchange programs and semesters abroad; joint/double degree programs; twinning[1] partnerships; and branch campuses.

This statement reiterates that internationalization should not only focus on climbing up the world university league tables, but also target the building of an international platform for the higher education sector.

One important aspect of the internationalization of higher education in East Asia has to do with the erosions of boundaries between different educational systems globally. This is reflected by the rapid growth of transnational/cross-border higher education, which is "the movement of people, knowledge, programs, providers and curriculum across national or regional jurisdictional borders" (Knight 2006a, 18). Though the cross-border education initiatives "can be an element in the development cooperation projects, academic exchange programs and commercial initiatives," in many cases they "are commercial in nature and are usually intended to be for profit" (18).

These activities can be understood as a movement along the "continuum from face-to-face (taking various forms from students travelling abroad and campuses abroad) to distance learning (using a range of technologies and including e-learning)... Cross-border education is such a modality in the continuum" (Knight 2006a, 19), and a result of being considered as a service industry under GATS (Knight 2006a, 2006b). As a consequence, many governments in the region, including Hong Kong and Singapore, have actively opened up their education markets to foreign education providers in various forms, such as the establishment of offshore campuses and twinning programs.

In the context of internationalization in higher education, all stakeholders are expected to respond to these changes proactively and strategically (UNESCO 2005). Given a shared vision of promoting the Hong Kong and Singapore as regional education hubs, this provides a strong rationale for the recent reforms of higher education. In this sense, by using the internationalization of higher education as a major strategy, it provides an opportunity to attract top talent and institutions from across the globe to study, work, and live in these regional centers.

Yet, it is noteworthy that the two cities have adopted rather different strategies in developing transnational/cross-border higher education. In the case of Singapore, the establishment of offshore campuses of foreign universities is a tactic used by the government in building "world-class universities." Hence, foreign education providers entering the market are usually elite universities who have been proactively invited by the Singapore government (Lee and Gopinathan 2007). As for the Hong Kong Special Administrative Region (HKSAR) of China, transnational higher education is taken as a sort of "supplement" to the local higher education sector (Huang 2006; Chan and Lo 2007; Chan and Ng 2008a, 2008b). Comparing their major differences, in terms of their policy approaches in the four major areas of concern, I will illustrate how the governments of the two cities employ this important strategy so as to develop themselves as regional education hubs, and thus reflect their fundamental mind-sets, underlying philosophies, and the style of governance of higher education.

Methods

This study employs a qualitative approach in analyzing the education policy in Hong Kong and Singapore by beginning with a systematic analysis of policies related to transnational higher education in the two cities, with a major focus on their strategies of internationalization. Attention was given to the specific socioeconomic and sociopolitical backgrounds of the two selected case studies.

The first part of the research consists of a literature review, historical survey, and documentary analysis. A fundamental source of data came from government documents and reports, official statistics, budget documents, reports of departments and of transnational higher education providers, as well as submissions to government inquiries and consultants' reports. Newspaper and magazine reports in the specialist columns of local and international press and professional journals were also important sources of contemporary information on educational issues. Thorough literature surveys of these principal sources were conducted during the first part of the study.

After a comprehensive policy analysis, a systematic survey of the different types of transnational higher education institutions and programs operating in these two cities were conducted. These critical and systematic policy analyses formed the basis for designing appropriate questions of semistructured questionnaires (Lewis-Beck et al. 2004) for in-depth interviews with key policy actors and education practitioners in the two places. Structured questionnaires for surveys and semistructured questions for focus-group discussions were also designed for students studying in transnational higher educational institutions.

The second part of the research consisted of fieldwork in both cities for in-depth interviews with academic staff, university administrators, and key government officials, as well as focus-group discussions with students studying in transnational higher educational institutions. As in much qualitative research, the sampling selection was deliberate rather than randomized (Lewis-Beck et al. 2004). Interviewees had official positions, either in the government or in public organizations responsible for transnational higher education policy and governance, or were major players of transnational higher education institutions operating their programs in the two places. Thus, the purposive sampling technique was adopted in choosing participants for the in-depth interviews. Toward the latter part of the process, a further type of nominated sampling technique, known as theoretical sampling (ibid.), was employed: I asked the original group of participants to nominate further participants with certain kinds of experience in transnational higher education for more intensive field interviews. About 8 key policy actors, with another 18 major players in offering transnational higher education, in each city were met, and a total of 52 people were interviewed.

At the same time, a series of structured questionnaires on student evaluations of their learning experiences in the different transnational higher education programs was conducted in each of the cities. One hundred students were selected in each society by convenience sampling technique (i.e., a total of 200). Some were drawn from programs based heavily on the virtual campus and e-learning, while others were identified from programs offered by overseas universities from the West with offshore campuses, private proprietors, public-private partnerships, or other forms of franchising, or twinning programs operating in the two places. These surveys were not meant to be representative, but enabled the development of student perspectives when analyzing the policy and operation of transnational higher education.

Furthermore, data were collected through focus-group interviews, which were purposely set so that "the explicit use of group interaction (can) produce data and insights that would be less accessible without the interaction found in a group" (Morgan 1997, 12). I found that the group situation stimulated participants to bring to the surface different situations that might not otherwise have been exposed, and to make explicit their views and perceptions (Punch 2005). Ten focus-group discussions (with five people per group) were conducted in each city (i.e., altogether 20 focus groups) for sharing their learning experiences, with all of them coming from the surveys conducted earlier.

Hong Kong

Vision of Government

Being the executive arm in managing higher education issues, the University Grants Committee (UGC) recently released a report that stated "the higher education system also needs to recognize and take up the challenge of the mutually beneficial relationship between Hong Kong, the Pearl River Delta and Mainland China" (UGC 2004a, 4), and more importantly "Hong Kong is too small a place to afford excessive overlapping of efforts in higher education" (8). Furthermore, the UGC seeks to develop a role-driven, yet deeply collaborative system (or a differentiated, yet interlocking system) of higher education in which each institution has its own role and mission, while, at the same time, being committed to extensive and deep collaboration with the other institutions in order that the system as a whole can sustain a greater variety of programs offered at a higher level of quality with improved efficiency (UGC 2004b).

This report turned out to be a roadmap for Hong Kong to become a regional education hub by providing quality-assured higher education for the Mainland. The UGC has further developed a role-driven strategy for the eight public-funded higher education institutions,[2] and encouraged them to develop their role missions freely. Ever since then, each has been working hard to promote their own internationalization agenda, together with their own ways of international benchmarking and the upgrading of their research profiles, so as to push themselves further up the world university league tables.

The Hong Kong Government Task Force on Economic Challenges (chaired by the HKSAR chief executive Mr. Donald Tsang) was set up in 2008 and aimed at assessing the economic challenges ahead in an attempt to propose different strategies in addressing those challenges. In terms of higher education, the committee raised various ideas for promoting the economic base of education, such as the increase on the provisions of land supply for international schools and a review of the postsecondary ordinance (Hong Kong Government Task Force on Economic Challenges 2009). Targeted at developing Hong Kong as a regional education hub, educational services were finally put on the agenda of the 2009 Policy Address (Tsang 2009).

As far as the vision of the Hong Kong government is concerned, this can be summarized as having three basic features: (1) the dominant belief on the philosophy of "small government, big market," (2) the internationalization of the local eight publicly funded institutions, and (3) its integration with the Mainland. In this way, the government's dominant thinking sees that higher education is crucial in developing itself into a regional education hub. It is clear that the initiatives, like the provision of suitable sites, review of the postsecondary ordinance, relaxation of immigration policy, and mutual exploration of quality higher education within the Pearl Delta River in Guangdong Province (Hong Kong Government 2010) are all centered around the philosophy of "small government, big market." The government tends to facilitate both the basis of its software (quality) and hardware (e.g., land supply) in providing more favorable environments for interested parties to offer self-financing programs without much intervention from the government.

As for the internationalization of higher education, the government believes that the existing eight publicly funded institutions should be the prime engine for developing Hong Kong into a regional education hub.[3] The achievements that local institutions have made in gradually moving toward being such a hub are quite evident, and the government has recognized their efforts by playing its role in a supportive, rather than a guiding, way.

Although the government keeps on with its philosophy of a "big market," it intends to have its position as a regional education hub to be backed by the Mainland. Furthermore, the HKSAR government has realized the imperatives of connecting the two places' higher education sectors, in order that Hong Kong can develop a unique education hub: "Our objective is to enhance Hong Kong's status as a regional education hub, boosting Hong Kong's competitiveness and complementing the future development of the Mainland" (Tsang 2009, 11).

The HKSAR government's initiatives have been to minimize the barriers by signing different Memoranda of Understanding with the Mainland, and yet it has tried to leave more room for local institutions to maneuver and decide on how they can make the best use of such opportunities. One recent example is that the University of Hong Kong will become the first university in Hong Kong to set up a branch-campus in cooperation with the Shenzhen municipal government (*Sing Tao Daily* 2010a), while the Hong Kong University of Science and Technology also intends to set up a research institute at Nansha (*Sing Tao Daily* 2010b).

Even though educational services are starting to be seen as a service industry in Hong Kong (Shive 2010), the current higher education system still relies largely on public funds, which may well serve as a barrier to future development. Now, local universities have to run all postgraduate programs on a self-financing basis as the HKSAR government has stopped funding such programs. In generating more income from the wider public, the universities are now offering more self-financing top-up degree programs in order to cater to the newly expanding demands of associate degree graduates coming from the new sector of community colleges. All these new initiatives are changing the overall landscape of higher education in Hong Kong.

The higher education sector in Hong Kong used to be characterized by a strong state dominance with a tiny private sector. However, the recent higher education reforms have provided room for the emergence of a stronger private sector. The newly approved Shue Yan University, which became Hong Kong's first private university in 2007, is a case in point. The government is interested in expanding the private sector's role as an alternative source of higher education (Tung 2000). Hence, the current stage in the privatization of higher education in Hong Kong is still characterized by a "public-aided" approach.

In view of its current development, Hong Kong's higher education seems to be splitting up into two parts: the first is the conventional sector that consists of the eight UGC-funded institutions that are mainly responsible for developing research and development areas in "Centres of Excellence," as well as for the training of both undergraduate and research postgraduate students; the second is the newly emerging private sector, comprising the only private university at present, with other privately run community colleges and tertiary institutions that offer sub-degree and other continuing education programs. While the HKSAR government sees the former as "the core" of its higher education and retains a strong steering role in it, the latter is regarded as "supplementary" and therefore the government is more relaxed and noninterventional toward it.

The rapid expansion of the private sector in recent years has further diversified the provision of higher education in Hong Kong. Consequently, a newly emerging higher education market has slowly taken shape. Basically, any institution, whether local or overseas, may enter the Hong Kong market with little government interference (Chan and Ng 2008a). Such an attitude is supported by the government's mind-set and underlying philosophy in believing in the efficiency and effectiveness of the market mechanism.

If seen in this light, then some kind of a *three-tiered* structure in Hong Kong's higher education may be slowly evolving, such that the eight UGC-funded universities (the "core") will form the *first tier*; with the other newly developed private universities and sub-degree community colleges ("supplementary") forming the *second tier*; while other postsecondary and tertiary institutions will slowly become the *third tier* of this new structural formation.

With the local institutions' eagerness in building further collaborations with foreign partners, the introduction of transnational higher education in Hong Kong is a further addition to the newly emerging "supplementary part" of its higher education, as well as a strategic move for Hong Kong to develop itself as a regional education hub, and can thus be seen as instrumentally "profit-seeking" investments (Yang 2006; Chan and Ng 2008b).

Cross-Border Education

Students

Among nonlocal students, Mainland students account for over 90 percent, while the remaining proportion is shared by other Southeast Asian and European students (Hong Kong Institute of Education [HKIEd] 2009; UGC 2009). The reason should be largely related to the close proximity of the two places. It is expected that the number of nonlocal students in each of the institutions will steadily increase with the target of the 20 percent admission quota. In terms of career mobility, Mainland students have been allowed to take up part-time, on-campus jobs for not more than 20 hours per week; and they are granted a one-year extension after graduation to seek employment in Hong Kong. As for other nonlocal students, there is no particular policy regarding their career aspirations in Hong Kong, since most of them are on exchange programs instead of being regularly enrolled full-time students.

Programs

The programs offered in Hong Kong are mainly from publicly funded institutions, self-financing community colleges, and other private institutions. It is normal that the publicly funded institutions try to develop collaborations with foreign universities, especially joint-degree programs. A recent example is the agreement between the Polytechnic University of Hong Kong (PolyU) and the Royal Veterinary College of the University of London, which introduced the first veterinary nursing degree program in Hong Kong (PolyU 2009), which is an exempted program under the 1997 Non-local Higher and Professional Education (Regulation) Ordinance (Cap 493) in Hong Kong.

As for the self-financing community colleges, all of their courses are accredited without establishing any cooperation linkages with foreign universities. There are currently at least 1,000 of such programs offered by these private institutions, and over 70 percent operate in collaborations with local institutions through various modes, like twinning, distance learning, or other supporting services.

Institutions

The current development of local higher education largely depends on the local publicly funded institutions as there is only one private university. Although the eight publicly funded institutions dominate the provisions of undergraduate programs, they still cooperate with over 70 percent of the privately run community colleges so as to guarantee the quality of their sub-degree courses with their international frame.

With its vision on the "internationalization of higher education," the HKSAR government may still need to put in extra efforts to attract foreign institutions to set up offshore campuses locally. Some local institutions have, in fact, started to export their educational services across the border. Such attempts will be a valuable experience for all, and will serve as the driving force in developing educational services as an industry.

In terms of both programs and institutions, undergraduate and postgraduate programs are typically provided by local publicly funded institutions, and few attempts have been made with other partnerships, except for particular subjects like the veterinary nursing program. Currently, there is not yet a foreign branch campus that has been set up locally, but it may happen as the government has allocated two plots of land for international schools as mentioned in the 2009 Policy Address. Some local institutions have established or plan to establish offshore campuses and/or research centers on the Mainland, and it is likely to expand further in the near future.

Marketing Strategies

The findings illustrate that the HKSAR government does not have a clear marketing strategy, not to mention the establishment of a specified agency focusing on the marketing of the local higher education. The Hong Kong Trade and Development Council (HKTDC) is the only formal organization dedicated to connecting different businesses both locally and overseas through doing different types of promotions, exhibitions, and/or various business services. It has developed its networks in almost every corner of the world through establishing 40 global offices, including 11 on the Mainland. In terms of higher education issues, HKTDC organized the first Hong Kong Higher Education Mini Expo in Central and South Asia in 2007, and invited the representatives of their local institutions to promote the higher education in Hong Kong (HKIEd 2009). For example, seven out of eight local institutions engaged in the International Education Expo in Jakarta, Indonesia, and met their

Indonesian counterparts for both cultural and business exchanges (Hong Kong Higher Education 2007).

Basically, the Chinese Education Bureau (C-EDB)[4] has not established any relationship with other economic agencies for the further promotion of local institutions. In fact, the C-EDB maintains its official duties on the quality assurance systems of local institutions, as well as seeking bilateral cooperation with different governments at the policy level. Yet, the C-EDB developed a deeper educational relationship with the Chinese government since 2004, known as the Memorandum of Understanding on Mutual Recognition of Academic Degrees in Higher Education (C-EDB 2010a). Under this kind of mutual cooperation, the holders of bachelor's and master's degrees from recognized higher education institutions can apply for admission to programs of masters or doctoral degrees in both places. This, then, is a large step in attracting Mainland students to study in Hong Kong.

The actual practice of marketing strategies, in fact, falls in the hands of the local institutions themselves, and so they need to participate in different kinds of education exhibitions, or simply through the raising of their international rankings in order to draw others' attention. Most local institutions have different strategies to draw the attention of the international students. For example, the City University of Hong Kong, the Hong Kong Baptist University, the Hong Kong Institute of Education, the Open University of Hong Kong, and the Hong Kong Polytechnic University all participated in the China International Education Exhibition Tour in 2010, which was held in some of the major cities in China, including Beijing, Chongqing, Shanghai, Qingdao, and Guangzhou, in order to spread their names across the Mainland. It was one of the largest education fairs in China, which was organized by the Chinese Service Center for Scholarly Exchange (CSCSE) and approved by the Chinese Ministry of Education, with around 90,000 visitors (C-EDB 2010b).

Despite the continuous efforts by local institutions, due to the lack of a specialized and centralized government agency to coordinate issues in relation to cross-border education, it is arguable that Hong Kong has yet to utilize the maximum potential of its resources in order to maximize its investment of human capital, and thus its economic returns and educational outcomes.

Its Steering Capacity through Quality Assurance System

The quality assurance system of local higher institutions can be categorized into three levels: (1) publicly funded programs, (2) self-financing programs, and (3) nonlocal programs. The publicly funded programs refer to courses offered by the eight publicly funded institutions, and so the UGC is mainly responsible for their quality assurance by conducting the Research Assessment Exercise, Teaching and Learning Quality Process Review, and Management Review aiming at assuring the quality of research, teaching, and management areas, respectively, of these institutions (Chan 2009).

In addition, there are currently 25 self-financing institutions that have been accredited by the Hong Kong Council for Accreditation of Academic and Vocational Qualifications (HKCAAVQ). It is a statutory board that is appointed by the secretary of education, and operates on a self-financing mode to provide relevant suggestions and accreditations to these local tertiary institutions. It is simply on a voluntary basis that these institutions seek such external accreditations from the HKCAAVQ, but the greater incentive is "for the sub-degree providers to join the qualifications framework will be eligibility for loan schemes for those offering higher-level awards such as associate degrees" (Leong and Wong 2004, 46).

As for the nonlocal higher and professional programs (sub-degree, degree, postgraduate, or postsecondary courses) offered by overseas institutions, they are all subject to the 1997 Non-local Higher and Professional Education (Regulation) Ordinance (Cap 493). Under this ordinance, they are required to either register or seek exemption by partnering with one of the 11 specified local institutions, and by now, almost 70 percent of the courses are being conducted in collaboration with local institutions (C-EDB 2010b; HKCAAVQ 2010).

Quality assurance is obviously an important dimension of cross-border education as this ensures that what the consumers (students) receive is accredited. Since most students are participating in publicly funded and self-financing programs, the government seems to adopt a more relaxed approach toward nonlocal programs. Regardless of whether they are either publicly funded institutions or privately run community colleges, their past experiences on the economic front has proven that the quality of education has become the most crucial aspect for keeping up its overall competitiveness.

In this regard, by examining the above observations, in terms of its vision and governance philosophy of a "small government, big market;" its cross-border education (students, programs, and institutions as the main "bread and butter" of the transnational higher education industry) that is quite loosely structured; its marketing strategies that are not well coordinated; and its steering capacity through quality assurance that is more well developed for the public sector (but not so for the private sector), it can be concluded that Hong Kong is still at a very rudimentary stage of its development to become a regional education hub.

* * *

Singapore

Vision of Government

The Global Student Mobility 2025 Report, prepared by Education Australia, predicts that the number of international students will increase from 1.8 million in 2000 to 7.2 million by 2025 (Knight 2005). According to the UK Vision 2020 Report, Asia is set to account for 70 percent of the global demand for international higher education by the year 2025 (Singapore Economic Development Board [S-EDB] 2009). Noticing this trend, the Singapore government is attempting to position itself as a regional education hub so that it can explore this potential market in advance. Singapore intends to become the "Boston of the East," that is, "a global knowledge-based hub associated with innovation, creativity, informed debate, and significant university-industry linkages" (Olds 2007, 960). It initiated the policy of "Thinking Schools, Learning Nations" in 1997, which aimed at raising the overall competitiveness of its citizens. With this, education becomes the prime tool to implement such a vision that "is interpreted and implemented as a move to enhance the publicly funded universities' autonomy and accountability" (Chan and Ng 2008a, 495).

At the strategic level, the Singapore government attempts to differentiate the role of each higher education institution in order to distribute public resources rationally. Hoping to capture a bigger piece of the estimated US$2.2 trillion world education market (Singapore Ministry of Trade and Industry—[MTI] 2002), it released a policy paper "Developing Singapore's Education Industry" in recommending the development of Singapore's economic potential into a "Global Schoolhouse" (MTI 2002).

In this regard, Singapore has creatively designed a *three-tiered* higher education system. The first tier are the elite universities (by inviting nine top "world-class universities" from overseas to establish their own offshore campuses in Singapore), which primarily aims to carry out "world-class" research and development (Chan and Ng 2008b). The second tier consists of the three main universities—the National University of Singapore (NUS), the Nanyang Technological University (NTU), and the Singapore Management University (SMU)—while the third tier consists of the five polytechnics and six other private specialized universities/institutions collaborating with local branches of foreign universities. The second and third tiers are the bedrock of the local university segment, and mainly focus on teaching and research to train the local populace.

The "Global Schoolhouse" project and "World-Class University" program launched by the government has strategically invited world-class universities to establish partnerships with local universities (mostly in the science, engineering, and business fields). In addition, the government has set up an international advisory panel to assist both NUS and NTU in their transformations into world-class universities.

The philosophy of governance of Singapore is active intervention and regulation, and thus it makes sense that its government targets the regional Asian market in a centralized direction. In this regard, education has been put under an industrial framework as educational services are being recognized as a profitable service industry.

The S-EDB, rather than the Singapore Ministry of Education (MOE), is responsible for inviting specific foreign universities to set up offshore campuses in Singapore, further proving that the whole higher education system is well articulated and shaped to connect to the global community. By adopting the alliance partnership model, local institutions can learn new administrative and teaching styles from foreign collaborators. Local institutions can make use of the power of their collaborators' "brand names" in empowering their own process of internationalization.

Generally speaking, the whole higher education system fits in with the government's ambition:

> The key idea is the creation of a virtuous circle: draw in the best university with global talent; this talent then creates knowledge and knowledgeable subjects; these knowledgeable subjects, through their actions and networks, then create the professional jobs that drive a vibrant local KBE [Knowledge-based economy] with profitable regional links. (Olds 2007, 973)

The Singapore government then acts as the designer of the game by directing all the other players (institutions) to make the right decisions.

Cross-border Education

Students

The Singapore government initiated the Global Schoolhouse Project in 2002, and it aims to attract 150,000 international students by the year

2015, mainly targeting the Southeast Asian region. According to statistics from the Singapore Tourism Board (STB) (2008), international students in Singapore are quite diverse, and this fits into the expectations of the government's targeting the Asian market. This successful scenario hinges on the attractiveness of the government's subsidy policy, which requires international students who receive a study subsidy to work in Singapore for three years after graduation. Gavin Sanderson concludes, "The only way to forego this legally binding commitment is either to pay the full tuition fee whilst studying, or pay out the balance of the tuition grant at some stage during the three years work in Singapore" (2002, 93). This "bonded" strategy demonstrates the way the Singapore government put the students' skills and knowledge into productive use, thus benefiting the whole economy.

Programs

The main features of cross-border education in Singapore can be characterized as follows: (1) the running of foreign offshore campuses locally, (2) collaboration on twinning programs, and (3) the distance-learning programs with other foreign universities. The Singapore Institute of Management and the TMC Academy are the main private institutions that offer a wide range of overseas-diploma programs to both local and international students in collaboration with foreign universities or academic organizations. In addition, different scales of private institutions also offer numerous specialized distance-learning diplomas, such as the Singapore Institute of Marketing and the Singapore Nurses Association.

Though there are many examples of the alliance-partnership model between local universities and world-brand universities in Singapore, the programs offered are, in fact, not twinning ones. This is because most of the foreign universities provide services that are supplementary in nature, like professors coming from overseas, enhancement of teaching techniques, and other administrative supports, but "the graduate from Singapore–MIT [Massachusetts Institute of Technology] alliance, for example, will be credentialed by the two local Singapore universities—NUS and NTU, not by MIT" (Sidhu 2005, 56).

The foreign offshore campuses and polytechnics also account for the contribution of providing diverse programs to the international student body. There are currently five polytechnics in Singapore that offer practice-oriented programs focusing on engineering and computing. For example, the Singapore Institute of Technology will partner with five other foreign universities to offer industry-focused degrees (Singapore MOE 2009).

Institutions

As Singapore aims to develop itself into becoming a leading regional education hub in Asia, it has invited "world-class" and "reputable" universities from abroad to set up their own Asian offshore campuses in the city since the mid-1990s. Two foreign business schools, INSEAD and the University of Chicago Graduate School of Business, have set up branches in Singapore. Along with the merit of international recognition, the presence of these foreign universities helps improve the image of Singapore in developing its higher education system to be the "Global Schoolhouse" (De Meyer et al. 2004, 108) in the long run.

The development of cross-border higher education in Singapore is strategically taken as a way to internationalize its higher education and to deem it "world class." These actions themselves have also diversified the provisions of higher education, thereby combining the public and private, as well as the foreign and domestic, in Singapore's higher education. In this regard, the new governance model promulgated by the Singapore government seems to be better suited to the new circumstances of the global competitive environment (Chan and Ng 2008b).

Marketing Strategies

The S-EDB, as one of the important statutory boards of the MTI, helms the strategy for the economic development of Singapore. Under the direction of S-EDB, the "World Class University" program has been articulated with the "Global Schoolhouse" project launched in 2003. Since the work of promotion is of paramount importance, several statutory bodies have been established for the implementation of these multidimensional strategies.

In 2003, a specialized agency, "Singapore Education," was established for the promotion of Singapore as an education hub by informing international students interested in studying in Singapore on such issues as immigration policy, information on schools, courses, and living conditions in Singapore. Strategically, it puts the Singapore MOE into a position of administrator, while the details and structure of Singapore's education system would be handled by "Singapore Education," so that international students can gain access to different kinds of information simultaneously (Singapore Education 2010).

A successful marketing campaign cannot be separated from the construction of marketing slogans. There is a general belief among Asians that studies can help one to have a stable life and better future. As the Asian region is the target market, the Singapore government uses the slogan "Springboard to a better future" to sell its higher education programs in order to gain traction with international students. Furthermore, "Singapore Education" also uses a number of different slogans to highlight the diversity of Singapore's lifestyle (Singapore Education 2010).

"Singapore Education" provides extensive details of both local publicly funded and private education institutions, and it is no different from the way that STB promotes its tourism. In other words, the Singapore government understands that it is not only the education itself that matters, but also how the buyers (international students) consume the product (educational services) in a comfortable way (sociocultural dimension). Therefore, it is not difficult to understand why the involvement of the tourism board and its slogans are crucial elements in its marketing process.

Its Steering Capacity through Quality Assurance

The Singapore government has adopted two different quality assurance frameworks for public and private institutions, respectively. For the public university sector (namely, NUS, NTU, and SMU), they are managed under the Quality Assurance Framework for Universities set up by the Singapore MOE in 2003. Under this framework, these three universities will be assessed by an external panel that regularly conducts "an on-site validation of each university once every three years to validate the university's self-assessment report, and to assess the university's strengths and weaknesses" (Singapore MOE 2003), and then "report[s] to the Minister for Education on its findings and recommendations for quality improvements by the university" in an attempt to ensure the proper use of public funds.

While the Singapore MOE is responsible for the quality assurance of publicly funded institutions, the SPRING Singapore (an official body in setting national standards and accreditation for Singapore enterprises) is charged with the duty of promoting internationally recognized standards and quality assurance infrastructure and regulatory framework for the private sector, such as the scheme of Singapore Quality Class for Private Education Organization (SQC-PEO). The recently established Council for Private Education, a centralized board to comprehensively monitor the quality of private education institutions (PEIs), takes on the role of regulation and promotion of the private education industry. The council is constituted by the representatives of S-EDB, STB, and Consumer Association of Singapore (CASE).

The PEIs are regulated under the framework of a new Private Education Act launched from December 2009. There are currently two quality schemes that aim to protect the interests of both local and international students studying in the PEIs. The first is the "CaseTrust for Education" scheme (CaseTrust), managed by CASE aiming at the protection of students' fees. The second is the "EduTrust for Education" scheme (EduTrust) launched in early 2009, and is the updated version of CaseTrust. These two schemes are now coexisting during this transitional period, as the Singapore MOE is undergoing an experimental stage in which it tries to replace the CaseTrust with the EduTrust eventually. The EduTrust requires private schools to maintain academic standards and protect students' interests, for instance, by having well-defined structures for program development, assessment, progression, and performance review, and protecting students by depositing fees into an escrow account or purchasing student insurance (Singapore MOE 2008). Any complaint made by students is directly reported to CASE and Singapore MOE.

In addition, one distinctive feature of the Singapore quality assurance system is that it is highly commercially related. The Singapore Quality Class sees education as a kind of business and extends a special SQC-PEO award to encourage outstanding quality PEIs. Hence, a clear distinction and division of labor on quality assurance, with detailed and elaborate mechanisms, is in place for both the public and private education sectors. These kinds of initiatives highlight how the Singapore government maintains a coherent economic policy for the development of its education industry with top-quality assurance in nurturing and upgrading human talents (Ng 2007).

Conclusion

Cross-border education is an important dimension of the "internationalization" of higher education, because it simultaneously improves and promotes the universities of a country in the globalized education marketplace. It is in this regard that the level of "internationalization" of higher education is critical to the success of developing and transforming this service industry into a regional education hub. According to Knight, "Internationalization at the national, sector and institutional levels is defined as the process of integrating an international, intercultural or global dimension into the purpose, functions or delivery of post secondary education" (2003, 3).

Governments are the most important influence on such processes of integration, and the importance of its vision for the development of higher education lies in its recognition of the value of education as an industry, as well as in what strategies and policies it adopts in response to the global market. Indeed, different governments will have varied interpretations about what internationalization entails, which reflects the government's basic philosophy of governance when putting its policy into practice. With the advent of globalization, the mobility of international students increases, and they are likely to choose to stay in a place where they can enjoy a truly international environment in terms of language, sociocultural environment, and diversified choices on programs of study, all of which are important dimensions of internationalization. English, as an international language, is the common medium of cultural and economic activities worldwide, and the prevalent use of English can raise the cosmopolitan character of a place.

Within the Asian region, there is no other city that enjoys the prevalent use of English like that of Singapore or Hong Kong, since both were former British colonies. Furthermore, as Hong Kong and Singapore are classified as advanced areas in Asia; they seem to have already achieved the mission of catching up and are now ready to go further ahead in their internationalization of higher education. It is in this sense that these two cities have comparative advantages over other places in Asia in becoming regional education hubs. Singapore has a more far-sighted and long-term vision of developing itself to be an education hub not only regionally, but also globally, while Hong Kong aims to develop itself to be an education hub mainly for the Greater China Region.

The contents of cross-border education itself will be the main focus for attracting international students. Next comes the quality assurance system, which is imperative for an education hub to guarantee the quality of its service provision, as well as the interests of its consumers (students). Therefore, when education is being viewed as a service industry, the quality assurance system is the prime safeguard on the "brand name" of such an education hub. Similarly, the marketing strategies that attract international students are also important in the process of internationalization, as they are the tactics and practices of its government in realizing its goal of becoming a regional educational hub.

Using the above discussions to look at the two cities in the context of transforming themselves to become regional education hubs, it is recognized that the higher education sectors in both cities are not merely developing toward a more diversified model, in terms of funding and provision, but are being transformed into a service industry for exporting their educational services so as to generate revenues to their national incomes. In order to distinguish the divided governing visions in the two places, it is suggested that Singapore adopts a "thoroughly-regulating approach" to drive its development of higher education, particularly by inviting world-class universities from overseas to set up their offshore branch campuses in Singapore.

In contrast, the Hong Kong government splits its higher education sector into two parts: the first part is the conventional sector, which is mainly responsible for research, and for undergraduate and research postgraduate programs; while the other part is the emerging sector, which mainly offers sub-degree programs, self-financing top-up degree programs, and continuing education. The Hong Kong government takes the former part as "the core" of its higher education and retains a strong steering role in it, while it regards the latter as a "supplementary" part and thus feels more relaxed and liberal toward it.

In this sense, the strengthened quality assurance mechanisms enable both governments to "govern at a distance" in a more decentralized governance setting (Jayasuriya 2005, 24). While the two governments share a similar role in terms of the stratification of their higher education sectors, it also reflects upon their different views and perspectives on their own roles as the "funder" and "provider" of higher education. While the Singapore government continues to take on a very proactive and regulatory role in shaping its higher education, the HKSAR government still believes in the philosophy of "the market knows the best," and thus allows the market to run its own course without much governmental intervention.

In view of these divided standpoints, it can be seen that these observations reflect the mind-sets of the government leaders of both places. On the one hand, for the leaders of Singapore, the internationalization agenda would merely be used as a rational policy instrument to streamline its higher education under the strong competitive tide of globalization, with quality control to be the prime consideration in its provision of educational services. On the other hand, within the mind-set of the HKSAR government, the internationalization of higher education would be for the attraction of nonlocal students in bringing about the maximization of "value for money" and cost-effectiveness in its higher education. "Academic entrepreneurship" (Leydsdorrff and Etzkowitz 2001) has been adopted by its leaders in order to transform its governance framework of higher education into that of the business sector, which has been underpinned by the "neoliberal" ideology and philosophy.

The argument that different local agendas have been implemented by employing similar global reform approaches can further be supported by looking at the underlying differences behind the attitudes and mind-sets of the leaders of the two places during the process of introducing overseas higher educational providers into their higher education sectors. In Singapore, the government proactively engages in developing this newly emerging part of higher education by linking up this "internationalization of higher education" with other strategic plans on the building of "world-class universities," in order to achieve its ultimate goal of becoming a "regional education hub."

Therefore, the number and the kind of institutions entering into Singapore's higher education market has been extremely limited, selective, and tightly controlled under strict government scrutiny. Only those regarded as world-renowned universities would be invited to set up their offshore branch campuses in the Singapore, while the government would close down those campuses seen to have "under-performed." The closure of the Division of Biomedical Sciences of Johns Hopkins University in Singapore in 2006 was such a case in point to demonstrate the strong government position on this important matter (Lee and Gopinathan 2007). This kind of provision in cross-border education, being the main bread and butter of the industry, is diversified and stratified, to be underpinned by a far-sighted and long-term global vision.

The Hong Kong government tends to see this newly emerging transnational higher education as only a "supplementary" part of its holistic landscape, and thus leaves it pretty much to the market to decide on its future existence and modes of delivery; while the major universities that are funded by the UGC still continue to remain as the "core" part of its higher education sector, upon which the government will continue to scrutinize more closely. It is in this sense that the introduction of transnational higher education in Hong Kong only serves as an incentive that the government uses to fuel its economic competitiveness within the region.

Nevertheless, despite their similar agendas, the internationalization practices of the two cities do not necessarily reflect that they have the same governing visions and missions. Indeed, present discussions have strongly and empirically reflected that different models of local dimensions and interpretations have been used in adopting the global practices, thus projecting different values into their governance systems and behaviors as a consequence. By putting the above discussions together, it is quite clear that the higher education systems of both Singapore and Hong Kong have been affected by the various policies and strategies of internationalization and their ultimate goals of developing themselves to become regional education hubs.

In conclusion, four major observations can be revealed from the present study. First, the process and strategy of the internationalization of higher education in the two cities take on rather different approaches, due to the fact that their overall developmental goals of aspiring to be "regional education hubs" are based upon very different mind-sets and visions of the two governments in terms of their governance of higher education. The HKSAR government officials took on a more "neoliberal" policy approach in managing its higher education (in the name of "small government, big market"), by allowing the market forces to play a much greater role in terms of provision and financing, while the government mainly plays the roles of "facilitator and moderator" through regulatory frameworks. The Singapore government officials saw themselves to be playing a major role in terms of provision, regulation, and financing of its higher education within a much more managed and regulated market by the state so as to boost up its overall competitiveness in becoming a "regional education hub."

Second, in providing the necessary policy frameworks for their further developments of the two cities as "regional education hubs," the two governments need to strategize and diversify their higher education sectors in order to bring about further economic development in the long run under the global "knowledge-based economy." The internationalization of higher education, particularly with cross-border education, has zeroed in for this game of global competition, such that all players will have to be compared and matched with quantifiable performance indicators, and be finally epitomized in the league tables of universities across the whole world, in the name of international benchmarking.

Third, under this strong tidal wave of marketization and managerialism in higher education, the universities in these two places have slowly perceived themselves to be "business enterprises" by adopting market values, principles, and mechanisms in their management, marketing and other ways of running their businesses. Thus, their educational administrators will have to be more sensitive to the changing market needs, and try to differentiate themselves from others through various mission statements, appraisal and auditing mechanisms, strategic plans, marketing strategies, public relations, and so on. Academics in the universities will feel the pressures to become more accountable and transparent, both professionally and managerially, in terms of their research and publication outputs, consultancies, evaluations of their teaching performances, involvements in various community and voluntary services, with characteristics such as performance-based merit systems. All of these are important factors in the new paradigm of the governance model.

Fourth, the higher education sectors in these two places are now facing much more pressures and competitions from their counterparts in the global marketplace of higher education. Hence, different higher education stakeholders, including governments, higher educational institutions, academic professionals, student bodies, and so on, all are now expected to respond to those changing demands and circumstances proactively and strategically, in order to increase their competitiveness and to be at the cutting edge. In this way, some kind of a stratification of higher education has slowly evolved, such that institutions of lesser status are trying hard to rise up in the international league tables, while long-standing institutions are now also trying hard to further demonstrate their overall competitiveness by exhibiting the so-called world-class attributes in order to win in this game of global competition.

Notes

1. Twinning is a collaborative approach that enables peer-to-peer exchange of knowledge and experience between two partners. In a twinning partnership, one partner seeks to improve its performance (recipient twin) and service delivery by pairing itself with a stronger partner (mentor twin) in order to learn from it. Twinning partnerships typically focus on selective performance areas in which the recipient twin aims to improve, and the mentor twin can provide the necessary knowledge for this kind of collaboration. Twinning arrangements follow a set of key principles to ensure that the partnership is mutually beneficial and results in tangible improvements of service delivery. For a four-year degree twinning program, it will usually be run on the basis of either a 2+2 mode, or a 3+1 mode.
2. Namely, the University of Hong Kong, the Chinese University of Hong Kong, the Hong Kong University of Science and Technology, the City University of Hong Kong, the Hong Kong Polytechnic University, the Hong Kong Baptist University, the Hong Kong Lingnan University, and the Hong Kong Institute of Education.
3. According to the latest figures of the *Times Higher Education* (*THE*) World Ranking of Universities in 2010, two of the local higher education institutions (University of Hong Kong-21 and Hong Kong University of Science and Technology-41) were among the world's top 50, while another two (Hong Kong Baptist University-111 and Polytechnic University of Hong Kong-149) were among the world's top 200 (*THE* 2010).
4. The original acronym for the Chinese Education Bureau is EDB. However, because the Singapore Economic Development Board also uses EDB as its acronym, the authors have slightly altered both acronyms in this chapter solely to avoid confusion. Thus, the Chinese Education Bureau acronym is C-EDB and the Singapore Economic Development Board is S-EDB.

References

Apple, Michael W. 2000. "Between Neoliberalism and Neoconservatism: Education and Conservatism in a Global Context." In *Globalization and Education: Critical Perspective*, ed. Nicholas C. Burbules and Carlos Alberto Torres. New York: Routledge.

Chan, David K. K. 2007a. "Global Agenda, Local Response: Changing Education Governance in Hong Kong's Higher Education." *Globalization, Societies and Education* 5 (1): 109-124.

Chan, David K. K. 2007b. "The Impact of Globalization on the Educational Developments in China: Policy and Challenges." In *Challenges and Policy Programmes of China's New Leadership*, ed. Joseph Y. S. Cheng. Hong Kong: City University of Hong Kong Press.

Chan, David K. K. 2009. "A Comparative Study on the Corporatization of Higher Education in Hong Kong and Singapore." *Social Transformations in Chinese Societies* 5: 191-224.

Chan, David, and Will Lo. 2007. "Running Universities as Enterprises: University Governance Changes in Hong Kong." *Asia Pacific Journal of Education* 27 (3): 305-322.

Chan, David, and Will Lo. 2008. "University Restructuring in East Asia: Trends, Challenges and Prospects." *Policy Futures in Education* 6 (5): 641-651.

Chan, David, and Ka Ho Mok. 2001. "Educational Reforms and Coping Strategies under the Tidal Wave of Marketization: A Comparative Study of Hong Kong and the Mainland." *Comparative Education* 37 (1): 21-41.

Chan, David, and Pak T. Ng. 2008a. "Similar Agendas, Diverse Strategies: The Quest for a Regional Hub of Higher Education in Hong Kong and Singapore." *Higher Education Policy* 21 (4): 487-503.

Chan, David, and Pak T. Ng. 2008b. "Developing Transnational Higher Education: Comparing the Approaches of Hong Kong and Singapore." *International Journal of Education Reform* 17 (3): 291-307.

Chinese Education Bureau (C-EDB). 2010a. *Other Information: Post-secondary Education, 2009*. Hong Kong: Education Bureau of the Government of the HKSAR. Available online at: http://www.edb.gov.hk.

C-EDB. 2010b. *Non-local Programs Statistical Information*. Hong Kong: Education Bureau of the Government of the HKSAR. Available online at: http://www.edb.gov.hk.

Coleman, James S. 1990. *Foundations of Social Theory*. Cambridge, MA: Harvard University Press.

De Vita, Glauco, and Peter Case. 2003. "Rethinking the Internationalization Agenda in UK Higher Education." *Journal of Further and Higher Education* 27 (4): 383-398.

De Meyer, Arnoud, Patrick T. Harker, and Gabriel Hawawini. 2004. "The Globalization of Business Education." In *The INSEAD-Wharton Alliance on Globalizing: Strategies for Building Successful Global Businesses*, ed. Hubert Gatignon, John R. Kimberly, and Robert E. Gunther. Cambridge: Cambridge University Press.

Denman, Brian D. 2002. "Globalisation and Its Impact on International University Cooperation." *Globalization* 2 (1): n.p. Available online at: http://globalization.icaap.org.

Gamage, David T., and J. Suwarnabroma. 2006. "Quality Assurance in the Context of Globalization and Its Impact on Higher Education." In

Globalization: Educational Research, Change and Reform, ed. Nicholas S. K. Pang. Hong Kong: Chinese University Press.

Gouri, Geeta, T. L. Shankar, Y. Venugopal Reddy, and Khalid Shams. 1991. "Imperatives and Perspectives." In *Privatisation and Public Enterprise: The Asian-Pacific Experience*, ed. Geeta Gouri. Oxford; New Delhi: Asian and Pacific Development Centre; Institute of Public Enterprise.

Hong Kong Institute of Education (HKIEd). 2009. *A Technical Research Report on The Development of Hong Kong as a Regional Education Hub*. Hong Kong: HKIEd.

Hong Kong Council for Accreditation of Academic and Vocational Qualifications (HKCAAVQ). 2010. *Assessment of Non-local Courses: Code of Practice for Non-local Courses Recommended by the HKCAAVQ*. Hong Kong: HKCAAVQ. Available online at: http://www.hkcaa.edu.hk.

Hong Kong Government. 2010. *Signing Ceremony of Framework Agreement on Hong Kong/Guangdong Co-operation held in Beijing, Press Release April 7, 2010*. Hong Kong: Government of the HKSAR. Available online at: http://www.gov.hk/en/residents/

Hong Kong Government Task Force on Economic Challenges. 2009. *Recommendations from the Task Force on Economic Challenges for Promoting the Development of the Six Economic Areas*. Hong Kong: Government of the HKSAR. Available online at: http://www.fso.gov.hk.

Hong Kong Higher Education. 2007. *Study HK*. Hong Kong: Hong Kong Higher Education. Available online at: http://studyinhongkong.edu.hk.

Huang, Futao. 2006. "Transnational Higher Education in Mainland China: A Focus on Foreign Degree-Conferring Programs." In *Transnational Higher Education in Asia and the Pacific Region: RIHE International Publication Series No. 10*, ed. Futao Huang. Hiroshima: Research Institute for Higher Education, Hiroshima University.

Jayasuriya, Kanishka. 2005. "Capacity beyond the Boundary: New Regulatory State, Fragmentation and Relational Capacity." In *Challenges to State Policy Capacity: Global Trends and Comparative Perspectives*, ed. Martin Painter and Jon Pierre. New York: Palgrave Macmillan.

Knight, Jane. 2002. "Trade Talk: An Analysis of the Impact of Trade Liberalization and the General Agreement on Trade in Services on Higher Education." *Journal of Studies in International Education* 6 (3): 209-229.

Knight, Jane. 2003. "Updated Internationalization Definition." *The Boston Centre for International Higher Education* 33 (Fall): 2-3. Available online at: http://www.bc.edu.

Knight, Jane. 2004. "Internationalism Remodeled: Definition, Approaches and Rationales." *Journal of Studies in International Education* 8 (1): 5-31.

Knight, Jane. 2005. "Cross-Border Education: Not Just Students on the Move." *International Higher Education: The Boston College Center for International Higher Education* 41 (Fall): 2-3. Available online at: http://www.bc.edu.

Knight, Jane. 2006a. *Higher Education Crossing Borders: A Guide to the Implications of the General Agreement on Trade in Services (GATS) for Cross-border Education*. Paris: UNESCO. Available online at: http://unesdoc.unesco.org.

Knight, Jane. 2006b. "Internationalization: Concepts, Complexities and Challenges." In *International Handbook of Higher Education, Part One: Global Themes and Contemporary Challenges,* ed. James J. F. Forest and Philip G. Altbach. Dordrecht, The Netherlands: Springer.

Knight, Jane, and Hans de Wit. 1995. "Strategies for Internationalisation of Higher Education: Historical and Conceptual Perspectives." In *Strategies for International Higher Education,* ed. Hans de Wit. Amsterdam: European Association for International Education Publications.

Lee, Michael H., and Saravanan Gopinathan. 2007. "University Restructuring in Singapore: Amazing! Or a Maze?" *Journal of Comparative Asian Development* 6 (1): 107-141.

Leong, John Chi-yan, and W.S. Wong. 2004. "The Accreditation and Quality Assurance of Sub-degree/Degree Qualifications in the Establishment of a Hong Kong Qualifications Framework: Local, Regional and Transnational Implications." *Quality in Higher Education* 10 (1): 43-49.

Lewis-Beck, Michael S., Alan Bryman, and Tim Futing Liao, eds. 2004. *Sage Encyclopedia of Social Science Research Methods.* Thousand Oaks, CA: Sage.

Leydsdorrff, Loet and Henry Etzkowitz. 2001. "The Transformation of University-Industry-Government Relations." *Electronic Journal of Sociology* 5 (4): 1-17.

Lo, Chun H., and Hui H. Tai. 2003. "Centralization and Decentralization in Higher Education: A Comparative Study of Hong Kong and Taiwan." In *Centralization and Decentralization: Educational Reforms and Changing Governance in Chinese Societies,* ed. Ka Ho Mok. Hong Kong: Comparative Education Research Centre, University of Hong Kong and Kluwer Academic Publishers.

McBurnie, Grant, and Christopher Ziguras. 2001. "The Regulation of Transnational Higher Education in Southeast Asia: Case Studies of Hong Kong, Malaysia and Australia." *Higher Education* 42 (1): 85-105.

Meyer, Heinz-Dieter, and William Lowe Boyd, eds. 2001. *Education Between States, Markets and Civil Society: Comparative Perspectives.* New Jersey: Lawrence Erlbaum Associates.

Mok, Ka Ho. 2003a. "Similar Trends, Diverse Agendas: Higher Education Reforms in East Asia." *Globalization, Societies & Education* 1 (2): 201-221.

Mok, Ka Ho. 2003b. "Globalization and Higher Education Restructuring in Hong Kong, Taiwan and Mainland China." *Higher Education Research and Development* 22 (2): 117-129.

Mok, Ka Ho. 2005. *Education Reform and Education Policy in East Asia.* London: Routledge Curzon.

Mok, Ka Ho. 2007. "Questing for Internationalization of Universities in Asia: Critical Reflections." *Journal of Studies in International Education* 11 (3-4): 433-454.

Mok, Ka Ho, and David Chan, eds. 2001. *Globalization and Education: The Quest for Quality Education in Hong Kong.* Hong Kong: Hong Kong University Press.

Mok, Ka Ho, and Jason Tan. 2004. Globalization and Marketization in Education: A Comparative Analysis of Hong Kong and Singapore. Cheltenham: Edward Elgar.

Mok, Ka Ho, and Anthony R. Welch, eds. 2003. *Globalization and Educational Re-structuring in the Asia Pacific Region*. Basingstoke: Palgrave Macmillan.

Morgan, David L. 1997. *Focus Groups as Qualitative Research*. 2nd ed. Newbury Park, CA: Sage.

Ng, Pak T. 2007. "Quality Assurance in the Singapore Education System in an Era of Diversity and Innovation." *Educational Research for Policy and Practice* 6 (3): 235-247.

Oba, Jun. 2004. "Incorporation of National Universities in Japan: Reform towards the Enhancement of Autonomy in Search of Excellence." COE Publication Series 11, Research Institute for Higher Education, Hiroshima University, Hiroshima.

Olds, Kris. 2007. "Global Assemblage: Singapore, Foreign Universities, and the Construction of a 'Global Education Hub'." *World Development* 35 (6): 959-975.

Polytechnic University of Hong Kong (PolyU). 2009. "PolyU and RVC Jointly Launch HK's First-ever Veterinary Nursing Degree." Press Release, September 16, 2009. Available online at: http://www.polyu.edu.hk.

Postiglione, Gerard A. 2007. "Expect Some Surprises in Second Survey of Hong Kong Academics." *South China Morning Post*, May 12, 2007, 4.

Punch, Keith F. 2005. *Introduction to Social Research: Quantitative and Qualitative Approaches*. 2nd ed. London: Sage.

Sanderson, Gavin. 2002. "International Education Developments in Singapore." *International Education Journal* 3 (2): 85-103.

Shive, Glenn. 2010. "Exporting Higher Education Services: An Engine of Growth for Hong Kong?" *Hong Kong Journal Archives* January 17. Available online at: http://www.hkjournal.org.

Sidhu, Ravinder. 2005. "Building a Global Schoolhouse: International Education in Singapore." *Australian Journal of Education* 49 (1): 46-65.

Singapore Education. 2010. *An Exciting City at The Heart of Asia*. Singapore: Government of Singapore. Available online at: http://www.singaporeedu.gov.sg.

Singapore Economic Development Board (S-EDB). 2009. *Industry Background*. Singapore: S-EDB. Available online at: http://www.edb.gov.sg.

Singapore Ministry of Education (MOE). 2003. "Restructuring of Singapore's University Sector," MOE Singapore Press Release May 28, 2003. Singapore: Singapore MOE. Available online at: http://www.moe.gov.sg.

Singapore MOE. 2008. "Enhancing Regulation of the Private Education Sector," Press Release March 4, 2008. Singapore: Singapore MOE. Available online at: http://www.moe.gov.sg.

Singapore MOE. 2009. "Singapore Institute of Technology Partners Five Overseas Universities to Offer Degree Programmes," MOE Singapore Press Release March 9, 2009. Singapore: Singapore MOE. Available online at: http://www.moe.gov.sg.

Singapore Ministry of Trade and Industry (MTI). 2002. *Developing Singapore's Education Industry*. Singapore: MTI. Available online at: http://www.mti.gov.sg.

Singapore Tourism Board (STB). 2008. *Singapore Tourism Board Annual Report on Tourism Statistics 2008*. Singapore: Government of

Singapore. Available online at: https://www.stbtrc.com.sg/images/links/X1Annual_Report_On_Tourism_Statistics_2008v3.pdf.
Sing Tao Daily. 2010a. "The University of Hong Kong Will Build A Hundred Hectares of Campus in Shenzhen." *Sing Tao Daily*, February 24, 2010, A1.
Sing Tao Daily. 2010b. "The Hong Kong University of Science and Technology Will Use Fund of 2 Billions to Build Research Institute at Nansha." *Sing Tao Daily*, April 29, 2010, F1.
Times Higher Education (THE). 2010. "World University Rankings, 2010." London: *THE*. Available online at: http://www.timeshighereducation.co.uk.
Tsang, Donald Y.K. 2009. *The 2009 Policy Address: Breaking New Ground Together*. Hong Kong: Information Services Department (ISD), the Hong Kong Special Administrative Region Government of the People's Republic of China. Available online at: http://www.policyaddress.gov.hk.
Tung, Chee H. 2000. *The 2000 Policy Address: Serving the Community, Sharing Common Goals*. Hong Kong: Information Services Department (ISD), the Hong Kong Special Administrative Region Government of the People's Republic of China. Available online at: http://www.policyaddress.gov.hk.
University Grants Committee (UGC). 2004a. *Hong Kong Higher Education: To Make a Difference, To Move with the Times*. Hong Kong: Government of the HKSAR. Available online at: http://www.ugc.edu.hk.
UGC. 2004b. *Hong Kong Higher Education Integration Matters: A Report of the Institutional Integration Working Party of the University Grants Committee*. Hong Kong: Government of the HKSAR. Available online at: http://www.ugc.edu.hk.
UGC. 2009. Statistics: *Non-academic Information of First-year Student Intakes of UGC-funded Full-time Sub-degree and Undergraduate Programmes*. Hong Kong: Government of the HKSAR. Available online at: http://www.ugc.edu.hk.
UNESCO. 2005. *Guidelines for Quality Provision in Cross-border Higher Education*. Paris: UNESCO.
Urry, John. 1998. "Contemporary Transformation of Time and Space." In *The Globalization of Higher Education*, ed. Peter Scott. Buckingham: Open University Press and Society for Research into Higher Education.
World Bank. 1995. *Higher Education: The Lessons of Experience*. Washington, DC: World Bank.
Yang, Rui. 2006. "Transnational Higher Education in Hong Kong: An Analysis." In *Transnational Higher Education in Asia and the Pacific Region*, ed. Futao Huang. Hiroshima: Research Institute for Higher Education, Hiroshima University.
Yonezawa, Akiyoshi. 1999. "Strategies for the Emerging Global Higher Education Market in East Asia: A Comparative Study of Singapore, Malaysia and Japan." *Globalisation, Societies and Education* 5 (1): 125-136.
Yonezawa, Akiyoshi. 2007. "Japanese Flagship Universities at Crossroads." *Higher Education* 54 (4): 483-499.

Chapter 2

Concepts, Contributions, and Challenges of the Contemporary University Community in Taiwan

Amy Roberts and Gregory S. Ching

The East Asia region—Mainland China, Taiwan, Hong Kong, Macau, Japan, Korea, and Singapore—is recognized for its cultural distinctiveness from the Euro-American sphere. Yet East Asia is linked to all world regions through its leading universities as producers, protectors, and inculcators of ideas and knowledge across both national and international boundaries (Mohrman 2003). Historically universities worldwide have been influenced by global trends while operating within broader international communities of academic institutions, scholars, and research. The impact of global events, however, on the structure and day-to-day functions of contemporary university communities is unique. In the contemporary era the growing impact of globalization is blended with the complexity of managing and governing universities. In East Asia, as well as other world regions, institutions of higher education are responding via a shift toward the image of the world-class university (Marginson 2000; Anderseck 2004). Philip G. Altbach argues that the paradox of the world-class university is that "everyone wants one, no one knows what it is, and no one knows how to get one" (2004, 1). As a concept, "world-class" calls attention to standards and improvement, the role of universities on the world stage, and the status of tertiary level institutions within international systems of higher education (Burbules and Torres 2000; Astiz et al. 2002; Breton and Lambert 2004).

In Taiwan, the transformation toward world-class status is led by the Ministry of Education (MOE) and the National Science Council program—"Promoting Academic Excellence of Universities." The aim is to improve infrastructure of leading universities and invigorate scholarly research (Taiwan MOE 2000). Recent initiatives at the leading National Cheng-Chi University (NCCU) in Taipei, Taiwan showcase these efforts; mindful of the importance of its international stature, the NCCU launched several initiatives in recent years to scaffold its status as a world-class institution. The rhetoric of the NCCU president exemplifies the institutional mission and strategic plans dedicated to development and sustainment of internationalization:

> We aim to serve as leaders in innovation and explore the new fields of knowledge in response to the changing times, in order to become the leading academic institution in Taiwan, Asia and even the world. We will develop our unique features in teaching, researching, and service, on campus and in internationalization. (Roberts et al. 2010, 151)

The president's vision is actualized through a range of NCCU international projects with more than 150 universities and research institutes. Opportunities for faculty exchanges and recruitment of international students are ongoing via a wide range of mutual cooperation agreements with institutions in Europe, the United States, Canada, Australia, New Zealand, Japan, India, South Africa, Korea, China, and Latin America. The population of foreign professors and international students is increasing across campus, as well as the offering of lectures from international speakers open to the university and local community on a weekly basis (ibid.).

Further processes of internationalization include commitment to English as the language of instruction (as opposed to Chinese Mandarin) for target programs and classes and encouragement of publication venues in international Social Science Citation Index (SSCI) and Science Citation Index (SCI) indexed journals. These initiatives transform the work of NCCU professors (Taiwan citizens) in the areas of teaching, research, and publication. Some scholars speculate that the professorate of East Asian institutions are committed to contemporary trends in order to raise the quality of higher education; others argue that academics are victims of an inescapable Western hegemony encapsulated in contemporary processes of globalization and internationalization (Mohrman 2003; Altbach 2006).

In response, the authors detail a mixed methods study profiling the transformation of the NCCU toward the status of being a world-class institution. The principal aim is to examine the concepts, contributions, and challenges of NCCU professors engaged in teaching and publishing within an institution striving for recognition as a world-class university. The expanding international student body, as a newly defined group adjusting to the academic and social patterns of the NCCU campus, is positioned as an overlapping focus of investigation. Key to this chapter, therefore, is attention to the events that reshape the work of professors—competition to establish publication records in leading international journals along with major modifications in pedagogy to amalgamate English-medium instruction and the diversities of increasing numbers of international students.

Features of the World-Class University

Examination of globalization and internationalization as distinct processes contributes to the overarching discourse on contemporary trends of higher education. The globalization of higher education is defined and shaped by the interconnectivity of world affairs specific to the integrated world economy, information and communications technology, the international knowledge network, the role of the English language, and other pressing forces beyond the control of academic institutions (Altbach and Knight 2007). Scholars agree that processes of globalization are unalterable, while those of internationalization remain fluid and changeable (Mok 2006). Internationalization is transparent through a variety of policies and programs that universities and governments implement in response to globalization.

Nearly all East Asian nations have deemed internationalization of higher education as paramount to education reform (Mok and James 2005). In Singapore, curricula have been redesigned with an emphasis on creative and critical thinking to offer a broad-based cross-disciplinary university education. In comparison, leading Hong Kong universities have introduced problem-based learning as a central thread of curriculum. Both systems introduced innovative teaching and assessment along with increased attention to the importance of leadership, community service and other nonacademic elements of student preparation (Mok and Tan 2004).

Increased attention to internationalization is also transparent on the NCCU campus through newly established degree programs including the: International Masters of Business Administration, International Masters Program in Taiwan Studies, International Masters Program in China Studies, International Masters Program in International Communication Studies, and English Taught Program. These programs are unique given that the language of instruction is English. Of the enrolled students and faculty, 50 percent are Taiwan citizens, while the remaining members represent a diverse mix of individuals from more than 20 countries. Beyond these programs is a broad array of more than 100 undergraduate and graduate English medium courses offered across campus annually.

Scholars suggest that the aura of the world-class university is a topic popularized worldwide within academic communities in response to the impact of globalization and internationalization. Henry M. Levin et al. (2006) reviewed key speeches and publications developed with reference to the label "world-class university." They evaluated criteria used in ranking universities internationally and provided comparative analysis of the determinants and outcomes of the world ranking system. World-class status according to these researchers is positional and subjective due to the lack of an absolute set of performance criteria and measures. While the term "world-class" is widely used within academic institutions, it has not been fully defined within discourses of theoretical or empirically based research.

The quest for world-class status is closely associated with the emerging global model (EGM) of the twenty-first century top stratum of research universities worldwide (Mohrman et al. 2007). The ethos of the EGM is aligned with the notion of the "super research university," defined as the leading edge of higher education in terms of international stature and scholarly output (Baker 2007). Seven characteristics developed by the New Century Scholars group denote the EGM:

1. Research intensive with the use of scientific methods in disciplines beyond the sciences.
2. Encourage faculty to assume new roles, shifting from traditional independent patterns of inquiry to members of team-oriented, cross-disciplinary, and international partnerships, with research focused on real-world problems.
3. Diversify financial base with funding from corporations and private donors, competitive grants for technology innovation, and creation of for-profit businesses as spin-offs of research enterprise.
4. Create innovative relationships with governments and corporations to advance economic development and to produce knowledge for the social good.
5. Adopt worldwide recruitment strategies for students, faculty, and administrators.
6. Require greater internal complexity directed toward research, such as interdisciplinary centers, integration of research elements in student training programs, and greater technological infrastructure for discovery.

7. Participate with international NGOs and multi-governmental organizations in support of collaborative research, student and faculty mobility, and validation of international stature. (Mohrman et al. 2007, 6)

Nearly all characteristics listed above are rooted in the United States education system, yet the EGM is embraced throughout the world (Altbach and Balán 2007; Mohrman et al. 2007). In response, East Asian academics report a lack of confidence in ability to meet the standards of leading international journals (Flowerdew 2001). In a seminal study, Rui Yang et al. (2007) emphasized that academics in China had negative reactions to the evaluation, performance, and assessment criteria imposed by and aligned with the EGM. Academics in Hong Kong universities, moreover, reported that the newly established weight attached to international publication venues created pressure to prioritize research and scholarly writing publication within the Institute for Scientific Information (ISI) database. The ISI has been criticized for a bias toward English language journals and, in particular, to those published in the United States.

Trends and Patterns of International Students

Internationalization of higher education through the movement of students from one country to another for the purposes of study has steadily increased since the mid-1990s. Statistics show that 2.9 million students studied abroad in 2006, compared to 1.3 million in 1995, and 0.6 million in 1975 (OECD 2000). Scholars estimate that the number of international students worldwide will expand to 7.2 million by the year 2025.

The examination of international student mobility trends and patterns is well documented within discourses defined by the push-pull framework (Fry 1984; Agarwal and Winkler 1985; Sirowy and Inkeles 1985; Cummings 1993; Altbach 1997). Researchers define "push factors" as conditions in home nations that engender interest in university education beyond national borders. Likewise, "pull factors" are host nation attributes that attract international students and influence their decision to study at particular institutions (Mazzarol 1998). As noted by a number of researchers, international students generally progress through levels of decision making that are initiated with a commitment to study internationally and end with the selection of a host institution.

Mary McMahon (1992) used a push-pull model to quantify mobility patterns of international students from 18 developing countries. Findings indicated that student flow was dependent on the level of economic wealth, the degree of involvement of the destination country in the world economy, and priority placed on education by home nation governments (McMahon 1992). McMahon noted a negative correlation between economic prosperity in home countries and the total number of students studying internationally. Significant pull factors included the size of host nation economies and associated political interests as evidenced by foreign assistance, transnational cultural links, and availability of international student scholarships.

Tim Mazzarol (1998) surmised that six key pull factors influence students' selection of host nations and institutions. The overall level of knowledge, access to information, and awareness of the destination nation within students' home country represented a critical pull factor. The reputation of host institutions for quality as well as the recognition of their degrees in students' home nations were significant attributes of this factor. The number of personal recommendations students received from parents, relatives, and friends were also influential (Garrod and Davis 1999). Additional factors included students' financial situation, perceptions about the host nation climate, the geographic and longitudinal proximity between home and host nations, and social links defined as family or friends residing in the destination country.

Andrew Garrod and Jay Davis (1999) refute generalizations regarding international students as a homogeneous group who share common experiences in host nations. Utilizing the intersections of students' educational experiences, Garrod and Davis conducted case study research to examine the international student experience. They emphasized the blending of diverse prior international student foundations with expectations for study in the global arena as a framework to evaluate the potential for growth manifested in contrasting differences of daily life and academic communities. All and all, they surmised that the international student experience offers potential for personal and professional growth to renegotiate identity and develop innovative habits of mind.

Overarching limitations of the push-pull research are noted in terms of the exclusion of international student samples from developed countries pursuing degrees in either developing or developed nations. The design of the push-pull framework categorizes national identities of international students as a reference for commonality, thus positioning international students as a homogenized group rather than as clusters of individuals with significant differences between and within nationalities. All in all the utility of the push-pull framework to examine complexities of the international student experience is limited.

Methods

Research Setting and Design

The research team is made up of authors Amy Roberts and Gregory S. Ching. The research evolved while Roberts completed a Fulbright award to lecture and conduct research at the NCCU in Taipei, Taiwan during the academic year 2007-2008. Ching worked for the NCCU Department of Education and was completing a dissertation in education policy studies examining factors affecting the internationalization of Taiwan's higher education system. The authors' shared a commitment to learning about the impact of globalization and internationalization within the university community. During the academic year a research assistant, Shirly Wang, participated in debriefing conversations with Roberts and Ching; she offered valuable additional insight and furthered reflection on the research process. Wang was also involved in transcription of interviews.

At the time of the study, the NCCU community included 15,255 students, 616 full-time professors, 70 researchers, and more than 200 part-time lecturers. Founded in 1927, the NCCU is recognized as a premier Taiwan university in the social sciences and humanities. The NCCU has a strong legacy of nurturing prime ministers, government officials, and an extensive network of alumni in various business fields.

In fall 2007 and spring 2008 the authors co-taught an NCCU doctoral course with a research component exploring the entity of higher education, as both mediators and reactors to contemporary processes of globalization. Nearly all students in the course were from various Asian nations other than Taiwan. As a group of researchers who were outsiders—guests in Taiwan and at the NCCU—the course research component unfolded as a tremendously challenging and engaging exercise consisting of a variety of individual and small group research projects. The methodological challenges of the projects resonated with innovative forms of comparative and international research bound by the importance of collaboration and partnership between insiders and outsiders; sensitivity to local, social constructions of reality; and emphasis on strategies that facilitated the strengthening of research capacity.

The research was designed as a mixed method study. Research methods from both qualitative and quantitative paradigms were systematically combined (Johnson and Christensen 2008) in an attempt to enhance the strength of data collection and to advance insights surrounding the complexities and patterns of the NCCU as an institution striving for world-class status. The rationale for mixing was to capture trends representing the affects of globalization and internationalization. When used in combination, quantitative and qualitative methods complemented each other and allowed for a more complete analysis (ibid.). Initial research questions included:

1. What are the views, strategies, and practices that professor participants adopt in response to teaching and publishing in an institution striving for world-class status?
2. What are the benefits and dilemmas associated with the NCCU international student population in terms of institutional commitments for the expansion of internationalization?
3. What are the interpretations of all participants in regard to the issues and dilemmas surrounding the NCCU international student experience?

Procedures for both qualitative and quantitative data collection and analyses were completed in sequential phases by means of a convenience sampling technique (Stewart et al. 2007).

Phase One

During the months of February, March, and April 2008 one-to-one voice-recorded interviews were conducted with 30 NCCU professors who held positions from assistant to full rank as well as deans, heads of departments, and center directors. Participants ranged in age from 36 to 65 years and were spread across faculties of the social sciences and the humanities. All participants had at least one foreign degree, most commonly a PhD from the United Kingdom, North America, Japan, Germany, or Australia. Participants were identified through snowball sampling emanating from professional and social network contacts during the 2007-2008 academic year.

Phase Two

In May 2009, focus group interviews were conducted on five consecutive days with NCCU international students. Development of the interview guide followed principles outlined by David Stewart et al. (2007) as the funnel approach; six unstructured, open-ended questions ranged from general to specific as a strategy to engage participants. We summarized key themes, reflections, and insights in a field log following each session. Minor adjustments were made for subsequent interviews based on the review of field logs. We then independently reviewed field logs and focus group recordings to generate a list of key themes. Biweekly two-hour researcher sessions were dedicated to identifying trends and patterns that reappeared within either a single or multiple focus group interviews.

Interview procedures included an introduction to the group discussion, overview of the topic, ground rules, and the initial question. All interviews were videotaped and voice recorded. A standardized written announcement was posted throughout the NCCU Mandarin Studies building and public student areas one week prior to scheduled focus group interviews. The announcement briefly introduced the study, included researchers' contact information, along with the dates, times, and locations of focus group interviews. Participation was voluntary. Each focus group included 6-12 students along with one bilingual Chinese-English interviewer and assistant. International student participants included 33 students ranging in age from 18 to 36; they represented 17 nations (Belgium, Brazil, Chile, France, Hungary, Indonesia, Iraq, Jordan, Kiribati, Korea, Mexico, Mongolia, Nicaragua, Philippines, Russia, Ukraine, and the United States). Interviews were conducted in English; participants responded using both English and Chinese.

Lawrence Stenhouse's (1988) categorization style of case data was used to document and analyze Phase One interviews and Phase Two focus group interviews. Case records were established for each professor participant interview and for each focus group session. Organization by case record was viewed as a strategy to keep data intact, to illuminate meaning and insights in relation to case-by-case processes, and to gleam themes and sub-categories across all cases under study. This approach limited the loss of potential contributions of each case (ibid.). Primary themes were determined after all data were transcribed as case records. Topics and emerging themes were recorded and a master list was generated. All participants were invited to complete member checks of the respective case records.

Phase Three

A survey questionnaire was developed based on key themes generated from analysis of focus group interviews and review of the push-pull model literature. A total of 45 participants representing 22 countries completed the questionnaire. English was the predominant first language of participants (27 percent), followed by Spanish (11 percent), and German (9 percent). Participants' second languages included English (44 percent), Mandarin Chinese (26 percent), and French (10 percent). Just over half of the sample (51 percent) consisted of international students studying abroad for the first time. Approximately one-third of participants were enrolled in NCCU degree programs; all others were full-time students in the NCCU Mandarin Studies program.

The questionnaire was written in English and required approximately 10-20 minutes for completion. A pilot test was administered to a small sample and minor revisions were made. The survey questionnaire was administered on a voluntary basis in June 2009 in a public area of the Mandarin Studies building during the student lunch hour. Data gathered from the survey questionnaire were encoded and analyzed using the Statistics Package for Social Science (SPSS) version 15. Internal consistency using Lee J. Cronbach's (1951) coefficient alpha (Cronbach's alpha) was computed at 0.89, suggesting a high level (Cronbach 1951; Nunnally and Bemstein 1994). Descriptive analysis included the mean, standard deviation (SD) and cross-tabulation of participants' multiple responses for identified questions.

NCCU International Students: An Overview

On a scale of 1 to 5, international student participants rated an overall satisfaction at 4.07, indicating a high level of contentment with the decision to study at the NCCU. International student participants identified the highly recognized NCCU Mandarin language program as a top pull factor. The significance of this factor is expected given that nearly all institutions of higher education receiving international students offer intensive courses in the primary host nation languages (Cummings 1993). Memorizing Chinese characters was ranked as the most challenging aspect of study:

> When I first got to Taiwan, it wasn't just getting used to a new culture, a new way to take out the trash, or figuring out how to navigate around Taipei, it went all the way to figuring out how to study this new language that had absolutely no similarities to mine except the Roman alphabet used in pinyin. In the beginning, I studied how I did in the States—with groups of people, talking about the class, going over notes. This didn't work because I was failing. I soon realized that Chinese required 100 percent dedication. I had to memorize the language instead of relying on the context to help me interpret. In place of interpretation I had to know exactly what I was hearing and speaking in order to be successful and progress in the Mandarin Studies Program. Most of my friends had a similar wakeup call.

As newcomers, participants arrived at NCCU with an established system for coping, studying, and socializing, yet often their strategies did not fit or conform to the standards of local cultures and the NCCU academic community. Many participants reported the need to make tremendous adjustments relative to study habits, differences in education systems, disparity in the philosophy and purpose of education, learning styles, and contrasting education values.

Nevertheless, international student participants reported that living and studying in Taiwan added a rewarding dimension to their academic programs and a valuable investment in future careers:

> Studying in Taiwan not only reinforced my intellectual capacity but through my Chinese studies I was given the opportunity to understand Chinese culture and the thought process of this area of the world. I am a person who wants to be connected to the world and able to truly identify with someone from another culture. This was an invaluable learning and growing experience and one that I hold as a landmark of my development as a capable and independent person in a globalizing world.

Additional factors identified as rewarding included: a sense of fulfillment and self-confidence initiated from the experience of living and studying at the NCCU, making new friends (17 percent); experiencing a new culture (12 percent); becoming a global citizen (11 percent); and becoming more mature (9 percent).

At the time of the study, 91 percent of international student participants received scholarships either through the Taiwan Scholarship Program (jointly funded by the Taiwan MOE, the Ministry of Foreign Affairs, the Nation Science Council, and the Ministry of Economic Affairs) or the Taiwan MOE Mandarin Enrichment Scholarship Program (funded by the Taiwan MOE). Of the international student participants, 27 percent rated the awards as critical to their decision to study in Taiwan. At first glance the Taiwan government scholarships appear as a significant pull factor that positively impacts internationalization in terms of expanding the NCCU international student population. Yet international student participants' rationale for dependence on scholarships was not directly linked to financial need in order to study at the NCCU. Approximately 87 percent of scholarship recipients identified themselves as either middle or upper socioeconomic status, and 30 percent classified their parents as professionals or self-employed business entrepreneurs.

The Taiwan scholarships highlight sharp contrasts in living standards between international students and Taiwan citizens. Newly graduated Taiwan college students earn beginning monthly salaries ranging from NT$26,000 to NT$28,000 (US$775-US$825) (Li 2008). In comparison the scholarships provide financial support from one to four years of study and range from NT$25,000 (US$800) monthly for undergraduate students to NT$30,000 (US$900) monthly for graduate students. Of international student participants, 32 percent reported that the scholarships were not sufficient for living expenses in Taiwan and 63 percent reported that the awards provided just enough in terms of financial support (ibid.).

Expanding international student enrollments for many newly emerging competitor nations represent the premier source for internationalization. In alignment with this trend, the Taiwan government and NCCU university policy makers identified the immersion of the increasing international student population in the local student body as a pivotal strategy for internationalization (Mok and Tan 2004; Lo and Weng 2005). The concept of immersion highlights the NCCU administrators' efforts to create and sustain a deep level of engagement between Taiwan and international students. Their efforts appear viable given that international student participants reported that traveling to, living, and studying in Taiwan at the NCCU set precedence for positive social and cultural encounters:

> I want to be part of an interconnected world; studying at the NCCU helped me realize that other parts of the world are real and that I am a part of them. Being here has helped me see progress in a positive manner and to operate within a system of connectedness. A lot of people in the world, in the United States, are losing consciousness, without this, without empathy and knowledge, we will never progress. I remember being reaffirmed of all this when I returned to my home for a visit. I realized you take the learning back home. I taught calligraphy to an art class in my old elementary school. Wow this really opened the eyes of not only the students but the teachers too.

The gap, however, between the large number of international student participant scholarship recipients and the lack of immersion within the NCCU campus sanctioned organizations is a point of contention. To date, seven NCCU sanctioned organizations on campus provide opportunities for the immersion of NCCU international students with Taiwan students. Strikingly, more than 70 percent of international student participants reported noninvolvement with the NCCU organizations.

Ron Barnett (2000) suggests that academics in contemporary universities, such as the NCCU, are called to critically reflect upon teaching and learning strategies that are most effective to facilitate practice and real-world experiences for all students. That said, attracting and defining the ideal international student candidates at the NCCU and determining standards for their contribution to campus life are more pressing concerns than the total number of international students. Based on this study, ideal incoming international student candidates enter the NCCU as a diverse group bound by positive and confident personal expectations of success; they expect a rewarding and enriching educational, cultural, and social experience in Taiwan. In addition, ideal international students are motivated to contribute meaningfully to the NCCU community, while also utilizing university support networks to address dilemmas associated with social adjustment.

Outreach, pre-counseling, and flexible support services should continue to be provided for all NCCU international students. A mandatory service-learning requirement, moreover, for international student scholarship recipients could serve as a platform to integrate academic and experiential learning involving the entire NCCU community. Rona Flippo (1993) noted that a compassion and concern for others in the immediate community increased for international students who participated in host nation service learning. Maggie Potthoff (2000) examined the effects of service learning on students' knowledge, skill, and attitudinal development as measured by the perceptions of their colleagues and participating community members. Findings suggested that overall participants were perceived to have achieved definite to significant growth associated with an ethic of care, warmth, and a willingness to serve others.

Core Faculty: Linchpin of World-Class Status

As in other world regions, curricular reform at the NCCU has advanced in recent years at an invigorating pace. The landscape of reform has included the rhetoric of student-centered learning, interdisciplinary, Information Technology (IT) literacies, cross-cultural competencies, interactive pedagogies and most importantly English as the language of instruction. In response a core group of professor participants defined their teaching as a global craft to enable new forms of community and knowledge.

Participants who shifted their teaching practices in order to incorporate the use of English were key agents in the internationalization of curricula and pedagogy at the NCCU. Through their day-to-day teaching, participants were mediators of the transitions from the standard Mandarin language medium classroom settings to using English in target programs and courses:

> I'm from Taiwan but I've spent nearly my entire career in Hong Kong with various responsibilities from instructor to dean. At NCCU we have the technology, transportation, infrastructure, and all the other stuff so the president wants to internationalize the university. My course is one example of these efforts. I was recruited to teach in the new masters' program—an international communication course taught in English. For this course we recruit 10 local students and 10 international students. I have students from Russia, Poland, Italy, Germany, Philippines, Malaysia, and Argentina.

> Regardless, it's tough. Some professors just can't deliver lectures in English. I often tell a joke that goes like this: When I teach in Chinese I drink one glass of water and when I teach in English I drink two. The point is that English is not my native language. I have to make a lot of effort.

The transition is noteworthy given that participants use English as a second or even third language. The role and function of English in Taiwan is still debated and questioned by some, yet it has been accepted by the public. English, a foreign language to the Taiwanese linguistic majority, has become an integral part of Taiwan's economic, financial, and technological development. It is also a leading factor in the educational success of students in Taiwan who are learning English from a young age.

The increasing population of NCCU international students in participants' classrooms also represented a shift in the complexities of teaching across nationality and language backgrounds as opposed to classrooms represented by groups of students from Taiwan. A core group of participants were in a position to understand what all students—national as well as international—needed academically, and to support the use of English to participate within the expanding global community:

> Two years ago I began teaching a comparative education course in English with about 24 students. I handed out the syllabus and began my lecture. The following class nobody showed up. I called the students and many said they had a conflict with schedules but finally some of them told me, "hey, this is too heavy for us—we can't do it in English." I learned that I have to use both languages—I am Chinese. I can be a model. So my ambition is to establish a comfortable community that is secure to teach in English. Many students will be intimidated and scared away because they are not used to instruction in English, the first class is critical for them. In the beginning I give options for language and assignments. Once we start building confidence, more English reading is added and I encourage them to respond in English. After the initial barrier English is no longer a big deal. They already have the foundation in English so it's really a psychological barrier to overcome. They have to understand we are learning content—through the use of English—not learning English grammar or reading comprehension. Using English is only a tool.

The use of English as a tool in NCCU classrooms became a reference point for participants committed to processes of internationalization. They identified themselves as curators of learning—encouraging students to collaborate among themselves and with others. For many, success was associated with the ability to transform teaching, to be innovative, to operate as problem solvers, and to lead change. In their roles as professors, participants represented the linchpin of development of the NCCU as a world-class institution.

Many reported that the threads of English in classroom settings and within the campus community created a paradox; for international students, English-medium instruction was an oasis from the struggle of courses instructed in Mandarin. For Taiwan students and some of the participants, the English-medium instruction was a confrontation—pressure to transfer or apply a grammar-based foundation of English to authentic use within the academic community. As such, English presented negative hurdles for those who struggled to bridge the domains of English in the classroom against their language in everyday life. The core faculty, however, intervened by bridging communication, not by privileging English against the use of Mandarin, but by supporting all students to interpret contemporary discourses of academic engagement as central to the university community.

International Mindfulness

Participants engaged in lively debate about the impacts of globalization within the NCCU academic community. Some argued that the forces of globalization inevitably led to a diminished capacity for freedom in research and publication. Indeed, all participants viewed academic freedom as a complex topic, central to the success of NCCU as a research institution. For many participants, the dilemmas surrounding academic freedom were defined by the pressure to write in English in order to publish in leading international journals:

> Some professors are losing [professionally] because they don't write in English. Years ago when faculty returned with degrees from the United States or Canada they weren't encouraged to write in English. But now times have changed. Faculty can still write in Chinese and the university will support the expense of translation to English. But this is problematic because translation does not mean revision. The Chinese manuscript translated to English is locally oriented. The audience won't understand the issues of Taiwan and won't be interested. The context is too different. Professors have to adapt; they have to have an international mind to capture the audience.

The majority of participants were trained in English-speaking countries. As such, they were accustomed to using English for academic purposes. Yet those who published in the leading international journals reported that writing in English required an exhaustive commitment and extra expense to hire professional English editing services. Others responded by ignoring the pressure with exclusive focus on domestic and indigenous issues published in national Mandarin-medium journals. A third group published in both international and national journals.

Many participants suspected that publishing in international journals (i.e., journals published in English) coincided with conformity to paradigms purported by the United States standard of excellence. Participants argued that Eastern and Western academia represented paradoxically opposing discourse communities (Kuhn 1970; Swales 1990). This point is aligned with scholars suggesting that patterns of research in social science and humanities are bound by national structures, policies, and scientific institutions as well as the respective languages and specific empirical worlds (Taylor 1985; Barnes 2001; Johnston and Sidaway 2004). Participants cited a number of contextual (social, political, economic, and cultural) reasons why the publishing practices of social science research was heterogeneous, context dependent, and linked to the Mandarin language. That said, participants reported that the trade-off of publication records in international journals was a disengagement with local-national issues; editors and reviewers of international journals would not recognize or validate their research and manuscripts grounded within East Asian paradigms.

In response to the phenomena of publish or perish in English-medium international journals, participants used a popular catchphrase—"the number of hits in top-tier journals." In some respects this catchphrase symbolized the quest for top-tier publications indexed with the ISI databases. The majority of indexed journals originated from English-speaking countries: 63 percent in the science database, 66 percent in the arts and humanities, and as many as 85 percent in the social sciences. The ISI indices cover more than 16,000 journals, books, and proceedings in the sciences, social sciences, and humanities; journals are categorized within the SCI, the SSCI, or the Arts and Humanities Citation Index (AHCI). The ISI requires all indexed journals to include articles with English-language titles, abstracts, and keywords (OECD 2000).

International publishing has a long-standing and prominent position within research practice (Merton 1973). Yet the increasing pressure for participants to publish in ISI English-medium international journals was viewed as a signpost of the changing demands in the production of knowledge and practices of the NCCU:

> At NCCU we have a team examine research production; in recent years they found that the overall production dropped based on total articles published in the SSCI and SCI. This information was posted and afterwards we were seriously criticized by the media. After that, everybody pursued publications in the SSCI or SCI. I don't think this is a healthy trend. If

everybody publishes in English there's no hope for local journals. It's a complex policy. The National Science Council encourages faculty to publish in local scientific journals but then we are encouraged to publish in English journals. I don't know how to help local journals to become international. If we want to impact local journals we have to publish in Chinese. So that's why some people are not happy. Like others, I'm confused.

The original intent of the ISI was to map publication activities and to manage the rising flow of knowledge. At the NCCU, the ISI has become a marker for the evaluation of the quantity and quality of scholarship. The number of ISI publications is used increasingly to monitor, rank, and govern the rank and status of professors (Yeung 2002).

The Taiwan SSCI was established to counterbalance pressures to publish exclusively in ISI journals; yet special weight is attached to international publication venues for promotion and research evaluation:

> Most people around me are writing in English. There is so much pressure and it's tough. The evaluations are very insulting; they ask how many journal articles I've published in SSCI and I have to answer zero. I haven't started yet so how should I be evaluated as an academic? How can I feel fulfilled as an academic with this pressure? What am I doing here? I chose a different path and now I am nobody, because I don't have articles in the indexed journals. I feel so ashamed when international scholars ask me to collaborate and I have to ask; "Will the article be published in the SSCI database?" How can I ask that? Nowadays my colleagues defer to the SSCI as a benchmark. It's ridiculous and contradicts my academic freedom.

The statement highlights the issues and dilemmas of publishing in an institution striving for world-class status. Participants noted commitment to an intellectual life adaptable to the changing world of higher education. That said, their traditional vision of the central university mission—teaching and research—has been redefined. In the contemporary era, participants confront tremendous pressure that is positioned as a priority to becoming entrepreneurial and proactive in order to compete for publication records in leading international journals.

Implications and Conclusion

This chapter draws attention to major areas of consideration for university professors and administrators engaging with processes of globalization and internationalization inherent to the academic arena. Implications emphasize the vibrant education paradox of the twenty-first century in terms of questioning the genuine improved quality in education and academic well being within institutions embracing affects of globalization and internationalization. The contemporary era offers extraordinary interest and possibilities of higher education side by side with the pressure to shift traditional perspectives and methods of instruction.

NCCU is adaptable to the changing world of higher education as evidenced by the infusion of English-medium courses within a wide variety of programs, shifting pedagogical teaching styles, increasing diversity sparked by rising numbers of international students, and new benchmarks for scholarship. While the shifts in participants' teaching were nearly seamless, the pressure to publish in international journals represented complex issues and dilemmas.

Participants illustrated the importance of the ability of academics to change in order to meet the needs of contemporary higher education. Key themes generated from the participants suggested that when change is embraced and paradigms shift, professorial teaching is transformed. Participants' views, strategies, and practices represented a blending of contradictory positions and discourses that were not uniform yet showcased an innovative and united ideology. In light of this, participants were situated as cultural conduits through which both global and local practices flowed (Appadurai 1996). They represented a national core of academics committed to both the global arena and the national intellectual capital. To nurture core faculty in terms of recognizing and authenticating their teaching practice diverts attention from the accepted discourse of the "world-class university" and at the same time offers stability as well as cultural and intellectual rootedness to the NCCU as an aspiring world-class institution.

References

Agarwal, Vinod B., and Donald R. Winkler. 1985. "Foreign Demand for United States Higher Education: A Study of Developing Countries in the Eastern Hemisphere." *Economic Development and Cultural Change* 33 (3): 623-644.

Altbach, Philip G. 1997. *Comparative Higher Education: Knowledge, the University and Development*. Chestnut Hill, MA: Center for International Higher Education, Boston College and Ablex Publishing Corporation.

Altbach, Philip G. 2004. *The Costs and Benefits of World Class Universities*. Washington, DC: American Association of University Professors. Available online at: http://www.aaup.org.

Altbach, Philip G. 2006. "Why the United States Will Not Be a Market for Foreign Higher Education Products: A Case Against GATS." In *International Higher Education: Reflections on Policy and Practice*, ed. Philip G. Altbach. Chestnut Hill, MA: Center for International Higher Education, Boston College. Available online at: http://www.bc.edu/content/dam/files/research_sites/cihe/pubs/Altbach_2006_Intl_HigherEd.pdf

Altbach, Philip G., and Jorge Balán, eds. 2007. *World Class Worldwide: Transforming Research Universities in Asia and Latin America*. Baltimore, MD: Johns Hopkins University Press.

Altbach, Philip G., and Jane Knight. 2007. "The Internationalization of Higher Education: Motivations and Realities." *Journal of Studies in International Education* 11: 290-305.

Anderseck, Klaus. 2004. "Institutional and Academic Entrepreneurship: Implications for University Governance and Management." *Higher Education in Europe* XXIX (2): 193-200.

Appadurai, Arjun. 1996. *Modernity at Large: Cultural Dimensions of Globalization*. Minneapolis: University of Minnesota Press.

Astiz, Fernanda M., Alexander W. Wiseman, and David P. Baker. 2002. "Slouching Towards Decentralization: Consequences of Globalization for Curricular Control in National Education Systems." *Comparative Education Review* 46 (1): 66-88.

Baker, David P. 2007. "Mass Higher Education and the Super Research University: A Symbiotic Relationship." *International Higher Education* 49: 9-10.

Barnes, Trevor J. 2001. "In the Beginning Was Economic Geography: Science Studies Approach to Disciplinary History." *Progress in Human Geography* 25 (4): 521-544.

Barnett, Ron. 2000. *Realizing the University in an Age of Supercomplexity*. Buckingham: Open University Press.

Breton, Gilles, and Michel Lambert. 2004. "Higher Education: Social Relevance and Collective Action." *Higher Education Policy* 17: 121-127.

Burbules, Nicholas C., and Carlos Alberto Torres, eds. 2000. *Globalization and Education: Critical Perspectives*. London: Routledge.

Cronbach, Lee J. 1951. "Coefficient Alpha and the Internal Structure of Tests." *Psychometrika* 16: 197-334.

Cummings, William K. 1993. "Global Trends in International Study." In *International Investment in Human Capital*, ed. Craufurd D. W. Goodwin. New York: Institute of International Education (IIE).

Flippo, Rona. 1993. "Literacy, Multicultural, Sociocultural Considerations: Student Literacy Corps and the Community." Paper presented at the Annual Meeting of the International Reading Association, San Antonio, TX, April 1993.

Flowerdew, John. 2001. "In Response East Asian Academics Report a Lack of Confidence in Ability to Meet the Standards of Leading International Journals." *Tesol Quarterly* 35 (1): 121-150.

Fry, Gerald. 1984. "The Economic and Political Impact of Study Abroad." *Comparative Education Review* 28 (2): 203-220.

Garrod, Andrew, and Jay Davis, eds. 1999. *Crossing Customs: International Students Write on US College Life and Culture*. New York: Flamer Press.
Johnson, Burke, and Larry Christensen. 2008. *Educational Research—Quantitative, Qualitative, and Mixed Approaches*. 3rd ed. Thousand Oaks, CA: Sage Publications.
Johnston, Ron, and James D. Sidaway. 2004. "The Trans-Atlantic Connection: Anglo-American Geography Reconsidered." *GeoJournal* 59 (1): 15-22.
Kuhn, Thomas 1970. *The Structure of Scientific Revolutions*. Chicago: University of Chicago Press.
Levin, Henry M., Dong Wook Jeong, and Dongshu Ou. 2006. "What is a World Class University?" Paper presented at the Conference of the Comparative and International Education Society, Honolulu, Hawaii, April 16, 2006.
Li, Judy. 2008. "Easy, Low Paying Jobs Gain Popularity in Taiwan." *China Economic News Service*, July 9. Available online at: http://www.cens.com.
Lo, Y. William, and Fwu Yuan Weng. 2005. "Taiwan's Responses to Globalization: Internationalization of Higher Education." In *Globalization and Higher Education in East Asia*, ed. Ka Ho Mok and Richard James. Singapore: Marshall Cavendish Academic.
Marginson, Simon 2000. "Rethinking Academic Work in the Global Era." *Journal of Higher Education Policy and Management* 22 (11): 23-35.
Mazzarol, Tim. 1998. "Critical Success Factors for International Education Marketing." *International Journal of Educational Management* 12 (4): 163-175.
McMahon, Mary E. 1992. "Higher Education in a World Market: An Historical Look at the Global Context of International Study." *Higher Education Policy* 24 (4): 465-482.
Merton, Robert K. 1973. *The Sociology of Science*. New York: Harper and Row.
Mohrman, Kathryn. 2003. "Center and Periphery: The Changing Relationship between the State and Institutions of Higher Education in China." Paper presented at Xiamen University and University of Hong Kong Conference on Higher Education Reforms in China, Xiamen, China, December 2003.
Mohrman, Kathryn, Wanhua Ma, and David P. Baker. 2007. "The Emerging Global Model of the Research University." In *Higher Education in the New Century: Global Challenges and Innovative Ideas*, ed. Philip G. Altbach and P. McGill Peterson. Rotterdam: Sense Publications.
Mok, Ka Ho. 2006. *Education Reform and Education Policy in East Asia*. London: Routledge.
Mok, Ka Ho, and Richard James, eds. 2005. *Globalization and Higher Education in East Asia*. Singapore: Marshall Cavendish Academic.
Mok, Ka Ho, and Jason Tan. 2004. *Globalization and Marketization in Education: A Comparative Analysis of Hong Kong and Singapore*. Northampton, MA: Edward Elgar Publishers.
Nunnally, Jum C., and Ira Bemstein. 1994. *Psychometric Theory*. New York: McGraw-Hill.
Organisation for Economic Co-operation and Development (OECD). 2000. *Science, Technology and Industry Outlook*. Paris: OECD.

Potthoff, Maggie, D. 2000. "Preparing for Democracy and Diversity: The Impact of a Community-Based Field Experience on Pre-Service Teachers' Knowledge, Skills, and Attitudes." *Action in teacher Education* 22 (1): 79-92.

Roberts, Amy, Chuing Chou, and Gregory Ching. 2010. "Contemporary Trends in East Asian Higher Education: Dispositions of International Students in a Taiwan University." *Higher Education* 59 (2): 149-166.

Sirowy, Larry, and Alex Inkeles. 1985. "University-Level Student Exchanges: The U.S. Role in Global Perspective." In *Foreign Student Flows: Their Significance for American Higher Education*, ed. Elinor G. Barber. New York: Institute of International Education.

Stenhouse, Lawrence. 1988. "Case Study Methods." In *Educational Research, Methodology, and Measurement: An International Handbook*, ed. John P. Keeves. Sydney: Pergamon Press.

Stewart, David W., Prem N. Shamdasani, and Dennis W. Rook. 2007. *Focus Groups - Theory and Practice*. 2nd ed. Thousand Oaks, CA: Sage Publications.

Swales, John. 1990. *Genre Analysis: English in Academic and Research Settings*. Cambridge: Cambridge University Press.

Taiwan Ministry of Education (MOE). 2000. *Education Yearbook of the Republic of China 2000*. Taipei: Taiwan MOE.

Taylor, Peter J. 1985. "The Value of a Geographical Perspective." In *The Future of Geography*, ed. Ronald John Johnston. London: Methuen.

Yang, Rui, Lesley Vidovich, and Jan Currie. 2007. "'Dancing in a Cage': Changing Autonomy in Chinese Higher Education." *Higher Education* 54 (5): 575-592.

Yeung, Henry Wai-chung. 2002. "Editorial: Deciphering Citations." *Environment and Planning* 34: 2093-2102.

Chapter 3

A Pearl on the Silk Road?
Internationalizing a Regional Chinese University

Anthony R. Welch and Rui Yang

Notwithstanding the burgeoning literature on the internationalization of higher education, a key paradox is evident. The internationalization literature is mostly quite ethnocentric, focusing on the experience of wealthy, White, and Western countries, especially the major, developed Anglophone nations. Less attention has been given to Asia, and even less again to Latin America and Africa. Within Asia, China remains little understood, despite some early work (Wang 1966; Hayhoe 1984, 1989; Hayhoe and Henze 1985) and a number of more recent studies (Hayhoe 1996; Yang and Welch 2001). Rarely is internationalization viewed from Chinese perspectives, with its powerful, long-standing philosophies of Confucianism, Buddhism, Taoism, and Islam, which are now mixed with almost 60 years of Communist ideology and nearly 30 years of a developing market economy that utilizes internationally oriented "Open Door" policies (Yang 2002). Such omissions in the scholarship are in part explained by the inequalities of the international knowledge systems. Indeed, the fact is that most of the major centers of scholarship are still in the English-speaking West, as are the bulk of major journals and books listed in internationally recognized citation indexes (Altbach 1994, 2003).

China, however, has its own long-standing traditions of internationalization, dating back to Confucius (551-479 B.C.), who had moved around different parts of what is now regarded as China. Confucius taught students in what were then different principalities or countries. Therefore, the Confucian system is inseparable from the history of higher learning in what is present-day South Korea and Vietnam, among other East Asian nations (Welch 2005, 2010; Welch and Cai 2010). Moreover, some of China's earlier modernization efforts were guided by the notion of dual influences, expressed in the principle *zhong ti xi yong* (Chinese learning as substance, Western learning for its utility). Yet today, China tends to look to the United States as the sole source of higher education reform and for developing institutional partners. This can, at times, blind Chinese educational leaders to useful reforms or partnerships from other locations, especially within the East Asian region.

The omission of a Chinese perspective and that of the global South is by no means the first time that such *lacunae* have occurred in the educational literature or the social sciences (Connell 2007). However, its continuation at the dawn of a new century, characterized at the theoretical level by an apparently greater acceptance and understanding of difference, and at the empirical level by China's spectacular economic and cultural rise, is nonetheless ironic. Compounding this failure to examine the rich and diverse experiences of many parts of the global South is the fact that the experience of internationalization is itself layered within the South, not merely between countries, but also within national education systems. Although the divide is not as sharp as it once was, the global South refers to less developed countries largely in the Southern hemisphere, with the exceptions of Singapore, Australia, and New Zealand, while the global North refers to developed world states, largely in the Northern hemisphere (Reuveny 2007). Thus, smaller and regional nonmainstream institutions in the global South are disadvantaged within the overall story of internationalization.

The picture of internationalization at regional institutions within China is often a rich and complex tapestry that offers fresh insights and an important counterpoint to both the experience of major, national institutions in the national system and to the experience of institutions in the developed world, the global North.

Our case study of Xinjiang University (hereafter XU [Uyghur: شىنجاڭ ئۇنىۋېرسىتېتى, Chinese: 新疆大学]) is a fascinating example of such differences, both from the Chinese experience more generally, and also from that of institutions in the North. In turn, it forms part of a much larger, ongoing study of internationalization in Chinese universities, currently being undertaken by the authors. This chapter then reports our findings from the case study and reveals a substantial contradiction between geographic and cultural location on the one hand, and the reality and aspirations for internationalization on the other hand.

XU was selected for two reasons, deriving from its special status within China and its location in Urumchi, the capital city of Xinjiang Uyghur Autonomous Region (XUAR) in the far west of China. Hundreds of years ago, the famed and fabled Silk Road formed an important cultural and trade bridge between China and the West, breaking down some of the barriers surrounding the "Middle Kingdom." An important staging post on the Silk Road and bordered by several key Central Asia states, Xinjiang remains a vast, sparsely populated, desolate, arid, and mountainous region. Its economic situation compares starkly with that in the coastal areas in China's east. Xinjiang's gross domestic product (GDP) was 26.9 trillion RMB in 2005, which ranked it 25th of China's 31 provinces. Some parts of the province are very poor, with average incomes of 1,482 RMB in 2003 (Kerr and Swinton 2008). Urban incomes are the highest in China's west, and its annual rate of increase and per capita GDP are higher than the national average due largely to the *Xibu Da Kaifa Zhanlüe* (Great Development in China's West) policy (ibid.), which exerts a significant impact on XU, as the province's leading higher education institution. Recently, XU has become a major development priority for the Chinese government, given both its strategic significance for China in the context of ongoing ethnic unrest, and the expectation of significant mineral riches, particularly oil and gas (ibid.).

Cultural diversity is the other reason for choosing XU as a site for our case study. Unlike most other regions of China, some 50 percent of the population in the region are designated as ethnic minorities, mostly Islamic, with Uyghurs comprising by far the largest group. In China, such groups are referred to as *shaoshu minzu*, which is usually translated as "minority nationalities" (Clothey 2005). Our previous Chinese case studies of internationalization have taken place in areas where Han Chinese formed by far the largest ethnic minority (Yang and Welch 2001). Equally, our former cases studies took place in elite national universities, located in major Chinese cities, with considerable drawing power, and substantial economic resources. But the "far-reaching differentiation and growing hierarchisation" (Henze 1992, 68) of Chinese universities over the past two decades have imparted specific qualities to XU. Although qualifying for additional funding as part of the prestigious nationwide 211 Project, XU's resources and facilities are significantly less than the other universities that we have examined. Indeed, XU was purposely selected because it contrasts so sharply with the situation of wealthier, elite universities in major cities, in the much more developed east.

Methods

The two researchers are Australians, even though Yang was born and raised in China. In this instance, therefore, neither could be termed wholly an insider researcher since the research context was significantly shaped by its minority cultural, religious, and linguistic setting. Specifically, a significant part of the data collection involved interviews with ethnic minority staff and students, cultures which we were not privy to prior to this study. Although we have worked together over a number of years and are familiar with the context of internationalization in Chinese universities, we consider ourselves to be outsider researchers when it comes to researching the minority cultures that were significant in this research project.

While the dichotomy between insider and outsider researcher has been recognized among sociologists since at least the work of Alfred Schutz, who pointed out that "any phenomenon of the social world has a different aspect for the sociologist and for the man [sic] who acts and thinks within it" (1964, 92), and such figures as William Foote Whyte (1943), whose classic *Street Corner Society: The Social Structure of the Italian Slum* involved discussing his interpretations with an insider (a gang leader) and hiring an insider as assistant, the difference is better described as representing either end of a continuum. Comparative researchers and anthropologists commonly confront the dialectic of insider and outsider directly in their research, as with classics such as Margaret Mead's (1973) *Coming of Age in Samoa: A Psychological Study of Primitive Youth for Western Civilization*, or Oscar Lewis's (1961) *Children of Sanchez: Autobiography of a Mexican Family* (Welch 2010).

Because we were well aware of these complexities, our main means of data collection in our initial field trips to Xinjiang consisted of questionnaires and interviews with Han Chinese and ethnic minority informants, as well a number of visiting scholars from abroad. Many items about international dimensions of academic life had to be adapted from the *International Survey of the Academic Profession: Portraits of Fourteen Countries*, sponsored by the Carnegie Foundation for the Advancement of Teaching (Altbach 1996). Our interview questions delved into the respondents' demographic data, including personal and professional background information, the factual aspects of their work concerning university internationalization, and their personal opinions on issues related to or affecting that work. The specific questions were chiefly prods to elicit information in these main areas and were often supplemented with follow-up questions.

Altogether 100 questionnaires were distributed. In order to obtain an adequate sample size that we believed could represent the population under survey (Bailey 1994) the final target sample size for questionnaires was 70 teachers and/or researchers and 30 administrators. Cooperation ensured a high response rate, giving considerable confidence in the authenticity of the results. Responses by academics numbered 50, yielding a response rate of 71.43 percent. Among the 50 respondents surveyed, 12 were full professors, 34 associate professors, and 4 lecturers. Of the 30 administrator questionnaires distributed, 26 were returned, with a response rate of 86.67 percent.

In addition, 17 interviews were conducted in 2000. Among them were one institutional leader, four directors of university administrative sections, four heads of research institutes or departments, and four academic staff (associate professors). Given that our first fieldwork at XU was five years earlier, and that there had been many subsequent changes in Xinjiang, in November 2005 we conducted follow-up interviews and gathered further documentation with a focus on new developments and minority and Central Asia issues. Also, in 2005, five interviews with seven informants were conducted, including the dean of Foreign Languages, the deputy director of Foreign Affairs, a professor of anthropology, and four lecturers.

Except for three interviews, respectively with a Russian academic, U.S. exchange academics, and four international students in 2000, which were in English, all the other interviews were conducted in Chinese. We felt that being able to interview in Chinese was beneficial, as some respondents indicated that while they were able to understand English, and respond to questions, their responses would be fuller and more nuanced in Chinese. Language is after all a powerful tool for constructing one's reality (Spradley 1979).

The Local Context

Situated in the center of the Europe-Asia continent, in the region commonly termed Central Asia, the most prominent feature of Xinjiang's local context is its geopolitical significance. It represents the northwest border of China. Its physical look and "feel" are immediately evident, with Arabic and Chinese characters on official buildings and stores, and at the entrance to XU, but also the distinctive physical appearance of the 12 different minorities (Hong 1998).

Xinjiang is among China's most politically sensitive regions. As a prime example, the riots in 2009 resulted in 197 deaths and 1,700 injuries, according to official reports (Dwyer 2005). Equally apparent are the tensions and lack of integration between Han and minority groups. The capital Urumchi, reestablished in 1763 by Emperor Qianlong, was originally named *Dihua*, which in Chinese means "enlightening and civilizing," signifying the contempt for local indigenous cultures that needed to be "enlightened" and "civilized." Today, the city is effectively divided into Han and minority areas. Ethnic Muslims who constitute the majority or a sizeable minority in the western provinces evince considerable self-confidence, assertiveness, and a rebellious spirit (Israeli 2002). Substantial economic disparities persist between Han and Uyghur. "In 2009, the average annual income in Southern Xinjiang (a Uyghur heartland) was only 3,142 RMB, which is less than one third of the average rural income for the greater Xinjiang region" (Yong 2010, 14). Recently, there has been a shift in attitude on the part of Beijing, which has pledged to increase financial support to the region from the wealthiest eastern provinces such as Guangdong and Shenzhen, to transfer more funds from Xinjiang's considerable oil and gas deposits to local government, to pursue a more softly stance on security, and to include more money for education in the region.

By 2004, Xinjiang's population had reached 19,631,100, comprising 7,802,500 Han Chinese and an ethnic minority population totaling 11,828,600, of which 8,976,700 were officially Uyghurs. Some estimate the population to be actually higher (Yong 2010). The significance of the rising Uyghur population becomes more apparent when compared with the total estimated Islamic population in China of between 20 and 30 million. The dramatic buildup of the Han population in Xinjiang occurred after the founding of the People's Republic of China (PRC) in 1949, and the establishment of the XUAR in 1955 (see Table 3.1). Internal migration from the majority Han areas of China's east is still encouraged with an expectation of exerting a civilizing influence (Kerr and Swinton 2008). In this sense, the *Xibu Kaifa* policy can be seen as an exercise in state-building and nation-building (Goodman 2004), in the context of Chinese concerns about pan-Turkism and pan-Islamism (Kerr and Swinton 2008).

The sharp decline in the proportion of the total population that is of Uyghur descent is the most notable demographic change and has caused significant resentment among locals. Although Uyghur still outnumber Han, non-Han locals have increasingly complained of Great Han chauvinism and racial and religious discrimination (MacPherson and Beckett 2008). Among the Han in Xinjiang, many have been assigned, rather than volunteering to live here, with a common feeling that Xinjiang is still a place of exile for them. The changing proportions of minority groups over the past half century are shown in the following table:

Table 3.1 Changing Proportions of Xinjiang Population by Principal Ethnic Minorities, 1948-2004

Principal Ethnic Groups	Percent in 1948 (estimated)	Percent in 1998	Percent in 2004
Uyghur*	75.0	46.58	45.73
Han	<6.0	38.58	39.75
Kazakh*	10.0	7.37	7.04
Hui	-	4.48	4.46
Kyrghiz*	<2.0	0.94	0.87
Mongolian	1.5	0.91	0.86
Xibe	-	0.23	0.21
Tadjikh*	-	0.23	0.22
Russian	-	0.05	0.06
Manchu	-	0.12	0.12
Taur	-	0.04	0.03
Tatar	-	0.03	0.02
Uzbekh*	1.0	0.79	0.07
Others	-	0.38	0.55

Note: Central Asian minorities are denoted by an asterisk.
Source: Data provided by Barnett (1993) and XUAR Government (2005).

Another change in the local context in Xinjiang, compared with other parts of China, is the rising influence of Islam. To some extent, this is explicable in terms of the collapse of the Union of Soviet Socialist Republics (USSR) and the subsequent establishment of separate Central Asian states with major Islamic populations on China's border. However, in this context, it is also an index of resistance to perceived Han domination, and an assertion of separatism (Barnett 1993; Barnett and Beahan 1995; Kerr and Swinton 2008; MacPherson and Beckett 2008). Chinese Islam, comprising the Hui (a diverse group of Chinese-speaking Muslims, inhabiting several parts of China, but who are nonetheless categorized as one of the 56 official minorities in China) and the Central Asian minorities listed in Table 3.1, has been sustained at least in part by "messianic yearnings, and a desire to live in a land of Islam" (Israeli 2002, 200). However, separatist tendencies are far more common among Uyghurs, who have rejected incorporation into mainstream Han culture, than among the Hui minority, who are more assimilated. In Xinjiang, Turkic-speaking Muslims are seen as "tied closely to separatist ideals." (Dillon 2004, 17; see also Kerr and Swinton 2008). Mosques are ubiquitous and are still being built. Adherence is another matter (Smith 2000). Certainly, most of the ethnic minority students to whom we spoke professed a more secular spirit, even though "increasing numbers of young intellectuals, including university professors, research scientists, and graduate students, who are usually antireligious, are attending mosques, both within and outside Xinjiang" (MacPherson and Beckett 2008, 114). Indeed, the rising number of mosques across Xinjiang is both an index of a resurgent Islam over the past decade and a half and a sign of rising cultural resistance.

Islamic fundamentalism is on the rise, fostered by the more militant mullahs, and undergirded by the increasing traffic of business travelers and others from neighboring Islamic Republics ostensibly on business trips (Shimin 1998; Kerr and Swinton 2008). The increasing number and rising prominence of fundamentalists lies behind China's membership, with Russia, Khyrghizstan, Tadhzikhistan, Uzbekhistan and Kazakhstan, of the security-inspired Shanghai Cooperation Organisation (SCO), founded in June 2001 with an explicitly antiterrorist and antiseparatist agenda (Kerr and Swinton 2008; Li 2010; SCO 2010). While it is hard to estimate either the number of such bands of fundamentalists or their total size, some of them are well armed and well connected to such groups in neighboring states, such as the Taliban, which for some time was reported to have local chapters in Xinjiang (Stobdan 2009).

This unique cultural and political environment has inevitably influenced international communications at XU. Compared with many of its counterparts in China's east and major cities, a majority of XU's staff possess an awareness of the necessity to develop mutual understanding among cultures. This is mainly due to their experience of getting along with various cultures; something little experienced by locals in most parts of China and particularly rare in the Han-dominated east and major cities. Such an experience has helped XU members to better understand the meaning of internationalization as a cultural and political connection (China TEFL 2007).

Several staff members articulated distinctive institutional goals for internationalization, as seen in the views of the following staff member, who argued that XU's goals should include incorporating Chinese, Central Asian, and other cultural perspectives:

> [To] become an institution that can incorporate different cultures, especially those of China's Central Plains [participant's definition of the traditional Chinese culture], Central Asia, and even Western countries and Russia, being located in a long-term mix of cultures, the more XU can display such characteristics, the better international status it has.

Such a cultural connection viewpoint is more widely expressed at XU than at many other Chinese universities in the coastal areas and cities and arguably internationally where, as we have reported previously, research level is accorded the single-most important element (Yang and Welch 2001). Nevertheless, despite XU respondents according internationalization a higher priority than at other Chinese universities where we had conducted similar research, and the fact that in nearly every questionnaire, and among almost all interviewees, internationalization was deemed a necessary, indeed, an urgent need, it remains questionable whether such an understanding has been incorporated adequately into XU's daily work.

The University

The early development of what is now termed XU illustrates most of the elements that continue to characterize the institution: (1) an important international dimension, (2) some tensions between internationalism and local demands, (3) ethnic issues, and (4) strategic concerns. From the very first, the institution displayed an international dimension. Reflecting its geographical proximity to the newly established USSR, it was founded by Yang Zhengxin, then governor of Xinjiang, in 1924 as the Xinjiang Russian Political and Law School. It was the only higher learning institution in Xinjiang and largely was responsible for training diplomats and personnel working in the legal system. While being renamed Xinjiang College in January 1935, it remained small, enrolling very few minority students and no females.

At the same time, significant local demands conflicted to a certain extent with internationalism. In June 1935, a newly appointed Soviet-educated Communist president of the College, Yu Xiusong, insisted that the development of the college be based on local demands. While his efforts laid the foundations for the later development of the college, he fell victim to local political struggles, and was sent secretly by the warlord Governor Sheng Shicai in 1938 to the Soviet Union, where he was executed during the Stalinist regime.

Xinjiang's position became even more strategically important when the July 7 incident of 1937 sparked the beginning of the Anti-Japanese War. In order to ensure safe passage between Communist Yan'an and the Soviet Union, the Chinese Communist Party (CCP) needed to maintain friendly relations with Sheng Shicai. At the invitation of Sheng, the CCP sent Lin Jilu to take charge of the college. Xinjiang's peculiarly violent brand of internecine politics continued. Lin was forced to leave the college and was killed by Sheng Shicai in early 1939 (his remains are still there in the Cemetery of Martyrs in Urumchi). His successor, Du Chongyuan, a fellow villager and former schoolmate of Sheng Shicai in Japan, was also arrested and killed by Sheng in 1943.

Du's death provoked the departure of significant numbers of the academic staff. The situation worsened after 1944, when its president went to Chongqing to seek donations and recruit academics but did not return, moving to Anhui College, a more congenial environment in the east of China. From May 1947, the final pre-communist presidency of Xinjiang College was held by Bao Erhan, concurrently with his other post as provincial governor.

Control changed again, just prior to the 1949 Revolution (XU 1995). One year after the CCP came into power, Xinjiang College was renamed Xinjiang Nationality College, training secondary school teachers, lawyers and professionals, and farming, forestry, and animal husbandry personnel. The college paid special attention to the recruitment of students from minority groups. By 1951, 90 percent of the students were ethnic minorities and much the same proportion was maintained in succeeding years. Heads of departments were drawn from minority groups (ibid.). Attention was also paid to political education. Indeed, it was accorded top priority at Xinjiang Nationality College, an index of the need to maintain political stability in a culturally diverse and volatile region (ibid.).

At the time of the Chinese-Soviet alliance in the 1950s, the college was renamed Xinjiang College in October 1954, at a point when the Chinese government was determined to spur industrialization, and higher education was urgently required to train specialists for China's social and economic development. All specialties, academic programs and administration were modeled on the Soviet experience. Teaching syllabi and textbooks were revised under the direct supervision of Soviet educational leaders.

XU was then officially established on October 1, 1960. In July 1962, Xinjiang Normal College was incorporated into XU (Xinjiang Normal University is now a separate institution). From 1963 to 1966, China's socialist education movement, a prelude to Mao's Cultural Revolution, emphasized class struggle and criticism of so-called capitalist roaders. The movement led to XU's suspension of teaching and research for six years. Normal order was not resumed until 1977, after Mao's death in October 1976.

In 1978, XU was listed as a national key university by the Chinese Ministry of Education (MOE), under the double jurisdiction of the Chinese MOE (academic affairs) and XUAR (administration). Similar to virtually all other Chinese universities in the 1980s and 1990s, XU developed rapidly in teaching, research, and international communications and, in the process, established significant strengths in the study of minority culture and history.

A milestone in its development was being chosen as a member institution of the 211 Project in 1997; however, that was more of an acknowledgment of its strategic significance and role in maintaining solidarity between minorities than a recognition of its academic achievements. Established in 1995, the 211 Project was a major initiative that sought to create an elite tier of 100 Chinese universities on which the government focused investment, in order to catch up with, or approach, the most advanced level, during the twenty-first century.

Unlike some of its more specialized regional counterparts, XU is a comprehensive institution. As of September 17, 2006, XU comprised 21 faculties, one graduate school, nine research institutes/centers, one center for teaching, four centers for teaching practicum, with 70 undergraduate majors including arts, science, engineering, law, economics, management, history, and philosophy. It possesses 12 doctoral programs, 3 postdoctoral stations, 79 master's programs, two national centers of excellence, a national philosophy and social science base, a national humanity base, three joint laboratories between the Autonomous Region and national ministries, and seven provincial key subjects. Locals are proud of their premier university, although some who are familiar with major universities in Shanghai, Hangzhou, and Beijing are a little more circumspect. Indeed, as seen below, some who visit other more developed parts of China, and their universities, do not return to Xinjiang.

Some 60 percent of XU's current students are designated "minority," with the largest contingent being Uyghur. This finding supports earlier research, which reported that in 1992, 56 percent of undergraduate students were ethnic minorities, while 20 percent of graduate students were ethnic minorities (Hayhoe 1996). More than ten nationalities are currently represented on campus, with the other ethnic minorities being Kazakh, Tadjikh, Mongolian, Kirghiz, Uzbekh, Hui, and Xibe. This rich cultural and ethnic diversity provides a distinctive regional flavor to the campus.

Academic staff numbers have more than doubled over the past 20 years. They are drawn from different ethnic groups, although Han and Uyghur predominate. While Han Chinese tend to dominate the senior levels of XU, the president is Uyghur; the director of Foreign Affairs, who also doubles as the assistant to the President's Office, is a Mongolian woman, and the (deputy) director of scientific research is Uyghur. The practice in Chinese universities sited in minority areas is for the president to be minority, while the party secretary, in practice at least as powerful, is Han.

XU is seeking to enhance foreign relations with Central Asian countries. Our interviewees, particularly those holding senior administrative posts, expressed strong support for this orientation, something further confirmed by questionnaire results. When asked whether XU could be internationalized while still maintaining a strong local/national identity, of the 50 returned academics/researchers questionnaires, only one answered "no" and one left the question blank. The view that internationalization should act in tandem with strengthened responsiveness to local conditions is a strong feature of our survey and interview results at XU. The response of a female associate professor and deputy dean of the graduate school was indicative of this global-local nexus:

> International communication helps us realize how far we are behind the world... Our established position is [that of] a provincial university. We feel that the more we communicate with the world, the more we can learn from them, and the better we can develop our own University.

Other respondents all emphasized the crucially important role of local conditions in responding to external/global forces. There is great scope for XU here, as a provincial university, a periphery within China's higher education, itself a giant periphery in the global knowledge system (Altbach 1994, 2003; Welch and Zhang 2005, 2008a, 2008b), to extend the scope of its operations in the international arena. This widespread commitment of the XU respondents and interviewees was also explicable in terms of their recognition of the increasingly extensive global-local nexus, which implies a certain reciprocity: on the one hand, denoting that local scientific and educational developments needed to employ the most advanced achievements of international research and, on the other hand, the application of knowledge derived from another time and space can contribute to advancing scientific knowledge from elsewhere (XU 1995).

While theoretical support for such reciprocity exists, empirical evidence at XU reveals the potential for further internationalization. While some examples were found—a visiting professor studied the local desert areas in 1990 and established collaborative research programs in desertification and dry-land biological environment studies—no evidence was found of follow-up activities.

Global forces often dominate (Yang 2000, 2002, 2004), and therefore increased interest and investment in the region, particularly in response to major oil and gas finds, as exemplified in the West-East Gas Pipeline project, has evoked more interest by agencies such as the World Bank, and there has been a growth in tourism. These developments may boost its international profile, something confirmed repeatedly and explicitly by both senior administrators and academics during our second site visit in 2005.

International Communications

Understandably, given geographical contiguity and political affinity, one of the more important channels of international dialogue was between Xinjiang and the then USSR; at least until the Sino-Soviet split in 1958. The Soviet government sent scholars to Xinjiang Nationality College in the early 1950s to train local Xinjiang academics, especially from ethnic minority groups. As was common at the time, sending Xinjiang academic staff to the then Soviet Union for further training was another major means of professional development for Xinjiang College (XU 1995). Although Soviet advice and experience was too often taken uncritically, the practice yielded more positive results than negative, particularly given the early stage of XU's development under Communist control. As exemplified in the Chinese aphorism *Xuexi Sulian Laodage* (Learn from Big Brother, Soviet Union) (Welch and Cai 2010), Soviet research and technology were at the time far more developed than that in China and especially in Xinjiang.

From the 1980s, in the post-Mao era, XU's international relations widened and changed direction, now exhibiting a greater focus on economically advanced nations, notably the United States, but also including Japan. Between 1980 and 1985, XU received visits and lectures from more than 12,000 "friends from overseas" (XU 1995, 117). During this period, XU established various institutional collaboration agreements with international counterparts and invited honorary guest lecturers and consultant professors from overseas. A further look at these foreign institutions and individuals reveals a phenomenon similar to many other universities in developing countries, which try to forge links with the most prestigious institutions in the advanced countries, without paying sufficient attention to the striking institutional and contextual differences (Altbach and Selvaratnam 1989; Yang 2003a).

In this sense, XU is no exception to the pattern found at other Chinese universities. It concentrated on the wealthier countries, notwithstanding its location in the middle of the Europe-Asia continent, bordered by eight Central Asian countries, several of which are also members of the Turkic linguistic family, and the "opening of the borders with former Soviet Central Asia and the increase in cross border trade in the early 1990's" (Dillon 2004, 76). What is strikingly different from many universities in China's east is that international communications at XU by the mid-1980s had not yielded substantive international collaboration, an indication of the relative underdevelopment of the region and its greater isolation from major centers.

The rich cultural diversity evident among its staff and students might well suggest that despite XU's relative lack of resources compared with many of its Chinese peers, its geography and ongoing cultural links with neighboring Central Asian republics could be a significant source of strength in building up international programs, including staff and student exchanges. All the more so given that Xinjiang, in terms of living standards, was "relatively well-off in comparison to ex-Soviet Central Asia and is generally more stable" (Sautman 2000, 454). While there was confirmation among our interviewees of a changing regional quality to XU's international relations, its 68 international enrollments at XU between 1978 and 1991 remained a modest one, especially in relation to major institutions in the eastern parts of China. No international students were listed as having come from the Central Asian region, despite linguistic, cultural, and religious affinities. On the contrary, the major source countries for international enrollments at that time were listed as Japan, the United States, Australia, New Zealand and (former West) Germany. The picture changed however, and as shown in Table 3.2, the United States, Japan, and South Korea accounted for some three-quarters of total international enrollments in 2000, even though the total number of international students remained relatively small (only 40 students in 2000). While this was similar to our findings at other Chinese universities, what was so distinctive was that a significant number of international students were learning Uyghur.

Table 3.2   Countries of Origin of XU International Students, 2000

Country	Number	Percentage
Japan	15	39.4
USA	9	23.6
Korea	4	10.5
Kazakhstan	3	7.9
Sweden	1	2.6
Norway	1	2.6
Czech Republic	1	2.6
Singapore	1	2.6
Philippines	1	2.6
India	2	5.2
Kyrghizstan	1	2.6
Other	1	2.6
Total	40	100

Note: Of the three Kazakhs, two were Russian speakers.
Source: Data compiled from internal XU data.

By 2002, international enrollments had risen to 65, and by 2008, it was reported that over 300 international students from more than 20 countries were enrolled at XU, perhaps an indication of the increasingly dynamic growth and development in the region and at XU. Agreements with 30 universities from a total of 20 countries were reported, including the United States, Japan, Russia, Germany, France, Italy, Kyrghizstan, and Kazakhstan (Study in China 2010).

Some examples of international collaboration, however, are more effective than others. One, with the private Oklahoma Baptist University (OBU) in the United States has proved to be one of the more long-standing and substantial collaborations, albeit rather anomalous, given the overtly religious charter of the institution and the equally overt antireligious orthodoxy of XU. Yet, it continues to work, reflecting goodwill on both sides, and a certain pragmatism by XU. A long-standing female administrator, a one-time deputy director, Foreign Affairs Office, reflected on her one-year experience at OBU, which she found somewhat provincial and isolated from the outside world:

> OBU was indeed very insular, with a strong religious atmosphere. My feeling was its international communication was not as good as XU. It was only interested in its own country, even its own local region. People there know little about the outside world. They were content with their life there.

Nonetheless, an XU vice president expressed satisfaction with the program, confirming that it was growing and and its benefits were more strongly felt in the social and economic spheres.

The collaborative training program, as two U.S. interviewees explained is well established:

> They have this exchange program for 13 years. It started in 1987. The primary focus of the exchange is the summer intensive English program that lasts for four weeks. Every summer, between 10 and 14 Americans [students from OBU] and two or three of their teachers come. They collaborate with Foreign Languages Department [at XU] to teach secondary school students from Urumchi for a four week intensive English class. Then one American [teacher] stays and teaches for a year. Then a Chinese professor would go to the States [to teach Chinese in Oklahoma], and completes that half. But this hasn't taken place for the last couple of years, primarily because of visa problems, but it is also a money issue.

Effects of international collaborations depend on the specific situations on all sides. The focus on the Central Asian region that was emphasized by our interviewees as a strategy for XU's medium-term future development is problematic in practice, mainly due to the great social, political, and economic instabilities in the region. A regional exchange and cooperation program with Novosibirsk State University (NSU) in Siberia revealed this problem clearly. As a major research establishment, NSU is a notable partner. But only one academic from NSU has worked at XU in the Russian Department in recent years. There had not been any examples of student exchange or research collaboration between the two institutions. The reasons for this apparent failure to establish an important international alliance are related to the catastrophic downturn in Russian higher education in the 1990s post-Soviet period (Sutherland 1999; Bain 2003).

By comparison, the expansion of relations with Japanese universities may be due to an increasing number of Japanese companies investigating Xinjiang's potential for investment. As a consequence, relevant issues regarding higher education are gradually put on the local agenda. Japanese academics are also keen to understand local minority cultures in Xinjiang and have initiated various forms of research collaboration. It has become a regular practice for XU to send minority staff to Japan to study for higher degrees; a practice occasioning resentment among some Han staff we interviewed. In such instances, Japanese institutions are responsible for all the costs. This support has had a strong impact on the strengthening of XU's teaching and research, as shown by the following comments by a Uyghur professor who studied in Japan for his master's and doctoral degrees and is now one of XU's top researchers:

> Through my study in Japan, I understand Japanese people and their life style. I could communicate with people from other countries, because my former institute in Japan had researchers from as many as 60 countries. I also learned how to live, do research and work independently. I still often communicate with my former supervisors and colleagues, and we collaborate a lot. Every two years I go back to Kyoto for conferences and other academic affairs.

Among the scholarship programs for top students, the most prominent is a Japanese scholarship. For years, it has selected the best students, mainly of ethnic minority status, to study in Japan. In one of our discussions with a female minority undergraduate student in her third and fourth year of study, she revealed that most ethnic minority students pay close attention to this international opportunity. Interestingly, an overwhelming number of minority students at the university are female. Indeed some of these young women had invested considerable hopes in attaining this particular scholarship.

Other partners, such as Taiwan, play an increasingly active role in XU's international communication. Reasons for Taiwanese interest in Xinjiang are not dissimilar to those for Japan. On March 16, 1993, a Taiwan delegation headed by the president of the renowned Taiwan Institute for Economic Studies, and containing several influential Taiwan businessmen, paid a special visit to XU. An agreement was reached, and an annual amount of 100,000 Yuan (at the time approximately US$12,500) was designated for XU scholarships, to encourage the best postgraduate and undergraduate students. Several interviewees indicated that more Taiwanese business associates were coming to Xinjiang to invest, and that current communication would be further developed; a sharp contrast with the lack of participation of Hong Kong and Macau in the internationalization of XU (Yang 2003b).

Brain Drain

International communication relies on willing and able academics, with established connections abroad. Clearly, the availability of this set of conditions varies considerably, even among academics in the developed world. Indeed, it is possible to clearly differentiate between more internationally oriented academic staff, and those who remain more rooted in the national context (Welch 1998). While international connections are an effective way to improve academic quality in China, they also contribute to the so-called brain drain (Guochu and Wenjun 2002; Welch and Zhang 2005, 2008a). XU faces a serious dilemma; while international communication is crucial to its intellectual vitality, it often contributes to the loss of its best academic staff.

The brain drain has caused staff losses to both overseas and other parts of China. Over the past 20 years, XU sent some 170 academic staff overseas for training, but only 45 have returned. Moreover, younger scholars are more likely to remain abroad (Hayhoe 1999). From 1990 to 1997, XU lost 294 academic and administrative staff. Among them, 159 were between 23 and 45 years old, 49 had senior academic titles (professors and associate professors), and 145 were lecturers (Zhou 1998). Such ongoing losses inevitably mean that some research projects are postponed, even suspended, and regular teaching and research in some areas are often seriously damaged. Almost every interviewee, particularly those with senior administrative positions, expressed their concern at this ongoing loss of talent. As one interviewee points out:

> Losing our brightest students and staff to the east [the wealthier and more built up eastern provinces of China] has always been a serious problem

for our university. It is even getting worse these days [as control from the governments loosens and market economy is being introduced]. We have to be realistic and acknowledge this. There is no way to avoid it. Many of our young staff [who are] sent to major cities in the east to study for degrees don't return, particularly those with doctoral degrees. The reasons are manifold, including our regional physical environment, economic situation, and the scholarly atmosphere within our university. We can't compete with universities in more developed areas in coastal regions and in the east. Honestly, if I had such an opportunity, I would have chosen to stay there. However, there are a few people with a spirit of giving. A professor in our Biology Department came back from Beijing Agricultural University after finishing his doctoral studies and some years of postdoctoral research there. But such people are very rare.

Although evident in other field research sites in China, the problem is particularly acute at XU. There is a form of double jeopardy with XU graduates commonly leaving for both the more prosperous eastern areas of China (Henze 1992) and overseas. While previous studies show that ethnic minority students are more likely to return than Han (Iredale et al. 2001; Iredale et al. 2003), the Uyghur students we met also expressed a desire to undertake study in the more developed regions of China or overseas. That ethnic minority students are more likely to return is indicative of a stronger regional attachment, captured in the traditional Uyghur saying, repeated by one of our interviewees: "Better a beggar in our own country, than a King in another's" (Hayhoe 1996).

XU's problem in this respect is frequently called in China "a loss of talented people," which is a real concern for the provincial government and the university authorities. Even though these leaders are keen for their students to take advantage of opportunities to study abroad or in more developed regions of China, they lament the significant loss of talent and investment that is entailed when a large proportion of students do not return to the area (Henze 1992). Xinjiang's arid environment, relative lack of wealth, infrastructure, and lifestyle attractions makes it relatively less attractive to live. Moreover, China's increasing unequal regional development (Kwong and Xiao 1989; Hannum 1999), paralleled by significant differences of rank and status among its universities, means that success stories of reversing brain drain (Choi 1995; Zweig et al. 2008) are far less likely at XU, than at Peking, Tsinghua, or Fudan Universities.

Overall, much of the earlier intention to develop the western regions of China and Xinjiang in particular, which seemed at times to be expressed largely at the rhetorical level, has now been overtaken by ambitious plans to exploit Xinjiang's large oil and gas deposits. Empirical evidence of substantial new resources from beyond the region being directed into actual schemes to develop industry in Xinjiang is changing the economic vista for Xinjiang, with reports of plans to build China's largest oil and gas production base announced recently (Li 2010; *People's Daily Online* 2010a, 2010b). According to these plans, the XUAR will become both a strategic route for oil and gas from Central Asia and Russia and "become the country's most significant base in oil and gas production, refining and chemicals manufacturing, oil storage, and engineering and technology services in the next 10 years, according to CNPC,[1] the nation's largest oil company" (*People's Daily Online* 2010b).

Notwithstanding such ambitious plans, until the serious and growing regional inequalities in development are addressed systematically, it seems unlikely that XU can profit much from efforts to lure overseas Chinese scholars and other highly trained personnel home. Until such time, the ongoing flight of highly skilled personnel from Xinjiang, both to the more developed regions of China and overseas, will persist.

Minority-Related Issues in Education

Internationalization of higher education is closely related to minority issues in Xinjiang. This is especially clear in political education. The maintenance of ideology is a more insistent feature of higher education institutions in Xinjiang than elsewhere in China. This may well have something to do with the widely acknowledged need for "stability," mentioned regularly by a significant number of our interviewees as the justification for many practices. At other campuses we have visited, political education has largely fallen into disuse, and, if not derided by students as outdated, attracts at most ritual support. Its strength and persistence at XU is likely an outcome, not merely of its distance from the more cosmopolitan and wealthier eastern regions, where there is a greater impact from outside influences, but also of the expressed need for political and cultural stability, especially among the different ethnic communities.

The strong minority presence at XU influences teaching practice, institutional administration, and research foci. While China's higher education system remains highly centralized, both the content of education and the means of teaching at XU are strikingly distinct. For the minority students who make up 60 percent of the student body, the length of undergraduate education is five years, with the first year mainly focused on Chinese Mandarin and making up for lack of basic knowledge in academic subjects. XU has a high proportion of minority academics, about 34 percent. More than 90 percent of minority senior secondary school graduates enter universities, compared with much more intense competition among Han students. Hence, to enter XU, the total entry scores for Han students are normally 200 marks higher than that for minority students. Language, too, is an issue: at XU, all instruction is either in Mandarin or in Uyghur, which means that Tadzhiks, Uzbekhs and some other minorities may not be able to study in their own languages.

For most minority students, proficiency in Mandarin remains a serious problem, which can limit their educational progress at XU. An earlier test by XU revealed that among 500 newly recruited minority students in the 1988-1989 academic year, the percentages of those who scored over 90, 80, 70 and 60 marks were, respectively, 0.6, 0.4, 13, 16.7, which meant that 70 percent failed to gain a pass score of 60 (Pan 1998). Considering the test was based on the level of the second year of junior secondary school, this result underlines the extent of difficulties faced by the institution.

Hence an issue that demands earnest consideration is the academic achievements of many minority students. The relatively poor elementary and secondary education in their hometown leaves most local minority students ill-prepared for university education. While the entry scores for XU are much higher than that for other universities in the region, results attained by minority and Han students are starkly different, as Table 3.3 reveals.

In 1998, XU required most of its new minority students to undertake a test of basic mathematics. The result was again considered "not encouraging," as shown in Table 3.4.

Previous studies confirm the finding that in China's northwest region, scores on the national entrance examinations have sometimes been lowered by as much as 200 points in order to secure a level of enrollments proportionate to the general population (Hayhoe 1996; Benson 2004). This casts some doubt on Barry Sautman's (2000) conclusion that levels of secondary and tertiary education among the Xinjiang workforce has been unproblematic, in comparison with other provinces. It also has implications for

Table 3.3 Highest and Lowest Scores at Entrance Examination, Minority Students of Class 2, 1992, Electronics Department

Scores	All subjects	Mother tongue	Mandarin	Politics	Maths	Physics	Chemistry	Biology
Highest	360	130	91	45	55	42	36	25
Lowest	253	75	54	15	17	16	18	9

Note: The Electronics Department boasted one of the highest entry scores in the university.
Source: Data compiled from internal XU data.

Table 3.4 Basic Mathematics Test Results, Enrolling Minority Students, by Departments, 1998

Scores	Selective (31)	Electronics (31)	Computing (32)	Maths (31)	Economics (36)	Physics (25)	Biology (29)	Chemistry (17)	Geography (37)
Highest	72	63	60	56	52	57	47	46	51
Lowest	19	10	7	9	6	7	5	1	5
Average	47.5	30.8	29	24.6	22.9	21.6	19.4	17	20.2

Note: Class size in brackets.
Source: Compiled from internal XU data. For more see Adonbieke (1998) and Yibuladin (2000).

XU's internationalization strategy, since minority students sent abroad may have more ground to make up.

Conclusion

Even more evident than other case studies we have conducted in China, the overall story of internationalization at XU is intimately bound up with its cultural history, regional political and economic development, and location. The predecessor to XU originally aimed at training diplomats, and was thus somewhat outward-looking from the very beginning. By 1934, when Xinjiang College was established, many of its institutional and departmental leaders already had substantial living and study experience overseas (XU 1995). Despite these advantages however, and although it has traditionally been the most important institution of higher learning in the region, it has lacked an entirely solid basis, right from the outset.

XU's case underlines the intricate dialectic between local and international contexts. In particular, internationalization at a regional university is closely related to the regional, national as well as the international situation. Our research confirms earlier work, revealing the desire for alliances with the most advanced and wealthiest systems, belying Xinjiang's location at the heart of Central Asia (Hayhoe 1996). Many of its strengths lie in Central Asia-related fields; yet, the United States remains the most influential institutional model, locus for international cooperation, and source of international students. This fact confirms both the role played by broader international power relations, in particular, the ongoing dominance of the wealthiest, most developed nations, In internationalizing universities, as Philip G. Altbach (1994, 2003), inter alia, has argued, but also the persistence of the belief on the part of Chinese university presidents that the United States is the single most important source of reform ideas.

In this sense, internationalization at XU does not differ much from many other Chinese universities, and perhaps those from several other developing countries. Judged, however, by the perhaps unduly harsh standards adopted by many of its international and domestic counterparts, the pace of international communication and collaboration at XU is evidently less, and slower, than at many other Chinese universities in the east, or central China.

In another sense, XU is very distinct. Its history and experience underlines the importance of ethnic tensions, geo-strategic concerns and the specific ways in which local conditions ultimately decide the extent to which provincial universities can internationalize themselves. Xinjiang's distinctive mix of cultures, and regional geography, imparts key social and cultural contextual advantages to XU, through which it may yet further develop its internationalization. Recent efforts to strengthen regional cooperation, economic development, security and human resource development, via the Central Asia Regional Economic Cooperation and the Shanghai Cooperation Agreement could assist in this regard (*China Daily* 2006; Zheng 2006). On the one hand, China's greater engagement with its Central Asian neighbors could offer further opportunities for international collaboration, and there is some evidence that some international students are from neighboring states: "Most students come from post Soviet Union" (*Global Times* 2010). Of the 400 or so international students that are listed by the Foreign Affairs Office as having enrolled at XU in recent years, Central Asian republics are among the sources, although precise numbers and proportions are not available (Wang and Zhang 2010; XU, Foreign Affairs Office 2011). However, notwithstanding Beijing's pursuit of more conciliatory policies toward the region, the fact that security concerns are paramount for China may, in practice, form something of a barrier to deepening academic relationships with surrounding Islamic states. China's determination to develop the western region, including the exploitation of substantial oil and gas deposits, possibly in partnership with Russian and other international investors, is perhaps more likely to yield promising opportunities for internationalization and development at XU, at least in the shorter term.

Note

1. China National Petroleum Corporation (CNPC) is an energy company covering oil and gas operations, oilfield services, engineering and construction, petroleum material and equipment manufacturing, and supply.

References

Adonbieke, G. 1998. "提高理科民族教育质量问题的探讨" ["Inquiries into the Improvement of Minority Science Education"]. 新疆大学高教研究 [*Xinjiang University Higher Education Research*] 3: 18-24.
Altbach, Philip G. 1994. "International Knowledge Networks." In *The International Encyclopedia of Education*, ed. Torsten Husén and T. Neville Postlethwaite. Oxford: Pergamon Press.
Altbach, Philip G, ed. 1996. *The International Academic Profession: Portraits of Fourteen Countries*. Princeton, NJ: Carnegie Foundation for the Advancement of Teaching.

Altbach, Philip G. 2003. "Centers and Peripheries in the Academic Profession: The Special Challenges of Developing Countries." In *The Decline of the Guru: The Academic Profession in Developing and Middle-Income Countries*, ed. Philip G. Altbach. New York: Palgrave Macmillan.
Altbach, Philip G., and Viswanathan Selvaratnam, eds. 1989. *From Dependence to Autonomy: The Development of Asian Universities*. Dordrecht, The Netherlands: Kluwer Academic Publishers.
Bailey, Kenneth. 1994. *Methods of Social Research*. New York: Free Press.
Bain, Olga. 2003. *University Autonomy in the Russian Federation Since Perestroika*. London: Routledge.
Barnett, A. Doak. 1993. *China's Far West: Four Decades of Change*. Boulder, CO: Westview Press.
Barnett, A. Doak, and Charlotte L. Beahan. 1995. "China's Far West: Four Decades of Change." *History: Reviews of New Books* 23 (4): 183-184.
Benson, Linda. 2004. "Education and Social Mobility among Minority Populations." In *Xinjiang: China's Muslim Borderland*, ed. S. Frederick Starr. Armonk, NY: M.E. Sharpe.
China Daily. 2006. "200 Officials to Attend 5th Ministerial Conference on CAREC." *China Daily*, October 19. Available online at: http://www.chinadaily.com.cn.
China TEFL Network. 2007. *Study in Xinjiang, China*. Zhejiang, China: China TEFL Network. Available online at: http://www.chinatefl.com.
Choi, Hyaeweol. 1995. *An International Scientific Community: Asian Scholars in the United States*. Westport, CT: Praeger Publishers.
Clothey, Rebecca. 2005. "China's Policies for Minority Nationalities in Higher Education: Negotiating National Values and Ethnic Identities." *Comparative Education Review* 49 (3): 389-409.
Connell, Raewyn. 2007. *Southern Theory: The Global Dynamics of Knowledge in Social Science*. Cambridge: Polity.
Dillon, Michael. 2004. *Xinjiang: China's Muslim Far Northwest*. London: New York: Routledge.
Dwyer, Arienne M. 2005. *The Xinjiang Conflict: Uyghur Identity, Language Policy, and Political Discourse*. Washington, DC: East-West Centre Washington.
Global Times. 2010. "Xinjiang University." *Global Times*. July 10, 2010. Available online at: http://forum.globaltimes.cn.
Goodman, David S. G. 2004. "The Campaign to 'Open up the West': National, Provincial-Level and Local Perspectives." *The China Quarterly* 178: 317-334.
Guochu, Zhang and Li Wenjun. 2002. "International Mobility of China's Resources in Science and Technology and Its Impact." In *International Mobility of the Highly Skilled*, ed. Organisation for Economic Co-operation and Development (OECD). Paris: OECD.
Hannum, Emily. 1999. "Political Change and the Urban-Rural Gap in Basic Education in China, 1949-1990." *Comparative Education Review* 43 (2): 193-207.
Hayhoe, Ruth. 1984. *Contemporary Chinese Education*. London: Croom Helm.
Hayhoe, Ruth. 1989. *China's Universities and the Open Door*. New York: M.E. Sharpe.

Hayhoe, Ruth. 1996. *China's Universities, 1895-1995: A Century of Cultural Conflict*. New York: Routledge.

Hayhoe, Ruth. 1999. *China's Universities: A Century of Cultural Conflict*. Hong Kong: Comparative Education Research Centre, The University of Hong Kong.

Hayhoe, Ruth, and Jurgen Henze. 1985. "Chinese-Western Scholarly Exchange: A Challenge for Comparative Bailey Educationalists." In *Education and the Diversity of Cultures: The Contribution of Comparative Education*, ed. Wolfgang Mitter and James Swift.: Köln, Germany: Böhlau.

Henze, Jurgen. 1992. "The Formal Education System and Modernization: An Analysis of Developments since 1978." In *Education and Modernization: The Chinese Experience*, ed. Ruth Hayhoe. Oxford: Pergamon.

Hong Qiu. 1998. "对我校民族文字教材建设的几点思考" ["Some Reflections on Minority Languages Textbooks at Our University"]. 新疆大学高教研究 [*Xinjiang University Higher Education Research*] 2: 16-22.

Iredale, Robyn R., Naran Bilik, and Fei Guo. 2003. *China's Minorities on the Move: Selected Case Studies*. New York: M.E. Sharpe.

Iredale, Robyn R., Naran Bilik, Wang Su, Fei Guo, and Caroline Hoy. 2001. *Contemporary Minority Migration, Education, and Ethnicity in China*. Cheltenham: Edward Elgar Publishing.

Israeli, Raphael. 2002. *Islam in China: Religion, Ethnicity, Culture, and Politics*. Lanham, MD: Lexington Books.

Kerr, David, and Laura C. Swinton. 2008. "China, Xinjiang and the Transnational Security of Central Asia." *Critical Asian Studies* 40 (1): 113-142.

Kwong, Julia, and Hong Xiao. 1989. "Educational Equality among China's Minorities." *Comparative Education* 25 (2): 229-244.

Lewis, Oscar. 1961. *The Children of Sanchez: Autobiography of a Mexican Family*. New York: Random House.

Li, Xiaokun. 2010. "Pilots Break New Ground in Anti-Terror Exercise." *People's Daily Online*, September 25, 2010. Available online at: http://english.peopledaily.com.cn.

Macpherson, Seonaigh, and Gulbahar Beckett. 2008. "The Hidden Curriculum of Assimilation in Modern Chinese Education: Fuelling Indigenous Tibetan and Uygur Cessation Movements." In *Cultural Education—Cultural Sustainability: Minority, Diaspora, Indigenous, and Ethno-Religious Groups in Multicultural Societies*, ed. Zivi Bekerman and Erza Kopelowitz. London: Routledge.

Mead, Margaret. 1973. *Coming of Age in Samoa: A Psychological Study of Primitive Youth for Western Civilization*. New York: Morrow.

Pan, Cong. 1998. "对我校民族文字教材建设的几点思考" ["Some Considerations of Reforms in Chinese Mandarin Teaching at Xinjiang University"]. 新疆大学高教研究 [*Xinjiang University Higher Education Research*] 2: 65-71.

People's Daily Online. 2010a. "CNPC Has Huge Plans for Xinjiang." *People's Daily Online*, July 20, 2010. Available online at: http://english.peopledaily.com.cn.

People's Daily Online. 2010b. "Xinjiang to Build Largest Oil, Gas Base over 10 Years." *People's Daily Online*, August 16, 2010. Available online at: http://english.peopledaily.com.cn.

Reuveny, Rafael X. 2007 "The North-South Divide and International Studies: A Symposium." *International Studies Review* 9 (4): 556-564.

Sautman, Barry. 2000. "Is Xinjiang an Internal Colony?" *Inner Asia* 2 (2): 438-471.

Schutz, Alfred. 1964. "The Stranger: An Essay in Social Psychology." In *Collected Papers II: Studies in Social Theory*, ed. Arvid Brodersen. The Hague: Nijhoff.

Shanghai Cooperation Organization [SCO] 2010. *The Shanghai Convention on Combating Terrorism, Separatism and Extremism*. Beijing, China: SCO. Available online at: http://www.sectsco.org.

Shimin, Chen, S. 1998. "试论中亚五国民族关系的发展前景" ["Prospects of Relations between Nationalities in Five Central Asia Countries"]. In 中国与中亚研究文集 [*Selected Articles on China's Relations with Central Asia*], ed. F. Wu and S. Chen. Urumchi: Xinjiang University Press.

Smith, Joanne. 2000. "Four Generations of Uyghurs: The Shift Towards Ethno-Political Ideologies among Xinjiang's Youth." *Inner Asia* 2 (2): 195-224.

Spradley, James P. 1979. *The Ethnographic Interview*. New York: Holt, Rinehart and Winston.

Stobdan, Phunchok. 2009. "China's Xianjiang Problem." *IDSA Comment*, July 9, 2009. New Delhi, India: Institute for Defence Studies and Analyses. Available online at: http://www.idsa.in.

Study in China. 2010. *Xinjiang University*. Zhejiang, China: Study-in-China.org. Available online at: http://www.study-in-china.org.

Sutherland, Jeanne. 1999. *Schooling in the New Russia: Innovation and Change 1984-1995*. London: Macmillan.

Wang, Yi Chu. 1966. *Chinese Intellectuals and the West, 1872-1949*. Chapel Hill: University of North Carolina Press.

Wang, Lili, and Xinjun Zhang. 2010. "新疆大学开设特色课程 外国留学生人数逐年增长." ["Xinjiang University Offers Featured Courses, Numbers of Foreign Students Increase Year after Year"]. *Bingtuannet.com*, October 22, 2010. Available on line at: http://bt.xinhuanet.com.

Welch, Anthony R. 1998, "The End of Certainty? The Academic Profession and the Challenge of Change." *Comparative Education Review* 42 (1): 1-14.

Welch, Anthony R. 2005. "Higher Education for a New Korea: Internationalized or Globalized." In *Globalization and Higher Education in East Asia*, ed. Ka Ho Mok and Richard James. Singapore: Marshall Cavendish Academic.

Welch, Anthony R. 2010. "The Challenge of Comparative Research: A Critical Introduction." In *Methodological Choice and Design: Scholarship, Policy and Practice in Social and Educational Research*, ed. Lina Markauskaite, Peter Freebody, and Jude Irwin. Dordrecht, The Netherlands: Springer.

Welch, Anthony R., and Hongxing Cai. 2010. "Enter the Dragon: The Internationalisation of Chinese Higher Education." In *China's Higher Education Reform and Internationalisation*, ed. Janette Ryan. London: Routledge.

Welch, Anthony R., and Zhang Zen. 2005. "中国的知识流散: 海外中国知识分子的交流网络" ["Communication Networks of the Chinese Intellectual Diaspora"]. 比较教育研究 [*Comparative Education Review, (Beijing)*] 26 (2): 26-32.

Welch, Anthony R., and Zhang Zen. 2008a. Higher Education and Global Talent Flows: Brain Drain, Overseas Chinese Intellectuals, and Diasporic Knowledge Networks. *Higher Education Policy* 21 (4): 519-537.

Welch, Anthony R., and Zhang Zen. 2008b. "Communication Networks among the Chinese Knowledge Diaspora: A New Invisible College?" In *World Yearbook of Education 2008 Geographies of Knowledge, Geometries of Power: Framing the Future of Higher Education*, ed. Debbie Epstein, Rebecca Boden, Rosemary Deem, Fazal Rizvi, and Susan Wright. London: Routledge.

Whyte, William Foote. 1943. *Street Corner Society: The Social Structure of the Italian Slum*. Chicago: University of Chicago Press.

Xinjiang University (XU). 1995. 新疆大学校史 1935-1995 *[Xinjiang Daxue Xiaoshi 1935-1995]*. Urumchi: Xinjiang University Press.

XU, Foreign Affairs Office. 2011. *International Students*. Xinjiang, China: XU.

Xinjiang Uyghur Autonomous Region (XUAR) Government. 2005. 新疆年鉴 2005 *[Xinjiang Nianjian 2005]*. Beijing, China: State Council Information Office and the China International Publishing Group. Available online at: http://www.China.com.cn.

Yang, Rui. 2000. "Tensions between the Global and the Local: A Comparative Illustration of the Reorganisation of China's Higher Education in the 1950s and 1990s." *Higher Education* 39 (3): 319-337.

Yang, Rui. 2002. *Third Delight: The Internationalization of Higher Education in China*. London: Routledge.

Yang, Rui. 2003a. "Internationalised While Provincialised? A Case Study of South China Normal University." *Compare: A Journal of Comparative and International Education* 33 (3): 287-300.

Yang, Rui. 2003b "The China-Hong Kong Connection: A Key to Internationalising Chinese Universities." *Asia Pacific Journal of Education* 23 (2): 121-134.

Yang, Rui. 2004. "Openness and Reform as Dynamics for Development: A Case Study of Internationalisation at South China University of Technology." *Higher Education* 47 (4): 473-500.

Yang, Rui, and Anthony R. Welch. 2001. "Internationalising Chinese Universities: A Study of Guangzhou." *World Studies in Education* 2 (1): 21-51.

Yibuladin, Abdul. 2000. "我校民族学生基础数学现状及对策简析" ["Some Analyses of Minority Students' Basic Mathematics at Our University"]. 新疆大学高教研究 *[Xinjiang University Higher Education Research]* 1: 10-16.

Yong, Liu. 2010. "An Economic Bandaid: China's New Approach to Xinjiang." *China Security* 6 (2): 13-23.

Zheng, Lifei. 2006. "Nation to Beef up Central Asian Ties." *China Daily*, October 19, 2006. Available online at: http://www.chinadaily.com.cn.

Zhou, Yao. 1998. "新疆大学人才流失问题的思考" ["Some Reflections on the Brain Drain at Xinjiang University"]. 新疆大学高教研究 *[Xinjiang University Higher Education Research]* 2: 42-49.

Zweig, David, Chung Sui Fung, and Donglin Han. 2008. "Redefining the Brain Drain: China's 'Diaspora Option.'" *Science, Technology and Society* 13 (1): 1-33.

Chapter 4

Minority Students' Access to Higher Education in an Era of Globalization: A Case of Ethnic Koreans in China

Heejin Park and W. James Jacob

The goal of this study is to investigate factors that influence minorities' access to higher education, taking ethnic Koreans' case in the People's Republic of China (PRC) in the context of rapid globalization and marketization. Geographical proximity to the land of origin and a relatively short history of immigration are some of the factors that distinguish ethnic Koreans from other ethnic minorities in China (S. Choi 2008). Also, the rapid marketization and globalization of the PRC and the growing interactions between the ethnic Korean society in China and South Korea are emerging factors that influence the lives of ethnic Koreans, in particular, their educational circumstances (Jacob and Park 2011).

Many researchers, including Nicholas C. Burbules and Carlos A. Torres (2000, 7), warn that subordinate groups have become more "fragmented and divided" as a result of globalization. Michael W. Apple (2005) points out the dark side of the globalization phenomenon as well, in that globalization ultimately accelerates the marginalization of the periphery peoples and countries of the world. In particular, Philip G. Altbach (2007) recognizes the important role higher education plays in developing countries to prevent the escalation of the marginalization the periphery world, since knowledge production has, for the most part, concentrated in developed countries because of the globalization process. The pressure of global competition tends to reshape the higher education subsector in many ways and often in ways that are not always positive. Universities often are forced to become more responsive to the demands of a global market economy (Hayhoe 1993), but less responsive to the missions of higher education institutions that traditionally emphasized common values of human beings (Altbach 2001).

In response to the discourse of global competency, universities around the world put internationalization as a top priority of their mission statement, even though the motivations of each institution would be different. Accordingly, not only developed countries, but also developing countries, including China, emphasize the importance of creating "world-class" research universities (Altbach and Knight 2007). In particular, having a strong drive to achieve world-class status, universities in East Asian countries such as South Korea, Taiwan, and China are keen to match the performance of their universities with that of the universities in developed countries (Mok 2003). University rankings and league tables are often regarded as criteria in determining world-class universities as well as policy criteria in these countries, even though it has been continually questioned whether these instruments are relevant evaluation tools that can be adopted universally (Proulx 2007).

Moreover, university ranking systems do not necessarily value the unique characteristics or missions of each university; rather, the rankings rely heavily on numerical standards such as the number of academic works published, mainly in English, or the amount of financial resources that each institution possesses (see Chapter 7). Nevertheless, world university ranking systems are adopted by many countries as the major criteria for the allocation of governmental financial resources. The Brain Korea 21 Project of South Korea and Projects 211 and 985 of China are examples of these policies. The drive to be considered a world-class university may have placed local universities at the periphery of the global society; local universities whose mission statement may be distinct from the world-class standards are unlikely to be eligible for financial support from the government (H. Park 2009). Ka Ho Mok (2010) also warns that the drive for global competition is dehumanizing higher education. Indeed, considerations of individual students' development become less visible in the important decision making process of universities.

On the contrary, the globalization phenomenon may have brought additional opportunities for people on the margins (Apple 2005). In the case of China, its transformation toward a market economy in the globalization era has enabled the country, which was not very active in the global market before, to become one of the major players in the world economy. Along with the rapid economic development, Chinese higher education subsector has developed dramatically (Jacob 2006; Mohrman and Wang 2010).

As the higher education subsector experienced an increase in the number of institutions, equity issues in education, particularly, in matters of equal educational opportunities and educational access, have emerged in China as well. In particular, studies show that there is a significant gap between the majority Han and the rest of the minority ethnicities in China in terms of academic achievement and higher education enrollment rate (Jacob 2004, 2006). However, history shows that not all ethnic minorities have fallen into the same category; some groups have faced more difficulties than others, whereas some have been regarded just as successful as the Han majority in various aspects, including political adjustment or language adaptation (Zhou 2000). Then, what are the changes in the educational situation for ethnic minorities at higher education level in China that have been brought by the globalization phenomena, particularly in the case of ethnic Koreans?

Based on the observation of the current educational circumstances in East Asia, mainly related to the marketization and globalization, this study investigates the changes and challenges that ethnic Koreans encounter in their attempt to gain access to higher education in China. Since the nature of current social and economic circumstances of ethnic Koreans is crucially related to the historical experiences of the group, we attempt to understand the group in the context of the broader Korean diaspora. Also, Chinese governmental policies that are in support of ethnic minorities are investigated. The guiding research questions are:

1. What are the historical, social, and cultural factors that have shaped the nature of ethnic Koreans' educational performance in the PRC?
2. What type of education policies does the Chinese government have to support minority populations' access to higher education?
3. What changes and challenges do ethnic Koreans face, caused by internationalization and marketization, particularly in terms of access to higher education?

By answering the questions listed above, this study contributes to the understanding of educational issues of the ethnic Koreans in the PRC at the higher education level. In addition, it provides a comprehensive understanding of minorities' educational issues in the PRC, particularly education changes and challenges in relation to the internationalization and marketization phenomenon.

Methods

An extensive literature review was conducted to understand the historical factors that influence the education of ethnic Koreans. Important terminologies such as "model minorities," "silenced minorities," or "middleman minorities" (Y. Park 1991; S. J. Lee 1996; Ogbu 2008) as well as "diaspora" and "nationality" were reviewed. Empirical data was collected mainly through interviews with contents area experts (CAEs) on Chinese minority education. Research team members—comprised of four individuals from the University of Pittsburgh, with the second author of this chapter serving as the principal investigator—believe that in-depth, oral interviews with experts on Chinese minority education are crucial to fill the gap that exists in the data regarding educational issues of China, since "so little information is publicly available" regarding higher education in China (Mohrman and Wang 2010, 175). Currently available data on ethnic minorities' educational issues in China are also very limited, and it is more so in the case of ethnic Koreans (H-R. Park 1996).

Researcher Identity

Open-ended interviews were conducted by four members of our research team using a semistructured questionnaire that was developed by the two authors of this chapter. We tried to minimize the influence of researchers' personal backgrounds in the process of data collection, since four people, who have various ethnic, cultural, and linguistic backgrounds, conducted the interviews of this study. The questionnaire is the major instrument of data collection for this study, and therefore, we decided to restrict any additional questions during the interview. Furthermore, we interviewed experts in the field in an attempt to compile knowledge and information from these experts; not necessarily focused solely on their personal experiences.

The ethnic background of the first author of this chapter might have influenced her understanding of the interview data; as a South Korean her analysis may reflect the perception of the South Korean society. However, as a team, we tried to balance the overarching standpoint of this study through continual communications. We also strived to validate our findings based on literature from various perspectives.

Procedure of the Research

The Institutional Review Board (IRB) of the University of Pittsburgh granted an approval for this research in April 2008. From April 2008 to April 2010, 32 CAEs were interviewed. CAEs on minority education in China were initially identified through an extensive literature review on the given topic and the number increased using a snowball sampling method.

Following the initial list of CAEs, we contacted scholars around the world including the United States, Canada, the United Kingdom, China, and South Korea. Once we started the interviews, we were able to increase the number of prospective interviewees on our list; again using the snowball sampling method, since the interviewed CAEs provided us with recommendations on prospective CAEs. We relied on the recommendations of interviewees to locate potential interviewees based on the belief that scholars, who have substantially contributed to a certain academic field, are important human resources to identifying other scholars in the same field.

The 32 interviewees consisted of a diverse population that included Han Chinese, ethnic Koreans in China, Korean-Americans, ethnic Mongols, and other ethnic minority groups in China. Most of the CAEs display language proficiency in English as well as either Chinese or Korean, and are researchers, faculty members, or educators who demonstrate a substantial level of expertise on ethnic minority educational issues in China, particularly on educational issues related to ethnic Koreans. The CAEs were interviewed in person, via phone, or via e-mail using English, Korean, or Chinese at individual interviewee's convenience. Interviews were recorded, transcribed, and translated into English, if necessary. Interviews lasted between 30 and 60 minutes.

Based on the analysis of the interviews, we discovered several important issues that influence ethnic minority access to higher education in China. When we quote some parts of any interviews, we cite them directly from the transcription/translation of the interview. To protect interviewees' anonymity, we do not reveal detailed personal identification information of each interviewee. For some cases however, we decided to provide background information on the interviewees that may help to better understand their perceptions on certain issues, such as ethnicity, citizenship, or educational background. Respondents provided important insights into the educational issues of ethnic minorities in China, and confirmed that many ethnic minority groups struggled with education issues at the higher education level. In particular, they helped to understand educational changes and challenges that ethnic Koreans face in the context of the rapid internationalization and marketization of the PRC and South Korea. Although the interviews mainly cover questions that relate specifically to the ethnic Koreans, the implications can be generalized to help better understand education issues of other ethnic minority groups.

Korean Diasporas and Ethnic Koreans in China

Ethnic Koreans are one of the officially recognized 56 ethnic groups in China (Zhou 2000, 2001; Jacob 2004; Mackerras 2004; de Varennes 2006; Ma 2007). We use the term *nationality* to indicate ethnic groups in China—a direct translation of *minzu*, which is an official term used by the Chinese government. Comprising about 10 percent of the total population of China, ethnic minorities makeup about 130 million people, whereas most of the countries in the world have less than 100 million people (World Bank 2008). Given the large number of the population as well as diversity in ethnic backgrounds, ethnic minorities in China portray various characteristics in terms of language, culture, economic status, and educational performance. More than 80 different minority languages are spoken (Zhou 2000), some among the 55 officially recognized ethnic minority groups have regional autonomy (Zhou 2000, 2001; Jacob 2004; Mackerras 2004; de Varennes 2006; Ma 2007), and several of them have higher education institutions in their autonomous regions (see Chapter 3).

The primary goal of universities in ethnic minority autonomous regions was to promote and preserve the respective ethic group's culture and languages, and these minorities' universities have played a significant role in the ethnic minority community by providing local cadres and leaders as well as by promoting minority students access to higher education (S. Choi 2010). In particular, ethnic Koreans have their own higher education institution, Yanbian University, which is the first university established for ethnic minorities in the Korean autonomous prefecture in the northeast region of China (Heo et al. 2003). Also, ethnic Koreans are believed to be successful in their children's education at every education level because of their "inherited zeal for education" (Cho 1998; Cai 2004), and they are even named as the "model minority" in terms of their heritage language preservation as well as their attitude toward *Putonghua*, which is the official language of the PRC (Postiglione 1992; Zhou 2000).

Steven K. Lee (2002) argues that minorities' heritage education and academic achievement have meaningful correlations, based on empirical research on Asian immigrants in the state of California. Although it is not clear whether the heritage education influences students' academic performance or vice versa, the study depicts the typical picture of the "model minority" very well. Nonetheless, the label of model minority can negatively affect minorities' lives as critical research has pointed out (S. J. Lee 1996). By labeling a certain ethnic group as the "model minority," the diversity that exists within the minority group can be easily ignored. It may also provide excuses for the receiving society and government not to provide policy support for an ethnic group that is regarded as the model minority, because the label gives an impression that these minority people are successful and therefore do not need any assistance. At the same time, it can be used to judge other type of minorities who do not comply with the norms and culture of the majority society.

In addition, the model minority terminology was adopted, in many cases, without recognizing various characteristics of minorities in different social contexts, including when it is used to identify ethnic Koreans in the PRC or the United States (S. J. Lee 1996; Zhou 2000; S. K. Lee 2002). Given the high average academic performance of the ethnic Koreans in some foreign countries and in their homeland, some researchers assume that the academic achievement of ethnic Koreans are due to the very nature of Korean ethnicity; the researchers argue that the intrinsic dedication of Korean toward their children's education has enabled them to become one of the most successful minorities in educational achievement in PRC (Postiglione 1992; Cho 1998; Zhou 2000).

To ensure the claim that ethnic Koreans' educational success is due to the very nature of the ethnicity (Cai 2004), the educational achievement of ethnic Koreans should be consistently high wherever they live. Even if ethnic Koreans constantly show successful educational performance wherever they live, it should not be attributed to the genetic characteristic of Korean ethnicity. To do so would make the claim no more than fanatical patriotism. On the contrary, factors that contribute their success need to be investigated so that the assertion could get some logical significance.

Korean Diasporas and the Model Minority Discourse

Several studies on ethnic Koreans in China and in the United States show results that confirm the model minority image imposed on the ethnic group (see Y. Park 1991 and Cai 2004). In fact, the model minority image is popular in the United States to label Asian populations, particularly regarding their children's educational achievement, and ethnic Koreans are considered as one of them (S. J. Lee 1996, S. K. Lee 2002). However, not all ethnic Korean minorities perform well at school.

In a comparative study on ethnic Koreans in the United States and Japan, Yongsook Park (1991) found that ethnic Koreans in Japan are regarded as a problematic ethnic group at school mainly due to their low academic achievement, whereas ethnic Koreans in the United States generally show high academic achievement (ibid.). However, the lower academic performance of ethnic Koreans in Japan should not be attributed to Korean ethnicities' relatively lower academic aptitude than that of Japanese students. In the international academic examinations, such as Programme for International Student Assessment (PISA), Korean students have performed equivalent or even better in comparison to Japanese students (OECD 2000, 2003, 2006). Then, what are the factors that explain the low academic performance of ethnic Koreans in Japan, which is distinct from the high academic achievement of ethnic Koreans in the United States?

Yongsook Park (1991) suggests a framework titled "Sociocultural Interactive Model for a Minority Group's Academic Achievement Process" and argues that events and factors at the macro level crucially influence minority students' academic achievement. Therefore, she contends that it is important to acknowledge the interactions occurring within the social structure of receiving countries and the responses of ethnic minorities regarding children's education in the foreign circumstances. In fact, factors that account for the movement of Koreans overseas vary, particularly among the three countries where the majority of ethnic Korean populations reside, such as the PRC, the United States, and Japan (Statistics Korea 2010). Historical events such as the occupation of the Korean peninsula by Japanese colonists and the Cold War in the beginning of the twentieth century are two major driving forces that pushed ethnic Koreans to move to China, Japan and the former Soviet Union territories in Central Asia (H-R. Park 1996).

Conversely, individuals' motivations to improve their socioeconomic circumstances are the major driving forces of recent Korean immigrants in foreign countries. Particularly, Korean immigrants in the United States are roughly categorized into two groups; immigrants pursing better living conditions, including better educational opportunities for their children or economic benefits (Kim et al. 2005), or settlers who initially entered the country for study abroad. The later type of immigration is considered as a problematic phenomenon in South Korean society, in that, it implies the brain drain of highly skilled human resources. Particularly since approximately 80 percent of South Korean PhD holders who graduated from the hard science programs at U.S. universities do not plan to return to Korea (J. Y. Lee 2006) and a half of them actually have settled in the United States after they obtained the degree (Kim 2007). Koreans who immigrate to the United States through investment, which requires a minimum of a half million USD, tripled last year compared to that of 2008 (C. Choi 2010). Accordingly, ethnic Koreans who settle down in the United States tend to be highly educated and financially wealthy, and their engagement in their children's education is active and effective (Y. Park 1991).

Different from Korean immigrants in the United States, however, most ethnic Koreans who initially moved to China were undereducated poor peasants who fled from colonizers' oppression (S. Choi 2008). Nonetheless, these ethnic Koreans became one of the most academically successful minority groups in China. Some of the reasons that explain ethnic Koreans' academic achievement might be geographical proximity to the motherland and cultural similarities between the two countries based on Confucian world order (S. Choi 2008; Jacob and Park 2011). However, ethnic Koreans in Japan, who share those characteristics listed above as well as those who immigrated to a foreign country in a similar period pushed by the Japanese colonization, are not academically as successful as ethnic Koreans in China.

Ethnic Koreans in China

Heh-Rahn Park (1996) and Sheena Choi (2008) provide meaningful insights to understand ethnic Koreans' successful settlement in China. The early Korean settlers in Manchuria, the northeastern regions of China, were mostly desperate, ordinary people whose educational level was not very high. However, there were other types of people who moved to the cold and barren land, such as political or military figures who were dedicated to the Korean independence movement against Japanese colonists (H-R. Park 1996). Ethnic Korean settlers in China were able to establish a very systemic ethnic community quickly because of these patriotic activists, educators and scholars, who sought asylum in this region. These ethnic leaders initiated key educational and military institutions for Koreans, such as military camps for independence movements and schools to preserve Korean ethnic identity and to promote patriotism.

Historically, the Manchuria region was governed by a few Korean dynasties tracing back to the Koguryo Dynasty (32 B.C. to 668 A.D.) (Gomà 2006). However, political disputes over the sovereignty of the region between the two Koreas and the PRC still continue. Moreover, the Manchurian region was not declared as Chinese territory at the time when ethnic Koreans moved there (H-R. Park 1996). Therefore, ethnic Koreans were able to establish their own communities and enjoy autonomy in Manchuria without much difficulty. At the same time, most Korean immigrants in Manchuria perceived themselves as temporal residents, at least in the beginning of their settlement (H-R. Park 1996; Cho 1998). Therefore, it was natural for the Korean ethnic community to put forth much effort to preserve their heritage language and culture, since they believed that they would return to the homeland someday, when it was liberated from the Japanese occupation.

Interestingly, however, what is recognized as "Korean culture" on the Korean Peninsula, particularly in South Korea, has changed dramatically with the marketization and globalization of the country. Accordingly, some cultural or linguistic components that ethnic Koreans in China have preserved can be perceived as "foreign" in South Korean society. Another reason that the cultural heritage of ethnic Koreans in China may be distinct from that of South Korea might be because of the fact that a substantial portion of ethnic Koreans originated from North Korea, which has had very limited interactions with South Korean society.

Recently, however, the interactions between the ethnic Korean communities in China and South Korea have increased dramatically. In only a three-year period, about 100,000 Koreans from China have entered South Korea by acquiring work permits (Jacob and Park 2011). The actual number of ethnic Koreans staying in South Korea is probably larger than the official statistics since many ethnic Korean workers in South Korea have failed to maintain proper immigrant status—in many cases, intentionally.

In addition, "marriage immigration" has become an important mode of interactions between ethnic Koreans in China and South Korean society. Initially, it was the idea of the South Korean government to arrange marriages between ethnic Korean women in China and South Korean rural men who were not able to find prospective brides within the country (Han and Seol 2006). The South Korean government and people believed that they might be able to preserve the originality of their homogenous ethnicity in this way (Freeman 2005). On the contrary, there have been numerous unintended outcomes of this policy such as issues of fraudulent marriages (Freeman 2006) and human rights violation issues. Furthermore, the massive emigration of young adult population either as "foreign brides" or "foreign laborers" has undermined the stability of ethnic Korean communities in China (You and Kwak 2004).

A substantial portion of ethnic Koreans from China living in South Korea serve in low-status occupations and make less money than native workers who are in the same occupation: these jobs include working as manual laborers, waitresses, nannies, and domestic workers. Their Korean language proficiency and cultural similarity may facilitate the adjustment to the South Korean society to a certain extent. However, the mass media reported that these Koreans are often exposed to cultural and social difficulties and discrimination in South Korean society, being considered as "second-class" people or "foreigners" (Freeman 2005). Similarly, although the South Korean government has kept compiling statistical data on ethnic Koreans in China by identifying them as Koreans and naming them as *dongpo* (overseas Koreans or Korean residents abroad), it does not guarantee any legal status (citizenship or resident permission) or provide special assistance for ethnic Koreans from China.

Furthermore, some scholars report that ethnic Koreans in China have encountered a number of educational challenges and changes in the last decade (Heo et al. 2003; Kim 2003; You and Kwak 2004). Ethnic Koreans in China have been able to receive formal education in Korean up to the higher education level thus far (Gao 2008) and are regarded as successful in education. However, the changing socioeconomic environment caused by the rapid globalization and marketization of China may or may not be working in favor of ethnic Koreans' educational success. For example, their educational performance in the national college entrance examination continues to decline (Cai 2004), and Yanbian University does not explicitly pursue its mission to contribute to the education of Korean descendants any more (Cho 1998; S. Choi 2010; see also Chapter 3).

Ethnic Minorities' Access to Higher Education in China

The proportion of minority students and faculty in higher education is not adequate in comparison to ethnic minorities' percentage in the Chinese national census data (Jacob and Park 2011); ethnic minorities comprise almost 10 percent of the Chinese population, while the proportion of minority students is 5.4 percent and that of faculty is 4.1 percent (Chinese Ministry of Education [MOE] 2005). While the percentage of minority faculty and students in Chinese higher education continues to increase (Sautman 1997; China MOE 2000, 2005), there may be diversity among minorities in terms of the numeric representation of each minority group in the higher education sector. Thus, further investigations may be required to understand the factors that influence the low enrollment rate of ethnic minorities in higher education.

However, given the obvious proportional disparity between ethnic minorities and the Han majority in terms of access to higher education, the Chinese government has implemented diverse policy instruments. In the following section we introduce the Chinese government's preferential policies for minority nationality students. In particular, we explore how these preferential policies have addressed the educational challenges that minority nationality students face.

China's Preferential Policies and their Limitations

In general, ethnic minorities are aware of the importance of higher education, particularly because of the economic returns that the education is expected to bring. Because of the popularization of higher education in China, as well as growing competency in the global market, Chinese young jobseekers are requested to attain college degrees to be successful in the expanding market. One of the CAEs interviewed, who is a Han Chinese scholar living in the United States, directly points out the fact that "Many of the minority members, they know that if they want to do well in communities in China in general, they need [higher] education." However, there are several obstacles that minorities face in getting access to higher education and the government has adopted several policies to address these challenges. The increasing tuition fee is just one of the obstacles that prevent ethnic minority access to higher education; W. James Jacob (2006) argues that the language barrier and geographic isolation are the two major hindrances.

Language Issues

Language is a critical factor that influences ethnic minority access to higher education in China. Most of the CAEs agree that the low enrollment rate in higher education is closely related to minorities' Putonghua proficiency. One CAE asserts: "Proficiency in Mandarin [Putonghua] seems to be the key factor [for minority nationality students to attend higher education]." However, no one mentioned the benefits that proficiency in ethnic language can bring to minority students' access to higher education, whereas most of the interviewees assert that proficiency in Mandarin Chinese is fundamental. One even asserted that "ethnic language proficiency is not generally regarded as a bonus." The majority of ethnic minorities, in particular who dwell in their autonomous regions, would feel more comfortable in their ethnic language, and the Chinese government allows ethnic minorities to educate their children in their own language in formal education settings, even though it does not necessarily mean that adequate supports are provided to actualize the policy goal. Also, the preferential treatment policy provides national college entrance examination in some ethnic languages.

In most cases, higher education is offered in Chinese language. Therefore, even though minorities are allowed to study in their native language until primary or secondary level, they need to have Putonghua proficiency to perform well in higher education (except for a limited number of ethnic universities that offer instructions in minority nationalities' languages). Nevertheless, the bachelor's degree, obtained in an ethnic higher education institution whose medium of instruction is the ethnic minority's language, does not guarantee success in the job market unless they search for a job exclusively within the ethnic society.

As long as the Chinese society operates in one language and the majority Han dominates the society, proficiency in Mandarin is a fundamental skill that all minorities need to master. It does not necessarily mean, however, that the Chinese society needs to operate in one official language. If the society is willing to pay the social cost, the Chinese society can recognize more than one official language as is the practice in other countries with multiple languages. Nonetheless, as long as ethnic language proficiency does not have equivalent relevancy to the dominant language proficiency in society as well as on campus, opportunity to learn the dominant language needs to be guaranteed by the government. Also, educational policies that do not support minorities in obtaining Mandarin proficiency, such as using ethnic minorities' languages as the medium of instruction without giving them adequate opportunities to learn Mandarin at school, do not promote a genuine sense of equal opportunities.

For the same reason, the preferential policy that offers college entrance examination in ethnic minority languages is just remedial in nature, since it does not address the fundamental issues of the challenges that minority students encounter. Minority students who are not able to master Mandarin, although they might have survived the entrance examinations, would be even more challenged when they enter the job market.

As a few interviewees mentioned, it may be very important to preserve minorities' languages and culture for the development of nationality communities. Some of the interviewees also argued that universities, particularly located in ethnic autonomous regions, should take the role to promote and preserve ethnic minorities' heritage. These interviewees made an important point that education is a crucial medium for the preservation and development of ethnic language and culture. However, if the knowledge of ethnic language and culture, for which ethnic minorities have to invest so much effort and resource to acquire, is not used in the dominant society, its utility needs to be reconsidered. No one can ask for the preservation of language or culture for the sake of preservation, since language rights (linguistic human right) is not the right of a language, but the right of the speakers of the language (Paulston 2003).

It seems that diversity is more appreciated than ever with the globalization movement, and so are indigenous culture and language. However, as Thomas Friedman (2005) ardently asserts, the degree of competition is intensified in this era of rapid globalization. Therefore, current globalization can be the cause of the marginalization of local communities and indigenous societies (Apple 2005), unless the locals can integrate as equivalent players to the dominant group in the global competition. In particular, the wide open opportunity in the "flat world" may threaten those who are not equipped with the means of global competition such as language, technology, and access to information (Friedman 2005). The encouragement to preserve indigenous language and culture, without ensuring that they have competency in the majority society, can worsen the marginal situation of local people.

We learn from the CAEs in this study that ethnic minority students have to confront discrimination on and off campus during their college life, mainly because of the issues related to their Mandarin language proficiency. Zhenzhou Zhao (2007) discovered that minority students experience difficulties in their adaptation to university life. To promote minority students' adjustment to higher education institutions, the Chinese government provides preliminary programs, which are mainly comprised of Mandarin language courses.

Besides, the Chinese government has enacted preferential education policies, though most of them are remedial treatments rather than fundamental solution. Examples of preferential policies are "preferential admissions, lowered school fees and boarding schools" (Sautman 1999, 174). Also, the lower minimum entrance score and quota system for minorities are some of the preferential policies acknowledged by most of the CAEs. However, the CAEs pointed out that only a few policies are adopted to address social, cultural, and economic obstacles other than that of language barriers. Therefore, some questioned the real function of preferential policies and were concerned with the gap between policies and the actual implementation.

Moreover, a high school teacher in the Yanbian region asserted that "universities prefer to accept Han students rather than minority students." She believes that universities would select a Han student rather than a minority student when the two students show equal academic grade in the application process, even though the universities may have preferential policies. An ethnic Korean faculty, who teaches Chinese language and literature at a university in South Korea, contended that the preferential policy exists, but it does not necessarily work as the government assumes:

> I do not think that the preferential policies in the higher education applications are actually helpful for minority nationality students. Even though minority students might get extra credits on the university entrance examination, it does not necessarily mean that these students are going to be accepted into the program because universities do not prefer to choose minority students who may not have fluency in Mandarin Chinese.

She also maintained that some ethnic minorities such as Tibetan and Uyghur might take advantage of the preferential policy, but not all minorities. As an ethnic Korean from China, she asserted that she did not benefit from any policy support.

All interviewees agreed that any barriers that hinder minority students from learning Putonghua at school should be removed, at least for pragmatic reasons. However, many of the interviewees disagreed with the government's policy to promote Putonghua as an exclusive national language. Several CAEs pointed out that a substantial number of ethnic minorities have very little exposure to Putonghua. They also claimed that it is the responsibility of the Chinese government to provide teaching materials and instruction in both Putonghua and the minorities' languages. However, it does not seem to be easy, or even unrealistic, to offer education in so many different languages for a country as large as China.

In reality, minority students have few opportunities to receive quality education in Mandarin since teachers who are fluent in Mandarin tend to find better job opportunities elsewhere rather than in the rural and hinterland regions where many minorities reside (Clothey 2005). One of the CAE interviewees mentioned, "The central policy neither encourages nor discourages the use of minority languages at school." The situation would be worse if the government prohibits certain languages to be spoken or used as the medium of instruction. However, if the government does not intervene in language matters by addressing properly the challenges that ethnic minorities face, minority language speakers would hardly avoid the disadvantages resulting from the inadequate proficiency in the dominated language.

Quota System

The Chinese government has a quota system that enforces universities to accept a certain proportion of students within the region where the university is located (Sautman 1997). In particular, universities in ethnic autonomous regions have quotas for the respective minority nationalities to promote minority access to higher education. The proportion of minority population in the region decides the quota size. Thus, the emigration of ethnic minorities from ethnic autonomous regions can result in the decrease of quota size for the ethnic groups in regional universities. For example, the Yanbian University had to cut its quota for Korean students from 50 percent to 40 percent, because of the massive emigration of ethnic Koreans both at domestic and international levels (Lin et al. 2011).

However, the decrease of ethnic Korean applicants and the reduction of quota size for ethnic Koreans generated an ironic response from the current president of the Yanbian University. He stated that he is satisfied with the lower proportion of ethnic Koreans because he believes that the university now admits better students (ibid.). Whereas the ethnic Koreans' university struggles to recruit highly qualified Korean students, ethnic Korean CAEs expressed their doubts about the quality of education at Yanbian University. One interviewee argued that as long as ethnic higher education institutions do not show excellence in education and high reputation, the quota system does not really provide opportunities for minority students to be successful in the Chinese society, particularly for high-achieving students. Given the importance of high quality education, one interviewee even argued that it is better for ethnic minorities to immigrate to metropolitan regions where they can have access to better education opportunities instead of relying on the quota system in ethnic autonomous regions.

Recently, Yanbian University was selected as one of the Project 211 universities, which is a Chinese ambitious policy drive to promote approximately 100 Chinese universities to the status of world-class higher education institutions. However, since it is a provincial level ethnic minorities' institution, the reputation of the institution as an elite university has not been established. Given the fact that the university is the oldest and one of the best ethnic higher education institutions, the quality education that minority students can access through regional quotas in minority regions must be even more limited (see Chapter 3).

Globalization and Marketization as a Threat and an Opportunity

Heritage Language Preservation, Bilingualism or Trilingualism?

The global influence of English language has made the language issue that ethnic Koreans face even more complicated. With the rapid globalization and marketization of the PRC, English has become increasingly important, especially in college and university admissions and the professional job market. For example, many higher education institutions in China set English language proficiency as one of the critical admission or graduation requirements. Therefore, there is a mutual understanding on the importance of English proficiency for young people in Chinese society.

One interviewee asserted that students who live in Han dominant regions learn English because it is required at school. Some CAEs argued that the same opportunities to learn English language at school should be ensured for ethnic minorities, as was reflected by an educational researcher we interviewed: "Everybody knows that one of the key factors in doing well in the entrance examination to get into the tertiary education system is English. English is one of the compulsory elements."

However, it is not that simple for ethnic minorities to focus on learning English because they have two additional languages to master. As many CAEs pointed out, a considerable number of minorities have already given up their native languages as a result of a national policy that promotes Mandarin Chinese as the official national language. Only one-third of ethnic minorities are bilingual—fluent both in Chinese and in their own language—six ethnic groups have converted into Chinese speakers and a majority of the ethnic minority groups use Chinese as a second language (Ma 2007). Given the challenges that minorities face regarding language, two CAEs argued that minorities need to prioritize acquiring Putonghua first:

> I would say, in terms of language choice, they [minorities] should choose Putonghua first. Once they are willing to learn Mandarin, they would be willing to learn English.
>
> For the Han majority Chinese, if they want to do well, they need to learn only two languages; which are Chinese and English. However, for minority students they have an extra language to learn. If they want to do well socially and economically, they may learn their native language after they master Chinese and English.

Fluency in languages other than Mandarin Chinese would not guarantee direct returns to minority students in most Chinese higher education institutions, because virtually most of the higher education is delivered in Chinese. Furthermore, it is hard for minority students to prepare for their future properly because they have few English learning opportunities at school, which is crucial to get into universities. It is not solely the minorities' willingness or unwillingness that prioritizes a certain language over another, but the accessibility of language programs, either English or Putonghua. In our interviews, we found that ethnic Koreans have rarely enjoyed opportunities to learn Mandarin language with quality teachers in primary or secondary schools and more so in the case of English language, as reflected in the following statement:

> I could not learn English at school because there was no teacher who can teach. So, I had to choose Japanese for my second language. It was not a problem for me while I was at school or when I applied for university.... However, I found that English is a very important language that I should have learned.

An ethnic Korean professor, now living in South Korea, explained that her lack of knowledge of English was not a problem when she applied to the university in China, because an entrance examination written in Japanese was offered to students who did not learn English. However, another educator argued that students need to show English proficiency to enter the top-tier universities and to perform well in universities for various reasons. For example, increasing numbers of English terminologies and expressions are used across disciplines. The ethnic Korean professor, who told us that she could not get quality English education in China, also stated that she encountered various difficulties in South Korea because of her lack of English proficiency: "Now, I am living in South Korea where people use a lot of English expressions in their daily lives. Therefore, I think the [Chinese] government should ensure equal opportunities for minority students to learn English."

Moreover, as the remark above indicates, because the proficiency in English language gains more significance, minority students face challenges, especially if they are seeking employment or education opportunities outside the country. In the case of one ethnic Korean professor now working in South Korea, she has confronted numerous unexpected challenges while she has held a professorship because of her lack of knowledge of the English language. Also, with the expansion of Korean firms in the Mainland China, there is an increasing demand to hire managers who have proficiency both in Korean and Chinese languages. Additionally, some knowledge of English is required to better understand contemporary Korean language because a substantial number of English expressions are used in the daily lives of ordinary Koreans, and more so in professions related to the international sector. However, not many scholars are interested in educational issues related to minority students' access to English language and the challenges or dilemmas that minorities face. It is also hard to find Chinese educational policies that address these challenges.

Globalization and the Identity Transformation

Most CAEs believe that ethnic Koreans are one of a few ethnic minority groups whose opportunities for better lives and education have increased through globalization and marketization of Chinese society. Domestically, ethnic Koreans have more job opportunities than other minority groups since Korean corporate branches have emerged in China. In addition, because of the huge popularization of Korean pop culture and music across Asian countries including China, referred to as *Hanyru* (Korean Wave), the image and status of the Korean culture and language has improved dramatically (Shim 2006). With the strong *Hanyru*, tourism, cultural or entertainment industries related to the Korean media culture continue to expand in Asian countries. Accordingly, the demand for Korean language learning programs and teachers have increased in China, which create more opportunities for ethnic Koreans to utilize their Korean language and culture proficiency. In particular, Yanbian University is a major provider of Korean language teachers across the country (Lin et al. 2011).

In addition, substantial numbers of ethnic Koreans have found career, matrimonial, and education opportunities in South Korea, although the quality of life that these ethnic Koreans enjoy in South Korea might be not necessarily higher than those in China. Interestingly, several of our interviewees pointed out that the professional careers that are available for ethnic Koreans in South Korea are usually related to their proficiency in Chinese culture and language. On the contrary, it is not easy for ethnic Koreans, who received their education in China, to compete with South Koreans in other fields, since the educational level of South Korean society is so high that there are already an abundant of well-educated and qualified human resources in most professional fields.

In other words, the opportunities that ethnic Koreans enjoy through the influence of globalization and marketization are created in a way that strengthens their transnational identity: both as Koreans and Chinese. For example, in most cases, ethnic Koreans' Korean language proficiency is very high, but they still stand out in South Korean society because of the unique accents and vocabularies that they have developed in Chinese society. One of our interviewees, an ethnic Korean from China currently living in South Korea, mentioned that she was frustrated when she found herself being treated as different in South Korea. Although she is not considered as a native Korean in South Korea, she proudly mentioned her involvement in a social network among Korean nationalities in South Korea, which promotes the preservation of Korean culture and tradition. Furthermore, she argued that ethnic Koreans' enthusiasm for preserving Korean culture and language should be appreciated by South Korean society.

However, there are substantial differences between Korean culture and language perceived as native by ethnic Koreans in China and those in the contemporary South Korean society. Although the two societies share the same heritage and ancestry, diverse inputs from the two distinct socioeconomic contexts, in China and South Korea, during the several decades of separation have resulted in two very different types of Korean culture and language. Quite often the different characteristics that ethnic Koreans portray in South Korean society are regarded as inferior or even as a sign of ignorance (Lee et al. 2009).

At the same time, the majority of the ethnic Koreans in China have specific characteristics different from the majority Han people. In most cases, the native language of ethnic Koreans in the Korean autonomous regions is Korean rather than Chinese. Ethnic Koreans are applauded as being *almost* invisible, in that their culture is similar to that of the mainstream Han Chinese. However, the fact that the relative "invisibility" of ethnic Korean is regarded as their major strength may indicate that ethnic Koreans' unique characteristics as one of the nationalities in China is not appreciated as a "significant" component that comprises the major society.

Any value judgment on the cultural and linguistic characteristics of ethnic Koreans compared to that of either South Korean or Chinese should not be accepted. At the same time, the differences that exist between ethnic Koreans and the majority Han or South Koreans should not be denied. Furthermore, the understanding of ethnic Koreans in China is important for both Korean and Chinese society and for ethnic Koreans themselves. In particular, what appears to assist ethnic Koreans in obtaining better opportunities in the globalization era is their transnational identity. Indeed, Korean proficiency helps them in China and Chinese proficiency in South Korea.

Transnational Identity and the Ethnic Korean University

Globalization has made more people who are identifying themselves as "transnational" and therefore have increased their career opportunities. One of the driving forces behind the transnational phenomenon is the increasing interactions and contacts of people and countries across borders. As a result, people who are capable in settings that involve diverse languages and cultures and therefore able to bridge different cultural groups together may assume important roles in the globalization era (S. Choi 2010).

Yanbian University has also been influenced by the globalization trend. In particular, the transnational identity and intercultural proficiency, which are crucial characteristics of Korean nationalities, create novel value for the development of the university in the globalization era. In the first couple of decades, the university was exclusively dedicated to recruiting ethnic Koreans and enhancing a Korean Studies Department. The proportion of ethnic Korean students has been dominant because of the regional allocation policy (quota system). Educating local ethnic leaders, the university has contributed to the development of the ethnic Korean community by providing local cadres and teachers. However, Korean high-achievers do not prefer to attend Yanbian University, although the number of qualified Han Chinese students has continued to increase. The average score of the academic aptitude of students has increased; leading to fewer ethnic Koreans but recruiting more qualified Han Chinese students than before (Lin et al. 2011).

Joining the Project 211, Yanbian University receives substantially increased supports from the central government; not only in the size of the revenue, but also the reputation of the university (Mok 2001). However, the transformation from an ethnic higher education institution to being one of the top 100 universities in China might not necessarily indicate educational improvement for the ethnic Koreans in China. The number of non-ethnic-Korean students has increased, while the proportion of ethnic Koreans in the student body as well as the emphasis on Korean language and culture have decreased. For example, the official website of the university is in Chinese, while the Korean version of the site is almost abandoned. Currently, most lectures are conducted in Chinese and the proportion of ethnic Korean faculty has decreased.

Ironically, however, the recently increasing opportunities that Yanbian University enjoys have been created in fields that are closely related to its Korean heritage. Yanbian University is located in a geographic region where the political tension of the northeast Asia is concentrated. Based on the geographical position, where Russia and China as well as the two Koreas are situated, the university is posing itself as a strategic research institution in the "Gold Triangle" (Lin et al. 2011). Therefore, the cultural and political implications are particularly meaningful to understand the current situation and challenges that the North Korean society faces.

The influence of communism and the relatively low economic development of both North Korea and ethnic Korean communities in China have made the two societies similarly distinct from South Korea. Therefore, cultural and economic challenges that ethnic Koreans face in the relationship with South Korea can partly illustrate the future that the two Koreas will face when they are reunited. Also, the borders between South Korea and North Korea are strictly closed, and interactions between the two Koreas are restricted. On the contrary, the northeastern region of China is where South and North Koreans may enjoy less tension and more opportunities to interact with each other. Moreover, the Yanbian region is the first destination for the increasing numbers of North Korean refugees.

Yanbian University also receives extra governmental support for research projects, which are mostly related to the university's characterization as an ethnic institution and for the local development of ethnic communities. Moreover, Han Chinese students are attracted to the university mostly due to the strong Korean language and cultural heritage. Furthermore, the graduates' success in the job market is related to the development of the South Korean economy: a large portion of graduates have been offered positions related to South Korea one way or the other (Jacob and Park 2011).

However, designated as a recipient of the extensive governmental aids through the Project 211, which forces Yanbian University to develop a comprehensive elite higher education institution, the traditional mission of serving ethnic Koreans tends to be compromised (S. Choi 2010). For example, conforming to the globalization trend, significant efforts have been made to connect to the rest of the world (Lin et al. 2011) in ways that are not necessarily related to the original missions of the university. Furthermore, the university is pursuing multiculturalism through building up partnerships with universities in Europe and North America to promote internationalization of the institution and its students (ibid.). However, it is not clear how the multilateral exchanges can contribute to the development of multiculturalism of the university. More importantly, it is hard to relate the efforts of the university to connect the intercultural characteristics of the university as an ethnic institution to their ambitious goal of internationalization or multiculturalization.

Yanbian University pursues academic excellence to become a center for studies on marginalized matters geographically and socioeconomically, given that the university is located in a remote area. To do so, the characteristics of the university as an ethnic institution should be in the center of the development strategies of the university. Most of all, the university can contribute to the development of the multiculturalism in the Chinese society by adding a strong understanding on ethnic Koreans and the intercultural and transnational experiences that students have within the institution. Therefore, the university's efforts to raise the overall academic scores of students by receiving more Han students while compromising the ethnic components of the institution appears ironic (Lin et al. 2011).

On the contrary, ethnic Korean students are crucial in the development of the intercultural and transnational characteristics of the institution, which may ultimately lead to the development of domestic as well as internal competency of the university. Therefore, efforts are needed to increase the recruitment of qualified ethnic Korean students and to understand the reasons that explain why qualified Koreans students do not prefer to attend Yanbian University.

Conclusion and Discussion

Comprised of 56 officially recognized ethnic groups, Chinese society has well over 100 million people of minority status. For the most part, ethnic minority students are underrepresented in China's higher education subsector. To address the numerical disparity of ethnic minority access to higher education, the Chinese government has adopted various preferential policies such as extra credits, lower requirements, or language choices in the college entrance examination, which have been deemed to be temporary remedies in nature, in that, these policies do not appear to address the fundamental challenges that ethnic minority nationalities have in gaining equal educational opportunities. As a matter of fact, the issue of minority students' access to higher education is not that simple, since so many factors are intertwined in the process of the preparation of the college and in the life on/off campus. The expectations on the prospect of success in the job market afterward are also important factors that influence the decision of minority students' access to higher education.

In our study, we investigated the broad historical, social, cultural, and economic factors that have influenced the educational circumstances of Korean nationalities, in particular, their access to higher education. We also addressed the challenges that Yanbian University has faced as an "ethnic Koreans' institution" in the context of globalization and increasing competitions. Most of our interviewees believe that globalization and marketization have brought more opportunities for ethnic Koreans than any other minority group in China. However, the belief of most of the CAEs in this study appears to accept the model minority stereotype in general: that is, Koreans are high academic achievers due to their inherent characteristics and therefore would be financially successful.

On the contrary, we argue that the applause for ethnic Koreans for being almost "invisible" in Chinese society illustrates the nature of struggles that Korean nationalities need to navigate as ethnic minorities in China. Our findings suggest that the globalization and marketization phenomena provide benefits for ethnic Koreans in China when they have both Korean and Chinese language and cultural proficiency, which ultimately allow them to locate better opportunities both in China and South Korea. However, it does not necessarily mean that ethnic Koreans can enjoy opportunities equal to those of the Han majority in China or native South Koreans in South Korea. It is not easy for them to compete with the majority populations in fields where they are not able to utilize their transnational identity. At the same time, the globalization and marketization of the Chinese society have brought different types of challenges to ethnic Koreans, such as the pressure to master three languages (Mandarin, English, and Korean) and to be successful in the higher education admissions and in the job market.

The Korean heritage is the asset that has enabled Yanbian University to recruit quality Han students as well as to obtain financial support from the government. However, only limited attention is given by the university to boost the development of ethnic Korean communities or to educate local Korean students by supporting their transnational characteristics. For example, an important figure of the university addressed the dilemma of recruiting more qualified Han students while at the same time fulfilling the mission to teach ethnic Korean students. However it is doubtful if having more Han high achievers without a strong academic Korean studies program will put the university in a better condition to become a world-class university. On the contrary, it is the Korean heritage that has brought not only financial opportunities from the government, but also attracted high-achieving Han students to the university.

Furthermore, as Daniel Schugurensky (2006) argues, on the one hand, pursuing the interests of a university by adding more success in business may not mean that the university serves the communities and regions successfully where they are located; on the other hand, the social responsibility of a university can be fulfilled through the conscious efforts to contribute to increase the public good. Therefore, Yanbian University may have to consider fulfilling its social responsibility as an ethnic institution focused on challenges and changes that ethnic Koreans face in the globalization era. For example, the continual brain drain of the ethnic Koreans from the local community to China's urban regions or to South Korea has resulted in the absence of parenting for primary and secondary students in local villages as well as in the shutdown of ethnic local schools (Cai 2004; Choi et al. 2004), which can be addressed by Yanbian University's mission statement.

Last, the transnational identity that ethnic Koreans have attained through their residency in China for several decades should not be subjected to any value judgment. To ensure equal opportunities for ethnic Koreans in higher education access as well as in their general lives, the characteristics of ethnic Koreans, such as their unique accent or cultural practices, should be acknowledged as they are. At the same time, the discourse on the preservation of heritage language or culture should be continued, keeping the balance between the development of ethnic communities and the fulfillment of individuals' pursuit of better opportunities. Thus far, however, both the Chinese and Korean societies where ethnic Koreans belong do not seem to properly recognize the uniqueness of ethnic Koreans.

REFERENCES

Altbach, Philip G. 2001. "Why Higher Education is not a Global Commodity." *Chronicle of Higher Education* 47 (35): B20.

Altbach, Philip G. 2007. "Peripheries and Centres: Research Universities in Developing Countries." *Higher Education Management & Policy* 19 (2): 111-134.
Altbach, Philip G., and Jane Knight. 2007. "The Internationalization of Higher Education: Motivations and Realities." *Journal of Studies in International Education* 11: 290-305.
Apple, Michael W. 2005. "Are Markets in Education Democratic? Neoliberal Globalism, Vouchers, and the Politics of Choice." In *Globalizing Education: Policies, Pedagogies, & Politics*, ed. Michael W. Apple, Jane Kenway, and Michael Singh. New York: Peter Lang.
Burbules, Nicolas C., and Carlos A. Torres. 2000. *Globalization and Education: Critical Perspectives*. New York: Routledge.
Cai, Mei Hua. 2004. "연변 조선족 중소학교 교육문제실태 조사연구" ["A Research on the Elementary and Secondary Education of Korean Chinese in Yanbian"]. 교육문제연구 [*Journal of Education Research*] 20: 93-111.
China Ministry of Education (MOE). 2000. *Bulletin for the National Educational Development Statistics*. Beijing: Chinese MOE.
China MOE. 2005. *Bulletin for the National Educational Development Statistics*. Beijing: Chinese MOE.
Cho, Yun Duck. 1998. "조선족 교육열과 한국인의 교육열의 비교연구" ["A Comparative Analysis on the Education Fever of Korean Chinese and South Korean"]. In *제124차 학술대회발표자료* [*The Korean Society for the Study of Sociology of Education the 124th Conference*]. Seoul: 한국교육사회학회 [The Korean Society for the Study of Sociology of Education].
Choi, Chul Ho. 2010. "美 투자이민에 한인들 크게 증가" ["The Number of Korean US Immigration through Investments has Dramatically Increased"], *Newsis*, January 11.
Choi, Sheena. 2008. "Korean Exceptionalism?: History, Culture, Politics, and Ethnic Relations in Northeast China." In *Cultural Education-Cultural Sustainability: Minority, Diaspora, Indigenous and Ethno-Religious Groups in Multicultural Societies*, ed. Zvi Bekerman and Ezra Kopelowitz. New York: Routledge.
Choi, Sheena. 2010. "Globalization, China's Drive for World-Class Universities (211 Project) and the Challenges of Ethnic Minority Higher Education: The Case of Yanbian University." *Asia Pacific Education Review* 11 (2): 169-178.
Choi, Sung Hak, Chul Hwa Kim, Man Seok Kang, Young Duck Kang, Soon Young Kim, Chun Bong Rah, Hae Sun Ryu, Doo Seok Ra, Chun Min Lee, Jung Hoo Park, Tae Soo Park, and Chang Hee Han. 2004. *21세기초 조선족 교육의 문제 및 개혁 연구* [*Educational Issues of Ethnic Koreans in China in the Early Twenty-First Century*]. Seoul: Korean Educational Development Institute (KEDI).
Clothey, Rebecca. 2005. "China's Policies for Minority Nationalities in Higher Education: Negotiating National Values and Ethnic Identities." *Comparative Education Review* 49 (3): 389-409.
de Varennes, Fernand. 2006. "Language Rights of Minorities and Increasing Tensions in the People's Republic of China." *Asia-Pacific Journal on Human Rights & the Law* 7 (2): 1-28.
Freeman, Caren. 2005. "Marrying Up and Marrying Down: The Paradoxes of Marital Mobility for Chosonjok Brides in South Korea." In *Cross-Border*

Marriages: Gender and Mobility in Transnational Asia, ed. Nicole Constable. Philadelphia: University of Pennsylvania Press.

Freeman, Caren. 2006. "Forging Kinship across Borders: Paradoxes of Gender, Kinship and Nation between China and South Korea." PhD diss., University of Virginia.

Friedman, Thomas L. 2005. *The World is Flat: A Brief History of the Twenty-First Century*. New York: Farrar, Straus and Giroux.

Gao, Fang. 2008. "What it Means to be a 'Model Minority': Voices of Ethnic Koreans in Northeast China." *Asian Ethnicity* 9 (1): 55-67.

Gomà, Daniel. 2006. "The Chinese-Korean Border Issue: An Analysis of a Contested Frontier." *Asian Survey* 46 (6): 867-880.

Han, Geon Soo, and Dong Hoon Seol. 2006. 결혼중개업체 실태조사 및 관리방안 연구 [*Matchmaking Agencies in South Korea and Government's Regulations*]. Seoul: Korean Ministry of Health and Welfare.

Hayhoe, Ruth. 1993 "China's Universities since Tiananmen: A Critical Assessment." *The China Quarterly* 134: 291-309.

Heo, Myung Chul, Gum Have Park, Hyang Hwa Kim, and Jung Lee. 2003. 연변 조선족 교육의 현황과 과제 [*Educational Issues of Ethnic Koreans in Yanbian China*]. Seoul: KEDI.

Jacob, W. James. 2004. "Marketization, Demarketization, and Remarketization: The Impact of the Economic Market on Higher Education in China." PhD diss., University of California, Los Angeles.

Jacob, W. James. 2006. "Social Justice in Chinese Higher Education: Regional Issues of Equity and Access." *International Review of Education* 52 (1): 149-169.

Jacob, W. James, and Heejin Park. 2011. "Language Issues in Chinese Higher Education : The Case of Korean and Mongol Minority Groups." In *China's Integrationist Language Policy: Impact on Social Harmony*, ed. Gulbahar H. Beckett and Gerad A. Postiglione. New York: Routledge.

Kim, Hong Won, Myung Lim Jang, Joo Hoo Kim, Hun Soo Kim, Hee Sook Lee, and Heejin Park. 2005. 조기유학에 관한 국민의식 및 실태 조사 연구 [*A Study on the Realities and People's Awareness on Secondary School Student's Study Abroad Issues*]. Seoul: KEDI.

Kim, Ik Tae. 2007. "한국인 美 이공계 박사, 현지 정착 절반 달해" ["Half of the Korean PhD Holders from the US Higher Education Institutions Major in Hard Science Settle in the US"]. *Money Today News*, October 3.

Kim, Yong Oak. 2003. "중국에서의 한국어(조선어) 교육에 관한 고찰" ["A Study on the Korean Language Education in China"]. 청람어문교육학회 [*The Society of Chongnam Language & Literature*] 26: 253-272.

Lee, Jae-Boon, Hyewon Kim, and Haeyoung Lee. 2009. "국제결혼 이주여성의 자녀 교육지원을 위한핵심역량 현황 및 인식" ["Core Competencies and Perceptions of Female Immigrants in International Marriages on Educational Support for Their Children"]. 한국교육 [*Journal of Korean Education*] 36 (2): 3-29.

Lee, Jae Yong. 2006. "美서 박사학위 취득 이공계 인력 74% 한국 안 돌아가겠다'" ["74% of Korean Hard Science PhD Who Received their Degree in the US Universities Say, 'I Do Not Plan to Go Back to Korea'"]. *Seoul KyungJae*, December 18.

Lee, Stacey J. 1996. *Unraveling the "Model Minority" Stereotype: Listening to Asian American Youth.* New York: Teachers College Press.

Lee, Steven K. 2002. "The Significance of Language and Cultural Education on Secondary Achievement: A Survey of Chinese-American and Korean-American Students." *Bilingual Research Journal* 26 (2): 213-224.

Lin, Jing, Jun Li, and Taizhu Piao. 2011. "Yanbian University: Building a Niche through a Multicultural Identity." In *Portraits of 21st Century Chinese Universities: In the Move to Mass Higher Education*, ed. Ruth Hayhoe, Jun Li, Jing Lin and Qiang Zha. Hong Kong; Dordrecht, The Netherlands: Comparative Education Research Centre, University of Hong Kong & Springer.

Ma, Rong. 2007. "Bilingual Education for China's Ethnic Minorities." *Chinese Education and Society* 40 (2): 9-25.

Mackerras, C. 2004. "Book Review: Multilingualism in China: The Politics of Writing Reforms for Minority Languages 1949-2002." *China Quarterly* (177): 238-239.

Mohrman, Kathryn, and Yingjie Wang. 2010. "China's Drive for World-Class Universities." In *Higher Education, Policy, and the Global Competition Phenomenon*, ed. Laura Michelle Portnoi, Val D. Rust, and Sylvia S. Bagley. New York: Palgrave Macmillan.

Mok, Ka Ho. 2001. "From State Control to Governance: Decentralization and Higher Education in Guangdong, China." *International Review of Education* 47 (1/2): 123-149.

Mok, Ka Ho. 2003. "Similar Trends, Diverse Agendas: Higher Education Reforms in East Asia." *Globalisation, Societies & Education* 1 (2): 201-221.

Mok, Ka Ho. 2010. "The Liberalization of the Privateness in Higher Education: Funding Strategies, Changing Governance and Policy Implications in Asia." A presentation delivered at the The Symposium of the Institute for International Studies in Education, Pittsburgh, April 28, 2010.

Ogbu, John U. 2008. *Minority Status, Oppositional Culture, and Schooling, Sociocultural, Political, and Historical Studies in Education.* New York: Routledge.

Organisation for Economic Co-operation and Development (OECD). 2000. *OECD The Programme for International Student Assessment (PISA).* Paris: OECD. Available online at: http://www.pisa.oecd.org.

OECD. 2003. *OECD The Programme for International Student Assessment (PISA).* Paris: OECD. Available online at: http://www.pisa.oecd.org.

OECD. 2006. *OECD The Programme for International Student Assessment (PISA).* Paris: OECD. Available online at: http://www.pisa.oecd.org.

Park, Heejin. 2009. "The Internationalization of Higher Education: Is Korea an Insider or an Outsider?" Paper presented at the Comparative and International Education Society Annual Conference, Charleston, SC, March 23, 2009.

Park, Heh-Rahn. 1996. "Narratives of Migration: From the Formation of Korean Chinese Nationality in the PRC to the emergence of Korean Chinese Migrants in South Korea." PhD diss., Department of Anthropology, University of Washington.

Park, Yongsook. 1991. "Koreans in Japan and the United States." In *Minority Status and Schooling: A Comparative Study of Immigrant and Involuntary Minorities*, ed. Margaret A. Gibson and John U. Ogbu. New York: Garland.

Paulston, Christina Bratt. 2003. "Language Policies and Language Rights." In *Sociolinguistics: The Essential Readings*, ed. Christina Bratt Paulston and G. Richard Tucker. Malden, MA: Blackwell Publishing.

Postiglione, Gerard A. 1992. "China's National Minorities and Educational Change." *Journal of Contemporary Asia* 22 (1): 20-44.

Proulx, Roland. 2007. "Higher Education Ranking and Leagues Tables: Lessons Learned from Benchmarking." *Higher Education in Europe* 32: 71-82.

Sautman, Barry. 1997. *Working Papers in the Social Sciences No. 32: Preferential Policies for Ethnic Minorities in China: The Case of Xinjiang*. Hong Kong: Hong Kong University of Science and Technology Library.

Schugurensky, Daniel. 2006. "The Political Economy of Higher Education in the Time of Global Markets: Wither the Social Responsibility of the University?" In *The University, the State and Market in the Americas: The Political Economy of Globalization*, ed. Robert A. Rhoads and Carlos A. Torres. Stanford, CA: Stanford University Press.

Shim, Doobo. 2006. "Hybridity and the Rise of Korean Copular Culture in Asia." *Media, Culture & Society* 28 (1): 25-44.

Statistics Korea. 2010. *Numbers of Ethnic Koreans Abroad. from Statistics Korea*. Daejeon: Statistics Korea. Available online at: http://kostat.go.kr.

Wan, Guofang, and Yang Jun. 2008. "How China Best Educates Its Ethnic Minority Children: Strategies, Experience and Challenges." *The Education of Diverse Student Populations* 2: 139-157.

World Bank. 2008. *World Development Indicators*. Washington, DC: World Bank. Available online at: http://data.worldbank.org.

You, Goon Sang, and Jae Seok Kwak. 2004. "연변 조선족 교육의 현황과 발전 과제" ["Ethnic Koreans in Yanbian China and Their Educational Issues"]. In *KEDI Position Paper 17*. Seoul: KEDI.

Zhao, Zhenzhou. 2007. "Ethnic Mongol Students and Cultural Recognition. *Chinese Education and Society* 40 (2): 26-37.

Zhou, Minglang. 2000. "Language Attitudes of Two Contrasting Ethnic Minority Nationalities in China: The 'Model' Koreans and the 'Rebellious' Tibetans." *International Journal of the Sociology of Language* 146: 1-20.

Zhou, Minglang. 2001. "The Politics of Bilingual Education and Educational Levels in Ethnic Minority Communities in China." *International Journal of Bilingual Education and Bilingualism* 4 (2): 125-149.

Chapter 5

Does Internationalization Really Mean Americanization?
A Closer Look at Major South Korean Universities' Internationalization Policies

John D. Palmer and Young Ha Cho

Since the last of the military governments in South Korea left power in 1992, the "people's government" has been pushing for globalization and internationalization throughout its government, economic, and education institutions. While the business world continues to charge ahead in developing relationships and partnerships with foreign investors and development agencies, universities have been called upon to produce graduates who are equipped with the abilities to succeed and lead in a globalized world. As a result, universities throughout Korea have been developing and implementing internationalization policies in an attempt to meet globalization's demands.

One of the major demands is the use of English language as the power language. Therefore, the use of English language has overwhelmed all levels of the Korean educational experience, especially at higher education institutions. For example, to gain entrance into a major university, a student must take an entrance examination, which includes a large section on English language usage; university students are taking regular courses through English language instruction; and most undergraduates and all graduate students are required to write at a minimum, an abstract of their graduating thesis in English. In addition, Korean universities have been offering Korean and foreign students an opportunity to study in Korea using English language throughout their studies. Most of these international programs were rather small entities within the larger campus and mainly admitted Korean Americans for their summer school programs, which focused on Korean language and culture and had lower enrollments for their MA degree offering Graduate School of International Studies (GSIS) program. It was not until more recently that other universities began offering GSIS programs; to date, 19 universities offer MA degrees and only Yonsei University offers BA, MA, and PhD through their international schools (J-H. Kim 2009).

Moreover, because of higher education's strong push to implement these types of internationalization policies, the K-12 system and students are also getting caught up in the globalization wave. The National Public Radio reported that "the number of South Korean students at US colleges and universities jumped by 11 percent last year [2008] to nearly 70,000. Only India and China send more, and they have far larger populations" (Kuhn 2009). The *Korea Times* published, "According to the Education Ministry, a total of 29,511 students under the age of 19 went overseas to study in 2006, up from 1,562 in 1998. Among them were 13,814 elementary school students, 9,246 middle school students, and 6,451 high schools students" (H-K. Kang 2008). The *New York Times* covered these same statistics and concluded that the 29,511 students studying abroad in 2006 was "nearly double the number in 2004 and almost seven times the figure in 2000, according to the Korean Educational Development Institute" (Onishi 2008, 1).

Most of these children are studying abroad with their mothers, while their fathers stay in Korea to work and financially support these efforts. This is such a widespread phenomenon that Koreans have given the title *gi leogi appa*, literally translated as "wild goose father," to the fathers living apart from their family, which has certain social and cultural implications (Palmer 2007). In other cases, students are living with relatives, host families, or living on their own in order to gain access to a "Western" education. These children have been dubbed "parachute kids" as they are literally dropped off in a foreign land, while their parents live in their home country (Zhou 1998). And in more recent years, there are a few situations where children are being adopted by a host family, sometimes a relative but also a certain trend that preferences White families, in the United States in order to gain access to public schools and even in-state university tuition, rather than paying the high costs of private boarding schools and international student tuition fees (A. Lee 2006).

In regard to the study abroad experience, in the past the typical student went abroad during her/his undergraduate years for a semester and/or as a full-time graduate school student. However, as indicated by the news reports cited above, in more recent years, there is a growing number of K-12 students leaving Korea. The authors saw this phenomenon as a major human capital and economic loss for Korea; in other words, "brain drain" for Korea and a gain of valuable educated professionals for already developed nations (Gribble 2008; Labi 2009). We considered these students as some of the best, brightest, and most highly educated Koreans and most, if not all, of these students are coming out of the upper-middle to upper-class of Korean society, which could also mean a drain on the Korean economy. It appeared that these students were staying in the host country (Labi 2009), due in part, as John D. Palmer (2001; see also Palmer and Jang 2005 and Palmer 2006) found, that these students no longer feel as though they are "real" Koreans, ultimately they have difficulty returning to a life in Korea and thus opt for careers and lives in the more developed countries. More important, these students may have found that the more lucrative career opportunities were located outside Korea as they perceived limited avenues in the Korean job market, especially as it related to their income potential and employment opportunities. We also believed that as these students assimilated in their new environments, they began to believe that the "traditional" ways of Korea were "inferior" to that of the "West" (Abelmann 2009).

In the midst of developing our research plan, South Korean President Lee Myung-bak announced, in the first months of his presidency, an English-only instruction policy that would be implemented throughout all the nation's schools (*Korea Times* 2008). The Lee administration made claims that it was attempting to lessen the financial costs to parents who were paying large *hakwon* (private cram school) and private tutor fees for their children to learn English. Since then, Lee has pulled back on this policy due to much resistance from teachers, parents, and citizens throughout Korea (Bae 2008), yet the desire for English language acquisition is still rampant throughout most of the nation. For example, the *Korea Times* reported that there are now 270 English kindergartens with tuition costs between 600,000 to 1.7 million Korean won per month—approximately US$505 to US$1,430 (S-W. Kang 2010). In addition, private institutions (e.g., taekwondo, yoga, golf) throughout Korea now offer instruction using the English language as a medium.

Delving deeper into Korea's leading universities' theory of globalization and internationalization policy, we ultimately concluded that both concepts could actually mean "assimilating" the more developed nations' ways into the everyday life of Korean universities; so much so that it appeared, at least on the surface, that Korea's most prestigious universities were in some ways surrendering not only their academic excellence but also their institutional identities in an attempt to gain perceived equal status with these world leading higher education institutions. Prior to gathering field data for this study we witnessed how Korean universities were attempting to recruit more foreign professors and students, who, in our perceptions, actually meant English language speaking and to a certain degree White, specifically from the United States and parts of Europe. In so doing, it appeared that Korean universities were accepting any foreign student or professor, no matter her/his academic credentials.

In the end, we see globalization's and internationalization's impact upon the Korean individual, institution, and society as being both benefitting but also inhibiting the nation's development, especially in the field of education. Yet, because globalization and internationalization were seen mainly in terms of "progress" within Korean society, the negative repercussions appeared to be overlooked and ignored not only within the educational system but by Korean society as a whole. We then set out to better understand the theory and practice of globalization and internationalization at the higher education level as we perceived this to be the site that had the most influence upon the entire educational system. Specifically, in this chapter, we attempt to reveal globalization's and internationalization's impact on leading university campuses through the views of both Korean nationals and foreigners. This chapter relies heavily upon interviews with government officials, national professors, staff, and students, and foreign professors and students as well as our on-site visits.

Theoretical Framework

Our study aims to uncover aspects of both globalization theory (Robertson and Khonder 1998; Jarvis 2000; Kim 2000; Giulianotti and Robertson 2006; Altbach and Knight 2007; Brown 2008) and internationalization theory (Bartell 2003; Kim 2005; Dixon 2006; Kritz 2006; Edwards 2007; Huang 2007; Healy 2008) to better understand the philosophy and practice of globalization and internationalization of Korean higher education. Specifically, when we began preparing for this study we perceived globalization as the interaction of different cultures, nations, peoples mainly through the exchange of products and technology. Globalization through an economic lens can be viewed as "the intensification of a global market operating across and among a system of national labor markets through international economic competition" (Astiz et al. 2002, 67).

We then view internationalization of higher education as the policies and practices of individual institutions in reaction to the increasing need to react to globalization's pressures (Altbach and Knight 2007). Through critical analysis of our data, we attempt to reveal how power and privilege are embedded within internationalization policies and procedures (Marginson and Mollis 2002; Ross 2002; Striano 2009; Noddings 2010). Taking aspects of George Ritzer's (2007) globalization theory that focuses on power and exploitation between the "core" nations and the "peripheral" and "semiperipheral" nations, we view the consumer/core nations as exploiting the peripheral and semiperipheral nations for its own benefits and advancements within the twenty-first century rules of globalization. Moreover, as this exploitation happens, "Globalization forces nation-states to focus more on acting as economic growth promoters for their national economies than as protectors of the national identity or a nationalist project" (Carnoy and Rhoten 2002, 3). Therefore, as peripheral and semiperipheral nations attempt to gain access to the core industrialized nations, they appear to be surrendering aspects of their cultural values in favor of developing positive relations with the core nations.

Indeed, we realize that higher education institutions are not completely independent from economic, social, and governmental pressures and therefore feel pushed to produce students who are suited to become leaders and contributors in a globalized economy. Consequently, as universities feel compelled to prepare students for this global leadership, it appears that they are sacrificing aspects of the cultural foundations in favor of a more internationalized look.

Internationalization of Higher Education

The internationalization of higher education is typically viewed as the exchange of students and faculty. We are aware that the exchange of students and faculty should be considered a two-way street; yet this exchange tends to be controlled by the economically and politically powerful nations and, therefore, students are largely moving from the periphery to the core. The number of "foreign-peripheral and semiperipheral" students, especially graduate students, studying in the United States to earn their degrees far outweigh the number of American students studying in "foreign-peripheral and semiperipheral" institutions of higher learning (Altbach and Knight 2007).

In reaction to the growing need for peripheral and semiperipheral nations to gain access to global leaders, higher education institutions are adapting to the current globalization environment. As will be seen in this chapter, Korean universities are developing innovative policies to attract foreign faculty and students. In other words, because only a small number of students are able to afford study abroad program costs, university leaders and government officials are now encouraging the recruitment of "foreign" professors and students and the development of "international schools" on leading campuses.

Methods

The research team is made up of authors John D. Palmer, a Korean adoptee, and Young Ha Cho, a Korean national. In the process of collecting data, two undergraduate research assistants from Colgate University, Soo Chin Lee, a Korean American, and Michael Tuan Kimura, a Korean Vietnamese American, were employed through the grant support of the Freeman Foundation. Palmer, Lee, and Kimura traveled to Korea to meet up with Cho to conduct field site visits and interview as many individuals as possible during the summer of 2008.

The universities were selected from the *JoongAng Daily's*, a major Korean newspaper's, rankings of the most successful universities for internationalization. We contacted the international divisions of the top ten universities, of which seven participated in the study. The staff members within these offices were essential in setting up interviews with faculty, students, and staff not only within the international schools, but also throughout the university.

During our site visits we conducted semistructured interviews. The interviews were conducted in Korean or English and sometimes both as the interviewee switched back and forth between the two languages. Certainly, those who spoke Korean and English as a second (or even third) language had some difficulty understanding the questions as well as in verbalizing their ideas (e.g., some of the students' first language was Chinese or Vietnamese and they were still learning both Korean and English). Here, we provided reassurance to the interviewee to take her/his own time in reflecting upon the questions and answering in whichever language she/he felt most comfortable. All interviews were recorded and then transcribed. The interviews conducted in Korean were translated into English by Cho. Our research included 49 interviews: 17 Korean professors, administrators, and government officials; 9 foreign professors from 4 different countries; 9 Korean students, and 15 foreign students from 10 different countries in East Asia, Southeast Asia, South Asia, East Europe, Africa, and the United States.

When we began discussing this project, we reflected upon the importance of this research project as well as on the need to be careful on how we focused upon the topic, as it would have a lasting impact upon our research design. Indeed, because the authors came into the project from differing, yet similar perspectives, we were sure to acknowledge how our insider and outsider researcher identities impacted how we would perceive globalization theory and internationalization policies and implementation (Palmer 2007). Specifically, both of us were international students at one point in our lives: (1) Palmer, a Korean American adoptee, attended kindergarten through to his bachelor's degree in the United States, earned an MA degree from Yonsei University GSIS in Seoul, and then acquired his PhD from the University of Iowa, in the department of educational policy and leadership studies, (2) Cho, a Korean national, attended kindergarten through to his bachelor's degree in Korea and then earned his MA and PhD from the University of Iowa, in the department of educational policy and leadership studies. Since our time together at the University of Iowa and into our roles as professors, we often discussed the differences and similarities in our international student experiences, mainly debating the fact that Cho was required to study in his second language of English when he came to the United States, while Palmer was able to continue his graduate studies in English even though he was in Korea and in the Korean Studies Program.

Internationalization (Americanization) of Korean Higher Education

From the very beginning of this study, we set out to explore the educational policies that were being implemented to internationalize Korean higher education. Our initial discovery, with the elite universities leading the way, supported our original thoughts that the policy shifts were geared toward assimilation through upholding the belief that English language was the privileged form of communication. We soon discovered that several of the campuses we visited mandated that all professors on the main campus offer courses taught solely in English; the international schools continued to conduct their day-to-day activities in English.

These initiatives then led to a belief that Korea's higher education institutions were becoming more internationalized. A student from the United States commented that "They are opening new English classes and recruiting more international professors.... In general, it's opening up to more international-based education. They are making more efforts to bring more English in the library, although it's kind of lacking, and even in classrooms and menus on campus." What struck us with this comment was the fact that the student equated the spreading of English language use with an "international-based education." This ideology of increasing internationalization quantitatively was widespread throughout our interviews and observations, which quickly led us to draw the conclusion that internationalization was linked to the implementation of English language throughout Korean campuses. Internationalization also meant the increase of a foreign presence in both the student body and faculty.

The Republic of Korea, Ministry of Education, Science and Technology (MEST) (2008b) stated that "Korean institutions of higher education are faced with increasing pressure to achieve international distinction in education and research.... Analysis has shown that the low number of foreign students and faculty at Korean universities plays a major role in hampering the development of many universities in Korea" (4). The Korean government began a concerted effort to recruit foreign students and faculty in 2001. The Korean Educational Development Institute (KEDI) reported that there were 11,646 foreign students studying in Korea in 2001. In 2005, the government initiated the Study Korea Project with the goal of South Korea becoming the higher education center for northeast Asia and, as a result, aimed to recruit 50,000 foreign students by the year 2010. It reached this goal by the year 2007 and then set its sights on recruiting 100,000 foreigners by 2012. The number of foreign faculty also rapidly increased from 1,220 in 2001 to 3,722 in 2008 and by far the majority of the foreign faculty members are employed by private universities (3,026).

Student Issues

Korean universities offered academic scholarships in an attempt to recruit more foreign students. According to the former MEST Minister Ahn, Byong-man (2010), MEST offered nearly 51.5 billion Korean won (approximately US$43 million) for 2,100 foreign scholarships in 2010 through its Global Korea Scholarship (GKS) program. When we asked foreign students why they chose to study in South Korea, by far the majority, especially students who are not from core industrialized nations, claimed it was the Korean government scholarship that lured them to study in Korea. Throughout our interviews, the rising foreign student presence was mentioned. A dean of international studies stated: "I am under tremendous pressure to increase the number of foreign students. I sent a few of my staff members to Beijing to recruit good Chinese students. We have several rounds of recruitment this year. We are trying hard to increase the number of foreign students."

Focusing our interview questions on the impact these internationalizing policies had upon both the integrity and identity of the institution, several of our participants discussed how the policies leaned toward "Americanization." A founder and president of an international education association questioned the teaching of courses in English:

> There was some objection by the faculty members at the beginning when we started teaching classes in English. Some people said, "You are losing your nationality or spirit of the nation." When we [Korean nationals] went to United States we had to learn English. Why not for them? Don't they have to learn Korean to study here?

And a Korean government official concluded that "In my view, many internationalization policies are too American-oriented. They do not consider other Asian countries even though Asian countries are more than one-third of the world's population and the Asian economy has rapidly developed." Both these quotes directly point out that the push to develop the surface aspects of internationalization through the increasing number of English courses and foreign faculty and students could be seen as disregarding Korea's integrity and identity. Some of the participants questioned the academic rigor of courses taught in English by both foreign professors (mainly native English speakers) and Korean professors (mainly English as a second language speakers). In that, some participants wondered if students were really gaining academic knowledge and understanding in classes taught in English, and told us that it is likely that some of the Korean professors ended up lecturing and discussing in Korean.

Moreover, the Korean college entrance examination is one of intense competition which forces high school students to endure tremendous amounts of stress (M. Lee 2003). However, foreign students are not required to take this examination as, most believe, they are accepted primarily upon their foreign status. While animosity toward foreign students was not obvious during our campus visits, several Korean students held both a negative attitude and a sense of resentment. Indeed, some of the Korean students we spoke to discussed how foreign students are provided with the best facilities (living and learning) on most of these campuses, leading some to feel as though Korean students were forgotten entities on campus.

In response to these charges of sacrificing academic standing in favor for internationalization policies, government officials and university leaders pointed to the fact that Korean language is not globally utilized and that in preparing Korean students for the globalized world of the twenty-first century, English language needed to be mastered in all areas—academically and practically—as well as in speaking, listening, reading, and writing. In addition, since most colleges and universities outside of Korea do not offer Korean language and literature as a major area of study, let alone Korean language courses, recruiting of foreign students and faculty would be even more difficult if Korean language skills are required for admission and employment. However, what was alarming to us was the fact that some university officials confided in us that the desire to recruit foreign students had led to a lowering of academic standards and in some cases forced admissions to accept *any* foreign student application. While this does not automatically mean that standards have been compromised due to the laxity in admission standards, it does imply that foreign students are admitted solely upon their foreign status. An administrator told us that:

> There is more focus on foreign students. It's not just [our] University but it's safe to say that most universities are really trying to bring more international students. When you are trying to increase the number, the quality of students can't stay the same.... I think that's definitely bringing the quality of our students downward overall. That's kind of scary. For the sake of [the] university and for the sake of students, you are almost positive that students won't be able to stay up with the rest of classmates but just for those [*Times Higher Education* (*THE*) World University Rankings] rankings, you sometimes have to accept the average students. This is a secret: The standard for admission for international students is slowly going down.

As mentioned above, we felt that there was some sense of animosity from the Korean students toward foreign students on these campuses, especially related to the admissions process. This, we concluded, was not the main cause of segregation between foreign students and Korean students, but we felt that it contributed to the growing distance between students.

Segregation on campus was a concern mainly for the foreign students. One student from the United States commented:

> I personally don't like how far international students are from the main part of campus. It's kind of a pain.... We are on [one] side of campus. Everybody else or the "natives" are down toward center or [the other] side of campus. If you really want to do a language exchange, you sign up for the program.... It's your own quest to branch out and meet other people. As far as meeting international students within your dorm you can meet people all over the world.

While administrators have attempted to develop spaces on campus that can bring the students together, such as a center on campus that is aimed at developing relationships, for the most part students were not taking advantage of these opportunities. There appears to be an actual physical distance between Korean and foreign students. During one of our campus visits, we witnessed what the student above stated about the actual distance between Korean and foreign students; foreign students mainly attended classes in a building directly adjacent to their dormitory and the foreign language school, while the Korean students remained in their student groups on the other side of campus.

In the students' statements, we discovered that while foreign students appeared to benefit from the internationalization within the international schools, the majority of the Korean students were less apt to engage with students from around the world due in part to the campus segregation. A student from India believed that the university needed to do more to bring students together:

> Somehow it [University] lacks the collaboration with foreign students and Korean students. I mean there should be more activities involving foreign students and international students. If I come to Korea, I should not be confined to only international students. I should be able to participate in any program with Korean students.

We delved deeper into this concern about segregation on campus because the divide between students appeared to hinder internationalization efforts. We soon discovered that the language barrier proved to be the most difficult aspect in bringing foreigners and Koreans together. Even though Korean students were well prepared in the form of reading and to a certain extent writing and listening in English, their speaking skills lagged far behind. A Tanzanian student believed that "there is a gap between international and Korean students. I think the reason behind this is the language barrier because sometimes they can't communicate and they feel shy." From this perspective, the Korean students must learn how to speak English better in order to develop stronger relationships with foreign students. However, taken from the belief that the foreign students need to learn Korean because they are studying in Korea then the foreign students were at fault for not speaking better Korean. A student from the United States also felt that the language barrier impeded foreign students from interacting with Korean students, "If you are not comfortable with speaking Korean, then you are at a disadvantage. If you got the means to speak [Korean], then it's more comfortable for you to meet Korean students."

We understood to a certain degree why Korean universities did not require foreign students to pass a Korean language examination for admissions. A Korean professor questioned: "How many students will come to Korea if they have to pass a Korean language examination?" And while he did not give a concrete answer to his own question, the conclusion was that very few foreign students would come if Korean language skills were required for admissions. However, we were not quite sure why foreign students were not required to pass a Korean language examination for graduation purposes.

In some cases, foreign students were not even required to take Korean language classes. A student from Uzbekistan attempted to clear this up for us:

> It's a problem for foreign students to use Korean here. Korean classes are not mandatory. It's my option... I know some students who studied Korean for two years, but they still don't know Korean. They [the administration] are not telling us that we need it [to speak Korean]. It's like a neutral position. But they'd better say that we need it.

On the other hand, several foreign students felt that since they were recruited to attend these universities in Korea through the use of scholarships, they should not be obliged to learn Korean language. It was quite interesting as some of the foreign students believed that more English needed to be made available throughout campus life, even though they were studying in Korea. A Cambodian student believed that "the education should be provided in English, not fully provided in English but at least like 70 or 80 percent of our courses are provided in English." In our conversation with a Tanzanian student, he provided his reasoning as to why more courses taught in English were needed:

> There is a limitation of English classes, so we are limited in some majors. I may prefer to take a certain major but because it's not provided in English, I can't take it. I think that's one of the problems. 90 percent of the international students are in Law and [Management], but the reason behind it is because the options are limited... [Management], almost 90 percent of international students are doing that. I think the reason is not that they aren't interested in other majors, but because of language barriers.... It's not easy because when you come here you don't know anything about [Korean] language. It needs time and then you have only four years to graduate. Maybe you can master the language in two years, but it's too late to take the major you want to take.

Through our study, we were better able to understand the debate over the usage of English language. On the other side of the campus, Korean students and faculty felt as though foreign students needed to learn Korean language as a basic foundation of being a foreign student studying in Korea. Most of these students and professors we met with made a comment such as: "When I studied in the United States, I had to speak English. All my courses were in English. I wrote my thesis/dissertation in English." In other words, these Koreans felt that foreign students in Korea were not abiding by the unwritten foreign student rules while studying in Korea. Moreover, they were questioning the internationalization policies being implemented by the administration that relentlessly drive toward more foreign students and increased use of English.

At the same time, foreign students bring ethnic, racial, and regional diversity to Korea, which in turn provides Korean students the opportunity to meet and interact with people from around the world. An administrator recognized that most Korean students are not able to afford the rapidly increasing costs of study abroad and therefore the university could bring parts of the world to Korea. She stated that,

> it's expensive for [our] University students to go abroad. But we are creating opportunities in which they can meet globally renowned professors or international students here. We are trying to give students the idea that you don't have to go abroad to be globalized. We are trying to get that to students but it's a little difficult. It means a lot to me that we are able to provide such a global program right here at [our] University for them to meet students from over 30 countries.

However, when interaction between Korean and foreign students are limited, it demands a further investigation of its internationalization policies. Indeed, when billions of Korean won are being spent on these internationalization efforts, there needs to be some understanding of the desired outcomes. It appears that foreign students were unclear as to why they were being recruited to study in Korea, and Korean students, at times, felt as though foreign students were provided with preferential treatment. However, most of these thoughts and concerns seemed to disappear under the belief that these internationalization policies were for the good of the university, the students, and the faculty.

Faculty Issues

As we moved deeper into the study it became clear that the internationalization policies were much more complex than the spreading of English language and recruiting of foreign students and faculty. Indeed, internationalization policies were not geared to emulate the "West," but rather, a way to gain global recognition as leading higher education institutes and, in order to gain recognition, it was concluded that more foreigners, in particular faculty members, were needed to have direct interaction with Korean universities. And in order to attract foreign faculty members to

Korea, the widespread usage of English language was necessary as most foreigners do not have access to the study of Korean language in their home countries.

We also discovered that this desire for more foreign presence (international mix) was based upon only one aspect of the *THE* World University Rankings, which only comprises a total of 5 percent of the total score. The other four main components of the teaching and learning environment (30 percent), research reputation and agenda (30 percent), citation impact (32.5 percent), and industry income (2.5 percent) certainly were being attended to and will be discussed below (*THE* 2010). However, at an initial glance, especially in regard to the teaching and learning environment, we believed that the recruitment of foreign students (described above) and faculty and the use of English was regarded as the first step toward global recognition as a leader in higher education.

One particular way the government was hoping to assist universities to recruit leading scholars was through the World Class University (WCU) Project. Launched in 2008, MEST (2008b) allocated 830 billion Korean won (approximately 692 million US dollars) over a period of five years to recruit "international scholars and researchers...to establish new academic departments or specialized majors in Korean universities; second, employing foreign scholars at existing academic programs; and third, inviting distinguished world-class scholars to teach and research in Korea" (6). According to a 2008 MEST report, 52 research teams and 18 universities were to be the beneficiaries of the WCU Project. A total of 284 "top notch" international scholars have been invited to teach and research in Korea, which includes two Nobel laureates; "Carlo Rubbia of the European Organization for Nuclear Research and George Smoot of UC Berkeley, winners of the 1984 and 2006 Nobel Prize in physics, will teach at Sungkyunkwan University and Ewha Womans University, respectively" (MEST 2008a).

It was determined that a foreign faculty presence could provide more than just English instruction and an international mix. In that, the government aimed to support foreign faculty recruitment and retention as a way to enhance Korea's research agendas and publications in order to gain global recognition as research/scholar leaders. According to a government official:

> There are reasons that the government has supported the World Class University Project that focuses on inviting foreign professors. I believe that increasing the number of foreign professors does not necessarily mean the advancement of Korean higher education and its internationalization policies. However, the government believes that competition-based excellence

is a key for global competencies of Korean universities. I expect that the presence of foreign professors will motivate Korean professors to actively jump into that competition.

We concluded that the competition the Korean government official is referring to above is directly linked to the academic/scholarly standing of the faculty, especially as it relates to active research reputation and agendas and the impact their research is having upon the field.

As a result, all of the universities we met with had made drastic revisions to their tenure and promotion policies in recent years. Korean universities have taken up the "publish or perish" motto. Specifically that meant publishing in Social Science Citation Index (SSCI) journals, the majority of which are published in English and mainly in the United States and Europe. Therefore, Korean scholars were now being required to publish and present their research in English as a way for Korean universities to gain global recognition of their academic standings. Moreover, the same government official believed that foreign faculty could provide Korean scholars with innovative research methods and skills, which would allow these scholars to conduct and produce groundbreaking studies:

> Korean universities should catch up to the skills and research capacities of advanced countries as quickly as possible so that we successfully obtain industrial skills and knowledge necessarily required for the twenty-first century's global competition. It is the solid first purpose that the government supports university's internationalization.

The government official recognized that increasing the number of foreign faculty was not the only aspect of internationalization policy, but rather the beginning of their support in developing globally renowned universities.

Similar to the issues raised by foreign students, foreign faculty recruitment as well as their lives on campus were points of concern for both Koreans and the foreign faculty members. The recruitment, tenure, and promotion policies for foreigners were not altogether clear as we received mix messages throughout our study. Some foreigners believed that the Korean government did not allow any foreign professor to stand for tenure. A foreign faculty was clearly upset with this policy:

> In Korea, they don't give tenure to foreigners... If I sit and think about the fact that I am not getting tenure and I'm not getting any research grants, then I will be miserable... Some of my other [foreign] colleagues are so frustrated because there's no equal treatment [for foreign professors]. We've got people with PhDs and we've got people that in any university in the west or any other university they would be tenured professors but they are not here. I think it's a law actually.

What is interesting here is the fact that this particular faculty member held an MA degree and was hired solely as an English instructor. During the faculty member's years of service, he took on other administrative duties, but was neither provided with a tenure-track appointment nor any of the benefits that come with being a tenure-track professor (e.g., research grants, research assistant). While we do not want to deny this faculty member's experience, during the course of our study we met with foreign faculty on the tenure track. We believe that the major difference in treatment is based upon whether one was an academic professor, who held a doctorate in his/her field, or an English language instructor, who for the most part held a master's degree in a variety of fields related to English language instruction. Academic professors were provided with similar type of duties (teaching and advising of students, conducting research, and providing service) and resources (research funds and assistants) as most Korean senior and tenure-track professors. However, English language instructors were hired mainly to teach English language courses.

Another issue that was raised by both academic professors and English language instructors was the point that they felt somewhat isolated on campus. Most English language instructors did not feel as though they were as full members of the faculty and community. Moreover, due in part to the language barriers, foreign faculty were rarely asked to sit in on committees and according to one participant, she was not even required to attend faculty meetings since they were conducted in Korean.

As for the academic professors, there seemed to be a lack of incentive to collaborate on research projects. While we believed that collaboration should have been one of the main outcomes of recruiting foreign faculty, there was no space or incentives made available to collaborate with foreign faculty on research projects. A government official suggested that the lack of collaboration was based upon "infrastructure, which means that even though they [foreign professors] come to Korea, few universities could provide a Korean colleague group that could collaborate on research agendas."

While we did not find any sense of animosity between foreign and Korean professors, and that, for the most part, they were being treated relatively the same in regard to duties and support, there were two obvious differences. Korean full-time, tenure and tenure-track faculty members were required to publish and teach in English and Korean language, while foreign faculty were required to publish and teach solely in English.

The division between faculty members goes beyond the differences in responsibilities. As we moved deeper into our project, we realized that internationalization in some ways did not necessary mean "Americanization" but rather nondomestic or non-Korean. Throughout our study we discovered that most of the people we talked with did not associate "Korean" with internationalization. For instance, the majority of Korean faculty members, in our opinion, are international scholars. The large majority have studied outside Korea, many earning their graduate degrees at prestigious schools throughout the United States and Europe. Some have earned tenure at various universities before opting to return to Korea. Others have held positions with international think tanks. Nearly all of them have traveled extensively for their research, lived in different countries at some point in time, and speak two or more languages.

Nevertheless, it was apparent that Korean scholars were not seen as international scholars by the government, university administration, and even students. For example, a student from India reinforces the notion that even though Korean scholars have studied outside Korea at some of the most prestigious universities, they are still not seen as international scholars:

> We have professors that are of top quality. They were studying in Harvard, some of them studied at Yale. The quality is quite good. All of them are Korean professors.... But I think there should be some international professors too so that they could give the international environment's opinion and that will help in terms of internationalization of Korea. Take the example of the US and UK, the environment now a days it is getting more cosmopolitan throughout all the campus and that's what attracts international students, isn't it? So, I think that would be a great help if they attract more international professors.

Throughout our conversations with government officials and university administration, the recruitment of international scholars was seen as a necessary step in internationalizing the schools. However, what we found as a terrible oversight was the fact that they did not recognize Korean faculty members as international scholars. Rather, these Korean scholars were required to prove themselves as international scholars, both through publishing and offering courses in English, while their foreign counterparts were granted international status based solely upon the fact that they do not hold Korean citizenship. In spite of all their efforts to "emulate the west in a mimetic and uncritical way," Korean scholars remain in the "shadow of the west[ern scholars]" (Nguyen et al. 2009, 111) due in part to the long lasting legacy of colonialism and neocolonialism.

As the recruitment of "top-notch" international scholars proved to be more difficult than originally planned, we were uncertain of the quality of foreign professors, especially in comparison to Korean scholars. However, we do not want to draw any conclusions at this time as tenure-track positions available to foreigners are still relatively new. We will need to wait to determine this upon the outcome of the foreign professors' tenure and promotion rates as well as their research outcomes.

Not Really Americanization, Rather Global Recognition and Local Aspiration

Speaking with deans, government officials, professors, and students we quickly determined that these institutions were developing internationalization policies that could benefit Korean and foreign students, the university, and the Korean nation as a whole. More importantly, as we began to critically analyze the data, it appeared that South Korea was at the forefront of internationalization policies, especially with the recruitment of students from developing countries. Indeed, their policies were far from the "Americanization" we initially believed them to be; we discovered that these institutions are attempting to become leaders not mimickers of the American higher education system. These universities were implementing policies aimed at gaining international recognition as leading higher education institutions and providing an international education for their own students and especially to students from developing countries to become global citizens and leaders. We consistently heard several mottos that leaned toward a social justice agenda while striving to become global leaders. "Global Excellence and Local Eminence" and "Glocalization" were two such phrases that were heralded by several participants.

It was then rather interesting to discuss and witness how these universities were developing policies that would place Korea as a leader among education institutions. It appeared that Korea recognized that it was not able to compete with the long history of prestige and economic power of the United States and therefore needed to find its own role in the globalized world. Our analysis revealed that there were four particular areas that Korean universities were directing their attention toward in order to gain global recognition as a leader in higher education: (1) rigorous publication records of its faculty, (2) recruitment of prestigious foreign faculty for visiting and summer positions, (3) the development of "dual degree-programs" with widely recognized universities throughout the world, and (4) recruitment of new foreign students as a way to impact the local area. These initiatives were in direct correlation with the *THE* World University Ranking Systems main criteria of: (1) research reputation and agenda, (2) citation impact, (3) teaching and learning environment, (4) international mix, and (5) industry income.

Research Agendas and Citation Impact

As mentioned previously, the tenure and promotion system for Korean faculty has made drastic changes in recent years. Even though each university maintains its own guidelines and regulations, overall Korean faculty members are required to keep an active research agenda and publish in leading journals. While there has been some resistance to these sudden policy shifts by the faculty, most of the faculty we met with accepted these changes as they believed the theory that in order to gain global recognition as a leading institute of higher learning, they need to improve their research capacities. Moreover, because Korean language is not widely studied, Korean scholars are forced to publish in the globally recognized and powerful language of English in order to gain international respect as not only contributors but leaders in their fields of study.

As a result, the Korean scholars are producing more and more research every year. MEST (2008b) reported that "the number of SCI-level Korean papers published in the fields of science and technology dramatically increased from 9,444 in 1998 to 23,515 in 2005, according to the Science Citation and Index report of Thomson Reuters. In terms of the country's ranking, Korea jumped from 18th in 1998 to 12th in 2005." Seoul National University (SNU) published on its university website that "As of 2008, it ranks 24th in the Science Citation Index, the worldwide standard for assessing research capacity" with a total of 4,291 publications (SNU 2010). However, MEST was still concerned that even though the number of publications is increasing, the number of citation referencing remains at a low level. Again, as was noted in a MEST (2008b) publication "when measuring the level of research quality, Korea is still far from world class. In 2006, Korea was ranked 28th in citations per paper while it ranked 11th in the number of SCI-level Korean papers."

Recruitment of Renowned Scholars and Top-Notch Students

During our site visits, we also witnessed the development of summer programs as a way to increase international recognition from leading universities throughout the world. These programs allowed foreign scholars and students to gain access to Korean universities without the long-term commitment as well as the need to master Korean as all courses were offered in English. Many of these programs hired foreign faculty members from the Ivy League and other leading institutes to teach the summer courses in a variety of fields. As we walked through several campuses it was hard to miss the larger banner advertisements for these programs that displayed, for instance, "UPENN professors" or "Ivy League professors." On Seoul National University's website they boast "Each summer course will be taught by a team of renowned international scholars from leading universities around the world as well as Seoul National University" (SNU, The Office of International Affairs 2010). Yonsei University claims on its website "Yonsei University has hosted the best International Summer School [YISS] since 1985. YISS is also administered in partnership with the University of California. Each year, key faculty and over 200 students from the UC system take part in YISS" (Yonsei University 2010).

University officials believed that by recruiting faculty members from internationally recognized universities would provide an image of academic credibility. This credibility would then lead to the recruitment of top-notch students from these elite schools as well as from around the world. Certainly, Korean universities benefitted a great deal from hiring faculty from highly renowned universities, especially in the recruitment of foreign students for both the summer and regular international programs. However, the interesting part of Yonsei's announcement is the mentioning of the development of a "partnership" with an elite higher education institution in the United States.

Teaching and Learning Environment: Dual-Degree Programs

For the most part, deans and faculty members discussed the creation of dual-degree programs with foreign universities as a way to recruit more foreign students. The basis of a dual-degree program allows a student to study at two institutions and then earn a degree from both institutions. SNU developed a dual-degree program with Duke University in 2007. The program is explained on SNU's website:

> In order to meet global standards, the SNU Business School has signed a comprehensive strategic alliance with the Fuqua Business School of Duke University, a leading U.S. business school.... The SNU Global MBA program provides an optional dual-degree program that allows students to receive a Duke degree and an SNU degree.... The students who enroll [in] the dual degree program will study 8-12 months at SNU MBA program and move to Duke University to study one more year. At Duke, the students will join other Duke daytime MBA program students and study

together. Students can freely choose one of the 12 concentrations that Duke offers...after finishing the study, the students will receive MBA degree from SNU and MMS [Master of Management Studies] degree from Duke. (SNU 2006)

Throughout our campus visits we heard about the development of partnerships with highly regarded colleges and universities. All of Korea's elite institutions and most of the major universities had established dual-degree programs throughout the world. These partnerships not only allowed for an increase in the exchange of students and faculty but, more importantly, provided Korean universities with an avenue to establish an equal standing with elite institutions in the United States and Europe.

Industry Income (Knowledge Transfer): Glocalization and Global Eminence

Korean government officials and leaders within the university illustrated for us how Korea can be a local leader through glocalization and global eminence. Indeed, recognized as one of the four Tigers of Asia due to its rapid economic development following nearly 40 years of colonization at the hands of the Japanese (1910-1945) and then caught in a devastating civil war (1950-1953), Korea can be a model for developing nations to look toward in developing their own countries. Indeed, the data implies that students from developing countries, especially Southeast and West Asia as well as parts of Africa (e.g., Vietnam, Cambodia, Tanzania, and Kenya) are looking to Korean universities to provide them with globalization knowledge and experience as they move to become key members of the globalized world. A dean provided insight into this aspect of his university's internationalization philosophy:

> We want to send our message toward those countries and people in those countries as a kind of voice here from Korea where we also went through all those hurdles and difficult times and challenging era. We went through those difficult times rather fast and rapidly within 30-40 years. So from their stand points, Korea has become a modern country that they want to follow.

And a Russian student claimed:

> I think nowadays Korean globalization has big power in the world. For example, if you look back on the history, Korea was trying to send students to other countries to know something about the whole world. But, now,

they are making more programs in Korea for foreigners to come here. It shows us that Korea is becoming a more and more powerful country in the world.

Providing opportunities for developing countries' students to study aspects of globalization in Korean universities played a significant role in supporting developing countries' inclusion into the globalized world. Therefore, Korean universities need to be careful not to exploit these new connections with developing nations, especially since these foreign students could prove to be valuable assets not only to the university but to Korea as whole as future trade partners and allies.

Moving deeper into our study, it became clearer to us that university officials were aware of the possibility of exploiting the less developed countries; that extending their power position over others is a reality as globalization has placed more pressure on universities to address issues related to educational and economic competition vis-à-vis limited resources. We were then impressed with the South Korean government officials and university deans who were attempting to carve out new internationalization policy that appeared to implement both glocalization and global eminence theory.

Conclusions and Suggestions

It was apparent that Korea's higher education internationalization policies leaned toward the development of partnerships with the powerful core nation university systems in order to advance their own financial and educational aspirations. Indeed, Korean universities are developing innovative programs and policies that should increase their international recognition, such as summer programs that recruited professors from highly recognizable schools in the United States, Europe, and some parts of East Asia, restructuring their tenure and promotion system that is weighted heavily upon publications in leading journals both in English and Korean, the expansion of international schools and GSIS, and more recently, dual-degree programs and other types of partnerships.

These initial policies proved difficult to fully implement as the recruitment of leading foreign scholars and top-notch core nation students proved difficult for most Korean universities. Therefore, Korean universities had to make sacrifices. The main sacrifice was to allow foreign faculty and students to work and study using English language as the medium of communication with the hope that they would study Korean language and eventually become proficient speakers. Another sacrifice was to admit foreign students on less stringent academic criteria in an attempt to increase the international presence on campus. Moreover, to a certain extent, some of the foreign faculty held substandard credentials in comparison to the Korean faculty.

Throughout this study, we began to see Korean universities on the cutting-edge of internationalization policy for higher education, not the assimilators we initially thought them to be, as they were creating policies that had the potential to boost Korea's international recognition while at the same time supporting the advancement of peripheral nations. We were particularly interested in the development of summer programs and dual-degree programs that provided several benefits to the host university. In regard to the summer programs, Korean universities were able to provide Korean students with an international experience without having to leave Korea. Moreover, the host university gained access to leading foreign scholars who were willing to come to Korea on a short-term basis. Even though these foreign professors were on campus for the summer program, exposure to the Korean university system, no matter for how short a time, was valuable in both gaining international recognition and building collaborative research relationships. The development of dual-degree programs was innovative in securing relationships with core nation university systems. Even though further research will need to be done to investigate the overall effectiveness and outcomes of these programs, these partnerships appear to be an effective way for Korean students to gain international experiences and for Korean universities to earn equal status with core nations.

We also discovered that while these universities were recruiting more foreign students and faculty, the campus remained physically segregated. On some campuses, the international schools were on the outskirts of the campus due to the construction of new buildings and dormitories (which also caused some resentment and therefore division on campus). While some campuses developed centers for international students to meet with Korean students, from what we gathered students rarely used these centers for these purposes. Foreign students remained isolated with other foreign students as long as they did not learn/study Korean language. Therefore, we strongly suggest that Korean language proficiency become a requirement, not necessarily for admissions, but for graduation or at least a two-year commitment to studying the language. These language classes could then be part of their graduation requirements rather than an added course load.

Moreover, foreign professors felt as though they were treated differently than their Korean colleagues. Some were not offered tenure-track positions, some complained of not receiving research grants to conduct research, and a few spoke of their isolation as English teachers. Therefore, we suggest that more needs to be done to improve these relationships. Indeed, internationalization is more than just numbers; foreigners and Koreans need opportunities to interact in well-defined spaces and encouragement to begin to interact and understand one another. We strongly believe that collaboration will allow foreign faculty to feel as though they are members of the community of scholars, not just teachers who can offer classes in English. First, develop research agendas with Korean and foreign faculty equally contributing. Second, while we do not believe that faculty meetings need to be held solely in English, it would be helpful for foreign faculty to receive the agenda and minutes in English. Third, foreign faculty, like any employee, need to have some sense of job security and acknowledgement of their work. It is our belief that universities could develop separate guidelines for tenure and promotion of its foreign faculty but needs to keep in mind the problems caused by a two-tiered system, which leads to our last suggestion in this area. Korean scholars are required to publish and teach in both Korean and English, while their foreign (English speakers and most of the time non-Korean speakers) colleagues are only required to publish and teach in English. This has potential to divide scholars, which in the end will possibly lead to resentment. Therefore, it is imperative for these universities to encourage and financially support collaboration across research, teaching, and service. It will not be an easy task to cross these cultural divides, but in order to become a truly internationalized campus, foreign faculty and Korean faculty will need to lead the way in developing cross-cultural relationships.

We believe that Korean universities can become leaders in the field of international studies, not just among developing nations but worldwide. We hope that Korean professors will develop research agendas aimed at understanding the purposes and outcomes of Korean graduate schools of international studies, the development and function of dual-degree programs, and the impact that the summer institutes have on both the Korean and foreign students. In short, what impact are these international programs having upon higher education access and outcomes? We strongly believe that developing nations as well as core industrialized nations can learn from Korea's innovative international policies.

References

Abelmann, Nancy. 2009. *The Intimate University: Korean American Students and the Problems of Segregation*. Durham, NC: Duke University Press.
Ahn, Byong-man. 2010. "'Study Korea' Emerges as New National Brand." *Korea Times*, July 21, 2010. Available online at: http://www.koreatimes.co.kr.

Altbach, Philip G., and Jane Knight. 2007. "The Internationalization of Higher Education: Motivations and Realities." *Journal of Studies in International Education* 11: 290-305.

Astiz, M. Fernanda, Alexander W. Wiseman, and David P. Baker. 2002. "Slouching towards Decentralization: Consequences of Globalization for Curricular Control in National Education Systems." *Comparative Education Review* 46 (1): 66-88.

Bae, Ji-sook. 2008. "President Lee Calls English Immersion Education 'Impossible.'" *Korea Times*, March 20, 2008. Available online at: http://www.koreatimes.co.kr.

Bartell, Marvin. 2003. "Internationalization of Universities: A University Culture-Based Framework." *Higher Education* 45 (1): 43-70.

Brown, Garrett Wallace. 2008. "Globalization is What We Make of It: Contemporary Globalization Theory and the Future Construction of Global Interconnection." *Political Studies Review* 6 (1): 42-53.

Carnoy, Martin, and Diana Rhoten. 2002. "What Does Globalization Mean for Educational Change? A Comparative Approach." *Comparative Education Review* 46 (1): 1-9.

Dixon, Mary. 2006. "Globalisation and International Higher Education: Contested Positionings." *Journal of Studies in International Education* 10 (4): 319-333.

Edwards, Jane. 2007. "Challenges and Opportunities for the Internationalization of Higher Education in the Coming Decade: Planned and Opportunistic Initiatives in American Institutions." *Journal of Studies in International Education* 11 (3&4): 373-381.

Giulianotti, Richard, and Roland Robertson. 2006. "Glocalization, Globalization and Migration." *International Sociology* 21 (2): 171-198.

Gribble, Cate. 2008. "Policy Options for Managing International Student Migration: The Sending Country's Perspective." *Journal of Higher Education Policy & Management* 30 (1): 25-39.

Healey, Nigel M. 2008. "Is Higher Education in Really 'Internationalising'?" *Higher Education* 55 (3): 333-355.

Huang, Futao. 2007. "Internationalisation of Higher Education in the Era of Globalisation: What Have Been its Implications in China and Japan?" *Higher Education Management and Policy* 19 (1): 47-61.

Jarvis, Peter. 2000. "Globalisation, the Learning Society and Comparative Education." *Comparative Education* 36 (3): 343-355.

Kang, Hyun-kyung. 2008. "New Administration Struggling to Tackle English Divide." *Korea Times*, January 23, 2008. Available online at: http://www.koreatimes.co.kr.

Kang, Shin-who. 2010. "English Kindergartens Thriving." *Korea Times*, October 5, 2010. Available online at: http://www.koreatimes.co.kr.

Kim, Ju-Hyun. 2009. 한국에서 세계를 품다: 국제대학원에 도전하라 [*The Inside Scoop on International Studies: A Complete Guide to the GSIS*]. Seoul: 에딧더월드 [Edit-the-World].

Kim, Samuel, ed. 2000. *Korea's Globalization*. Cambridge: Cambridge University Press.

Kim, Terri. 2005. "Internationalisation of Higher Education in South Korea: Reality, Rhetoric, and Disparity in Academic Culture and Identities." *Australian Journal of Education* 49 (1): 1-28.

Korea Times. 2008. "English-Only Classes: President-elect's Immersion Drive Sparks Debate." January 27. Available online at: http://www.koreatimes.co.kr.

Kritz, Mary M. 2006. "Globalisation and Internationalisation of Tertiary Education." Final report submitted to the United Nations Population Division, New York.

Kuhn, Anthony 2009. "Korean School Preps Students for Ivy League." *National Public Radio*, July 2, 2009. Available online at: http://www.npr.org.

Labi, Aisha. 2009. "Global Survey Finds Shifts in Universities' Internationalization Priorities." *Chronicle of Higher Education* 56 (6): A23.

Lee, Aruna. 2006. "New Immigration Strategy: Koreans Send Children to America for Adoption." *New America Media*, January 25, 2006. Available online at: http://news.newamericamedia.org.

Lee, Meery. 2003. "Korean Adolescents' 'Examination Hell' and Their Use of Free Time." *New Directions for Child and Adolescent Development* 99: 9-21.

Marginson, Simon, and Marcela Mollis. 2002. "'The Door Opens and the Tiger Leaps': Theories and Reflexivities of Comparative Education for a Global Millennium." *Comparative Education Review* 45 (4): 581-615

Noddings, Nel. 2010. "Moral Education in an Age of Globalization." *Educational Philosophy & Theory* 42 (4): 390-396.

Nguyen, Phuong-Mai, Julian G. Elliott, Cees Terlouw, and Albert Pilot. 2009. "Neocolonialism in Education: Cooperative Learning in an Asian Context." *Comparative Education* 45 (1): 109-130.

Onishi, Norimitsu. 2008. "For English Studies, Koreans Say Goodbye to Dad." *New York Times*, June 8, 2008, Section A, 1. Available online at: http://www.nytimes.com.

Palmer, John D. 2001. "In the Midst of Two Cultures: 1.5 Generation Korean Americans' Acculturation Process and Ethnic Identity Development." PhD diss., University of Iowa.

Palmer, John D. 2006. "Negotiating the Indistinct: Reflections of a Korean Adopted American Working with Korean Born, Korean Americans." *Qualitative Research* 6 (4): 473-495.

Palmer, John D. 2007. "Who is the Authentic Korean American? Korean-born Korean American High School Students' Negotiations of Ascribed and Achieved Identities." *Journal of Language, Identity, and Education* 6 (4): 277-298.

Palmer, John D., and Eun-Young Jang. 2005. "Korean Born, Korean American High School Students' Entry into Understanding Race and Racism through Social Interactions and Conversations." *Race Ethnicity and Education* 8 (3): 297-317.

Republic of Korea, Ministry of Education, Science and Technology (MEST). 2008a. "284 Top-notch Scholars Invited from Overseas under the WCU Project." Press Release, Academic Research Promotion Division. Seoul: MEST. Available online at: http://english.mest.go.kr.

Republic of Korea, MEST. 2008b. "National Project toward Building World Class Universities: 2008-2012." Seoul: Academic Research Promotion Division, MEST.

Ritzer, George. 2007. *The Globalization of Nothing 2*. Thousand Oaks: Pine Forge Press.
Robertson, Roland, and Habib Haque Khondker. 1998. "Discourses of Globalization." *International Sociology* 13 (1): 25-40.
Ross, Heidi. 2002. "The Space between Us: The Relevance of Relational Theories to Comparative and International Education." *Comparative Education Review* 46 (4): 407-432.
Seoul National University (SNU). 2006. *Dual Degree Program*. Seoul: SNU Graduate School of Business. Available online at: http://gsb.snu.ac.kr.
SNU. 2010. *SNU in the World: Global Standing*. Seoul: SNU. Available online at: http://www.useoul.edu.
SNU, The Office of International Affairs. 2010. *About ISI*. Seoul: SNU, The Office of International Affairs. Available online at: http://snuoia.snu.ac.kr.
Striano, Maura. 2009. "Managing Educational Transformation in the Globalized World: A Deweyan Perspective." *Educational Theory* 59 (4): 379-393.
Times Higher Education (THE). 2010. *Robust, Transparent, and Yours*. London: *THE*. Available online at: http://www.timeshighereducation.co.uk
Yonsei University. 2010. *Introduction: Yonsei Advantages*. Seoul: Yonsei University. Available online at: http://summer.yonsei.ac.kr.
Zhou, Min. 1998. "'Parachute Kids' in Southern California: The Educational Experience of Chinese Children in Transnational Families." *Educational Policy* 12 (6): 682-704.

Chapter 6

What It Takes to Internationalize Higher Education in Korea and Japan: English-Mediated Courses and International Students

Jae-Eun Jon and Eun-Young Kim

Globalization has been one of the most influential forces on higher education, and its implications have indicated inequalities for universities in the "centers" versus the "peripheries" debate (Altbach 2006). In the cases of Japan and Korea, they have several top research universities, according to the university ranking systems of Shanghai Jiao Tong University and the London *Times Higher Education Supplement*. However, the position of Japan and Korea as non-English speaking countries in Asia, combined with the predominance of English in higher education, appears to place them both on the peripheries of the elite higher education institutions. One example that may indicate their peripheral position is the mobility of international students. With respect to international student mobility, Korea has been one of the top sending countries globally for many years, particularly to the United States, while it has been the lowest among developed nations as a host country (Davis 2003; Institute of International Education [IIE] 2009). Similarly, Japan has been a major sending country, while it is recently emerging as a study abroad destination (IIE 2009, 2010).

In the context of globalization in higher education, the governments and universities in Japan and Korea have made efforts to strengthen the global competitiveness of their universities. One of their strategies has focused on internationalization of higher education, which has brought concerns that it may lead to the Westernization, Americanization, or Englishization of Korean and Japanese universities (Tsuneyoshi 2005; Mok 2007). For example, Ka Ho Mok (2007, 438) points out, regarding the internationalization of universities in Asia and Westernization, that

> the introduction of English as the medium of instruction; the adoption of curricula from Australia, the United Kingdom, and the United States; the sending of students for overseas studies and international exchanges; and the quest for world-class universities as predominately defined by the Anglo-Saxon world have not only created a new dependency culture but also reinforced the American-dominated hegemony.

Similarly, Philip G. Altbach (2006) notes that globalization is unavoidable in higher education, but working toward reducing the inequalities in global higher education is important, while challenging the system, to prevent neocolonialism.

Therefore, the issue of the dominating Western model and possibly the dependency of universities in Asia on it need to be studied for their implications in individual countries, as well as in the context of international higher education. However, it is required first to understand the realities in each country, particularly from the insights of individuals at universities, who have been directly impacted by the internationalization efforts on campus. In this regard, this chapter delves into the issues that Korean and Japanese universities have faced by using internationalization strategies, from the perspectives of students, faculty, and staff. In other words, our chapter investigates how students, faculty, and staff perceive issues of internationalization at their universities and discusses the implications for Japanese and Korean higher education.

Internationalization Strategies at Korean and Japanese Universities

In this chapter, we examine two East Asian countries, Korea and Japan; two major players in international higher education as sending countries to top study abroad destinations in the world. According to the IIE (2009), Korea and Japan were the top third and fifth countries respectively, in sending students to the United States in 2009 (the top two countries are China and India whose populations exceed a billion each while Korea and Japan are both below 50 million). In internationalizing higher education, Korean and Japanese universities also share their main internationalization strategies of recruiting international students and increasing the number of courses taught in English.

International Student Recruitment—Japan

In the case of Japan, government-initiated policy has played an important role in internationalizing higher education. In particular, it includes the government plans to recruit international students, who have been pivotal for internationalization (Lassegard 2006; Ninomiya et al. 2009). Following the plan established in 1983 to recruit 100,000 international students by the year 2000, the Japanese government announced a new plan to recruit 300,000 "high quality" international students by 2020 (Ninomiya et al. 2009). Over the years, the number of international students increased rapidly from 10,428 in 1983 to 22,154 in 1987 to 41,347 in 1990 and to 109,508 in 2003. Most recently, in 2007, there were 118,498 international students, exceeding their original goal (Japan, Ministry of Education, Culture, Sports, Science and Technology [MEXT] 2008). The backdrop of Japan's 300,000 international students by 2020 plan includes the need to address the issue of international students' quality. This issue of quality will be discussed later in this chapter. Other reasons include the decreased population of high school graduates in Japan and increasing competition with Western European and U.S. higher education institutions to attract talented Chinese students (Kuwamura 2009).

International Student Recruitment—Korea

The Korean government initiated a plan in 2004 to recruit 50,000 international students by the year of 2010, known as the Study Korea Project (Republic of Korea, Ministry of Education and Human Resource Development [MOE and HRD] 2004). As shown in Table 6.1, the Korean government needed to address the large discrepancy between incoming and outgoing students, which led to a financial deficit in the educational sector amounting to US$4.5 billion in 2008 (Lee 2009; Byun and Kim 2010). Following the early achievement of this goal by 2007, the Korean government raised the number of international student recruits to 100,000 by 2012 (Republic of Korea, Ministry of Education, Science and Technology [MEST] 2008c).[1] Similar to Japan, the need to check the quality of international students has been emphasized as a new focus at this stage.

With regard to the composition of the international student population in Japan and Korea (see Tables 6.2 and 6.3), the vast majority of international students in both countries came from Asian countries. In

Table 6.1 International Student Mobility in Japan and Korea

		1999	2001	2003	2005	2007	2009
Japan	International students	55,755	78,812	109,508	121,812	118,498	132,720
	Japanese students abroad	75,856	78,151	74,551	80,023	–	–
Korea	International students	6,279	11,646	12,314	22,526	49,270	–
	Korean students abroad	120,170	149,933	159,903	192,254	217,959	243,224

Source: Data from MEST (2008a, 2008b, 2009a); MEXT (2004, 2008); MOE and HRD (2003).

Table 6.2 Number of International Students in Japan by Country of Origin, 2007

	China	Korea	Taiwan	Vietnam	Malaysia	Thailand	US
Japan	71,277	17,274	4,686	2,582	2,146	2,090	1,805
	60.2%	14.6%	4.0%	2.2%	1.8%	1.8%	1.5%

Note: Total=118,498.
Source: Data from MEXT (2008).

Table 6.3 Number of International Students in Korea by Country of Origin, 2008

	China	Japan	US	Vietnam	Taiwan	Mongolia
Korea	44,746	3,324	1,481	1,827	1,158	2,022
	70.0%	5.2%	2.3%	2.8%	1.8%	3.2%

Note: Total=63,952.
Source: Data from MEST (2008a).

particular, the largest share of the international student body came from China, which comprised 60 percent of the international student body in Japan and 70 percent in Korea.

Using English as a Medium of Teaching—Japan

As a package of the government's plans to recruit international students, the Japanese government also encouraged universities to provide non-degree short-term programs or graduate-level programs with courses taught in English (Huang 2006; Ninomiya et al. 2009). The strategy of insisting on the use of English in universities by the Japanese government had multiple purposes. Those short-term international programs using English are especially aimed to attract international students and intended to internationalize universities in Japan. The Japanese government also believed that using English at universities and adopting an American model of evaluation and coursework would facilitate partnerships with overseas institutions. It also attempted to increase international transparency by using English in Japanese universities (Tsuneyoshi 2005). In reality, however, Akira Kuwamura (2009) noted that Japanese universities have not been active in hiring international faculty.

Using English as a Medium of Teaching—Korea

In the case of Korea and its use of English in universities, not only has the government encouraged universities to hire international faculty, but many Korean universities have also stipulated that newly hired faculty should be able to teach classes in English. In addition, Korean universities have taken more active measures to expand courses taught in English, including in top research universities in Korea. For example, Korea University has mandated undergraduate students to take five courses in English for graduation and plan to increase the ratio of classes taught in English up to 50 percent by 2010 (H-K Kim 2008). Korea Advanced Institute of Science and Technology (KAIST) has announced its plan to teach the entire undergraduate curriculum in English by the year 2010 (Yoo 2007). This plan has created a controversy about its utility and effectiveness, not only among students, but also in the public at large.

In providing English-mediated courses, similarities exist between Korea and Japan. In Korea, existing universities have mainly expanded the number of English-mediated courses offered or have transformed the entire undergraduate curriculum to be taught in English. And in Japan, several universities have undergraduate programs that teach the entire curriculum in English and confer degrees in English. They include Sophia University, International Christian University, and the Asia Pacific University of Ritsumeikan.

These two common strategies in Japan and Korea to internationalize higher education, that is, English-mediated courses and international student recruitment, have been pinpointed for risking Westernization and Englishization in the literature (Tsuneyoshi 2005; Mok 2007).

Accordingly, this chapter explores how these internationalization strategies of the Western model have unfolded, and how they are perceived by stakeholders at universities in Korea and Japan.

Methods

Data for the Korean case were collected using individual interviews at two stages. During the first stage, interviews with Korean faculty and administrators at multiple universities in Korea were conducted. All of the participants were selected from 23 universities in Korea. They consisted of administrators and faculty members who served in varying capacities throughout the university. In the selection of participants, special consideration was given to institutional diversity, such as institutional status, geographic location (metropolitan, near-metropolitan, and regional), governance styles (public or private), and religious affiliation.

During the second stage, Korean students at one private university in Seoul were interviewed. They were all students participating in a short-term international summer program at this university. This six-week program included courses all taught in English mostly by international faculty invited for this program. In total, 15 Korean students who attended this university and participated in this short-term summer program were interviewed. These students were recruited as a targeted sample due to their experience of taking courses taught in English by international faculty along with international students. All interviews were recorded with participants' permission, and conducted and transcribed in Korean language.

The interview data were analyzed based on interview questions related to internationalization: (1) What do you think about the internationalization of universities in Korea? (2) How do you think internationalization efforts may influence Korean students? (3) How do you think increased international students on campus may influence Korean students at your university? At an early stage of data analysis, codes based on the categories of interview questions were created and then revised after initial coding.

For the Japanese case, research papers on the internationalization of Japanese higher education, especially related to the issues of using English and recruiting international students, were reviewed. Journal articles in English, published in international journals, were chosen for this study. The authors were based at Japanese institutions, including Japanese and international faculty, and journals included the *Journal of Research in*

International Education and *Journal of Studies in International Education.* In this chapter, the study of the Japanese case was limited to the literature review. The number of journal articles was also limited for the specific focus of this chapter. Future research needs to expand its scope to use empirical data, and include journals published in Japanese language from Japan's national journals.

Researcher Identity

Regarding authors' researcher identity in conducting this qualitative study, the fact that both researchers completed their education through college (Eun-Young Kim) or graduate education (Jae-Eun Jon) in Korea as Korean nationals allowed them to have insider perspectives into the portion of the study on Korean higher education. However, due to the multiple internationalization policies that had been implemented in Korean universities during their doctoral education in the United States, they were left feeling that they were outsiders. Moreover, they are not affiliated with the universities that they visited for this study. For Kim, faculty and administrators often hesitated to criticize their universities in front of her. The fact that she was conducting a doctoral research study made her an instant outsider for some participants in administrative sectors. Her outsider identity prompted her to feel a bit detached (not intentionally) from her participants and as a result, her explanations tend to be based on an outsider's position. On the other hand, Jon's student participants were more open in sharing their positive and negative views about internationalization. She believes that her gender, seniority by age, and shared Korean identity and language contributed to building rapport with the student participants. Her experience of taking classes in English during graduate school in Korea and the United States also helped her communicate with Korean students about internationalization.

Findings: Korean Case

The findings from the two sets of interviews with the Korean students, faculty, and staff demonstrated their views on internationalization efforts at Korean universities. Their opinions concentrated on two main internationalization strategies that emerged from the interviews. They include teaching courses in English and recruiting international students, especially focusing on the issues of using English in class.

Use of English as a Medium for Teaching: Students' Voice

With regard to using English as the medium of teaching in class, many students, faculty, and administrators expressed their concerns about it. One of the main problems that faculty and administrators noted, with respect to offering courses in English, was the dearth of faculty members who are able to lecture in English. One professor said that most Korean universities currently only employ new faculty who are able to teach courses in English.

For the students, they perceived that the use of English as the medium of courses gives English predominant status. One student called it "Americanization," as her university used English only for internationalization, and continued to argue that internationalization should rather mean using diverse foreign languages. This student added, "If courses in philosophy are going to be taught in a language other than Korean, German would be appropriate [instead of English]." Another student took the example of France, as he thought that French universities may not try to teach courses in English as much as Korean universities. He perceived Korean universities as attempting to institutionalize curricula in English beyond the students' capacities, even ignoring subsequent issues.

In addition, one student pointed out that creating courses taught in English has caused the "English-divide" between students who are good at English and those who are not. Those English-mediated courses normally use a fixed grading scale while courses taught in Korean language normally used grading on a curve. Students emphasized that those students who are not good at or who are reluctant to take courses in English typically earn much lower grades than those who are English proficient. On a related note, one professor said:

> Teaching courses in English has a lot of problems. First of all, most students' English proficiency is not high enough to understand lectures, so they tend to do poorly in evaluations. Thus, students try to avoid courses that are offered in English. In addition to students' language proficiency, faculty's language proficiency is also problematic. Those older professors cannot teach a course in English. And I'm sure you understand what I'm saying, but not every professor who received their degrees in the US can teach courses in English.

Students' overall English language proficiency has improved in Korea, but academic terms, abstract concepts and academic theories require more advanced language ability. Since, students' grade point average (GPA) could be an important component in his/her employability in the competitive job market, students then tend to take courses that are less academic rigorous and challenging. As the number of courses offered in English is one of the main criteria for university evaluation (especially in the case of international rankings, see Chapter 7), universities are forced to follow the trend. This gradual but significant change suggests that external forces, such as government regulations and public views, influence the ways in which universities operate (E-Y Kim 2010).

In relation to the "English divide," some students were critical that using English may lead to the issue of inequality among students in class, even beginning from the college entrance exam. For example, one student voiced the concern that average Korean students who have not lived abroad prior to college tend to be disadvantaged from the beginning in taking English-mediated courses, compared to those who are more capable in English from their pre-college experience. A student informed us that:

> There are many students who have lived abroad for quite some time. And that is how they could enter the university [for being qualified to take a separate entrance exam from their number of years schooling and living abroad]. Those who lived [abroad] even for a little bit or those who graduated from high schools for foreign languages. I graduated from a normal high school. That is all good. But asking us to take courses taught in English with those who exceed in their English or foreign languages. It is good that it is helpful to take classes [with them]. But the level of language ability is totally different, and we cannot play a game on the same ground. The university should not just do good things for them, but I believe that they should support those native Korean students who have lived [in Korea only] for 20, 30 years? It may be inappropriate to call it a separate support [for us] because it depends on individuals' efforts. However, with all these, I felt it is unfair.

Another student raised the issue of inequality related to internationalization in the sense of providing opportunities to a wider range of students. He explained that his university has represented students from a regional area for a long time, normally those who may be less economically and socially privileged than those from a metropolitan area in Korea. However, as the college entrance exam has changed to focus on English competence, it appears to have resulted in recruiting students from economically wealthy backgrounds as these students tend to have more access to various types of education (e.g., opportunity to study abroad, private tutoring, and cram schools) and therefore have higher levels of English competence. His concern was that internationalization may lead to inequality in providing opportunities for higher education:

> I have participated in the protest against internationalization. My university has been a leader of internationalization, but from when?... Then universities begin to admit students from rich families, those who did schooling abroad, because they are good at English. Students from a regional area can have good high school GPA, but they may be relatively bad at English. My university has traditionally been a symbol for students from a regional area. As many poor students were present on campus, we discussed our era of drinking *makkuli*;[2] when did we start to advocate internationalization over wine! I have heard this side of the story. As everyone has different values, we cannot say who is right. But over-internationalization could cause inequality [among students].... I hope the institution provides opportunities to everybody.

Many students expressed concerns that using English as the medium of teaching may hamper their understanding of the course content, especially when courses carry critical knowledge for their academic major programs. One student pointed out that Korean professors' teaching in English is not as effective as that of the international faculty because they are not native speakers in English either. Another student expressed discontent that one course in her major was offered only in English as the following quote aptly describes why she raises this concern:

> If I am going to take courses taught in English for my major, I think I had better not take them at all. When I cannot understand something, I would not be able to pursue it further [in class]. Because professors do not let students do challenging tasks.... People say, "Take classes in Korean if you want to know your major better." I believe that professors would be able to have a good class when students are at some level. Wouldn't they have such struggles?

Students added that some instructors may end up mixing Korean language for a large portion of teaching instead of using English only because it can help Korean students understand the course better. This practice questions the purpose of using English for the medium of teaching in a non-English speaking country. It is critical to reconsider why English is necessary if it inhibits teaching and learning in class. It is important to note that teaching is one of the fundamental activities in higher education; its core essence is the transfer of knowledge from professors to students (Clark 1983).

Many students criticized that it is inappropriate to mandate students in academic programs, such as Korean literature and Korean history, to take the same number of courses in English as those in other programs. They perceived the university policy as injudicious and did not consider that it fit at the disciplinary level. As the institution claims, opening courses in English may help recruit international students and diversify their choice of courses. Taking courses in English could also enrich Korean students' classroom experience by learning from a variety of teaching materials and working with students from other cultures. However, flexibility in implementing the policy, such as the number of courses needed and the field of courses taught in English, is necessary. One such change at their institutions included the approval of courses taken in other foreign languages that can count towards the mandated number of courses taken in English.

Impact of English-Medium Teaching on Faculty

With regard to faculty and internationalization, the cultural and traditional notions of what a professor is, as well as conflicts among faculty members (e.g., over salaries, courses offered in English) appear to have hindered incorporating international components into the curricula. Some administrators interviewed criticized faculty members who did not want to accept new values and practices. For example:

> We want more professors to teach courses in English. To encourage them to do so, we [the university] even offer financial incentives for professors to teach courses in English. First of all, faculty members are not willing to teach courses in English. When some professors do and take the incentives, others started to criticize, saying that providing financial benefits only to the professors offering courses in English [foreign languages] was an unfair treatment.

Salary differentials among professors at the same level with similar experience did not exist in the previous Korean higher education system, regardless of the area of studies. Providing a financial incentive for teaching courses in English appears to be recognized as a threat to this traditional practice. At the same time, the concept of financial incentives conflicts with the organizational culture at Korean universities. The following comment from a former teaching assistant at an elite university aptly illustrates the mentality of some professors who are resistant to offering lectures in foreign languages: "I remember a professor told me that he felt that offering financial incentives for giving lectures in English is an insult to educators. He said that it was like trying to buy the professor's authority and right."

For some faculty members, such changes as seeing student as clients, conducting course evaluations, and being paid based on their performance, might be a culture and reality that are hard to understand or accept. The above quote illustrates that while the old university culture that romanticizes the role of professors may still exist; it is definitely receding, suggesting the emergence of a new rules and approaches (E-Y Kim 2010).

The Korean government has announced that faculty members at national and public universities should be paid bonuses based on their performance (i.e., teaching, research, and services). This announcement was met with resistance and criticism from professors. One criticism stated that professors are not laborers, therefore, providing an additional benefit based on their performance would only discourage faculty morale (Choi and Kim 2000).

Nevertheless, other students shared their positive views on English-mediated courses, based on their experiences. For example, one student stated that classes in her discipline involve the frequent use of terminology in English. She felt that using English as the medium of teaching worked well for her. Another student described a course that he took about nuclear energy and understanding science by a Korean professor during a semester. He liked the fact that the class used materials at a "world-class" level, and that he learned about international organizations and what may not be carried, even in the media. He explained that the professor successfully integrated an international dimension in class by taking examples outside of Korea. He explained that he had learned to take what happens in Korea and apply it to the international level. He also felt that he needed to broaden his perspectives after taking this course.

Other students also mentioned that they learned the practical use of English from taking courses in English and felt the need to work more on their English capability. A case in point, Jon (2009) found from the same group of interviewees that Korean students had started to perceive English as a tool rather than only as an experience of taking courses in English from a native English-speaking professional and alongside international students. Indeed, Jon discovered that most students viewed their study of English as useful, solely for getting good scores and a better job qualification and therefore felt a considerable pressure to be proficient in English.

International Students on Campus: Separate from Us

With regard to the growing number of international students, Korean interviewee students noted that the university isolated international students, or even some Korean students from the rest as it created a separate space for international students, such as their separate dormitory and lounge.

Interestingly during the interviews, many students described international students' presence on campus by using the Korean proverb, "Just as a cow looks at a chicken." This expression indicates indifference to others.

In other words, Korean students are indifferent to international students on campus and do not interact with them. Some Korean students also complained about the unfamiliar presence of international students on campus. While there is a campus program that teams up international and Korean students to promote relationships between them, one student pointed out that this kind of program can also divide Korean students by those who were given the opportunity to participate in the program and interact with international students and those who were not.

A couple of other students also believed that the university tends to dedicate more of its resources for incoming international students than for Korean students. They felt that new facilities, such as the dormitory and lounge, targeted and served international students alone and that international students are treated better. They felt that international students are provided with a space separate from the Korean student body. However, some Korean students perceived it positively that facilities on campus have improved, and utilized these facilities and related services.

In addition, students were aware that international students may not have come to Korea voluntarily, or with high education qualifications. Rather, the move could be due to the international student quota that the Korean university aimed to fill or increase; several Korean students remarked that the university was accepting any international student who applied. One of the students indicated:

> One of my friends took a course in English and did a team project with an international student. My friend has talked to this student and this international student did not know a thing about the course. It was a very difficult course in international management and many students must have taken that course because this course that is taught in English is less challenging [than that taught in Korean]. I do not think this international student would have wanted to come to Korea. Korea could have been the fourth choice. I suppose that this international student's qualification is questionable. Otherwise, this student may have gone to Japan or China.

In other words, Korean students felt that international students chose to come to Korea because they could not go to their first or second choice such as universities in Japan and China. Their level of academic achievement did not convince Korean students of the need to recruit international students who did not appear to have a high standard of education. This phenomenon comes from the emphasis of the government and many universities on increasing the number of international students, but not so much on what happens afterward on campus. This is related to our discussion later in this chapter on the lack of substance in internationalization and the so-called quality of international students in the context of both Korea and Japan.

A professor also described problems caused by international students at one small private university that has recently been established. His description characterizes his university as being "China specialized:"

> This University admits many Chinese students. I heard that the school suffers from problems caused by those students. Once they enter Korea with a student visa, quite a number of those Chinese students flee from school in order to find jobs and work. They come here [Korea] for the student status, but their main purpose of coming to Korea is not education.

This interview reveals that the student visa (D-2) is used as an excuse for entering Korea and that quite a lot of Chinese students' main purpose of coming to Korea is to earn money. As such, it is hard to expect them to make significant academic achievements or to bring a cultural contribution to the campus (E-Y Kim 2010).

However, including courses in English, Korean students also felt a positive impact of having international students around. Korean students often mentioned that international students motivate and stimulate them in their own studies and language learning. They also said that Korean students appear to have begun to open their minds to international students and show interest in making friends with them. They noted the possibility of intercultural learning from interacting with international students. Jon (2009) focused on this aspect of Korean students' intercultural learning from the same data. Interestingly, one student stated that increased international students on campus could contribute to developing respect for diversity when her university has a reputation for its own strong identity:

> The identity of my university is very strong, as you are well aware of it; like bonding among us. As international students increase on campus; accordingly, as such an aspect [a strong identity] diminishes, we may come to respect diversity more. It may function to relax [the campus atmosphere and identity]. In the past, we pushed things through by "we are from this university!" But now more diverse things are possible on campus; we have foreigners like this. In this respect, I suppose people may become more relaxed.

Internationalization for Whom?

Regarding how internationalization efforts are perceived by Korean students, many students criticized that the university focuses on how it looks to the outside world rather than what it really means to those involved on campus. They claimed that the university tends to use internationalization efforts for its publicity. Students added that the number of international students, faculty, and courses taught in English could be useful in raising the university ranking in domestic or international ranking systems. They explained that the university uses internationalization strategies to be ranked internationally as the top university in Korea, while their university has been traditionally regarded as the second or third top university in Korea:

> I take it [as a] positive to have courses taught in English and internationalization itself. Exchange [among students and faculty] may be necessary. However, I feel skeptical that my university must be internationalized. Because my university is not a top in this country yet, but I think my university is trying to make up for it by internationalization. Even though we see an apparent barrier to entry, SNU[3] to become a perfect top university, my university seems to try to make up for it by getting good scores from evaluation by international university ranking systems. I don't quite remember their standards, but I heard that they count the number of international faculty and courses taught in English, apart from their quality.

Similarly, a couple of students summarized that internationalization efforts lack substance; for example, in not going beyond merely hosting international students. They particularly raised the need to facilitate academic exchanges among Korean and international students so that they could share academic interests and could help international students learn Korean studies when that was their purpose in coming to Korea. Other examples included building a support system for international students, providing enough information in English, and helping them integrate into campus life.

Korean students also expressed the positive impact of internationalization efforts on themselves, which may have been originally designed to create an appearance of internationalization. For example, internationalization of their university has provided Korean students with more diverse opportunities, such as taking courses in English and interacting with international students or faculty. Moreover, students felt that internationalization could help them progress beyond narrow perspectives, which they expressed by using the Korean proverb of not being "a frog in a well" any longer. One student shared that initially he only felt the pressure about the trend and requirements to use English on campus imposed by internationalization efforts at his university. However, having realized what he wants to do in the future, he began to feel the need for internationalization on campus and tried to utilize this opportunity for himself. He then emphasized the need to ease tensions and resistance in introducing change associated with internationalization to general students. Another student explained how internationalization could become meaningful to individual students:

> If internationalization inside the university comes true, it is not internationalization that I used to hear only from the media, but it is really the part of our life. Accepting it as reality... it seems that I get an opportunity to think more about what I am going to do in the future."

Overall, most of the students perceived the direction that their institution set to internationalize the university in a positive way. Nevertheless, they pointed out that its method in implementing internationalization on campus has entailed problems, as discussed above.

In summary, Korean students perceived the negative consequences of internationalization efforts at their university in providing courses in English and recruiting international students. They raised the issues of English-mediated teaching, such as the predominance of English, the English divide and inequality in educational opportunities among students, and hindrance to content understanding. For the issues of international student recruitment, they pointed out international students' separation from Korean students by institutional setting. Korean students also questioned the purpose of internationalization, whether it is for how the university looks to the outside world, or for the students on campus. In addition, faculty and administrators noted that teaching courses in English may conflict with the traditional notion of being a Korean professor. However, it is also important to note that Korean students acknowledged the positive sides of internationalization, including intercultural learning and having diverse educational opportunities.

Findings: Japanese Case

Research papers on the internationalization of higher education in Japan discussed the issues of using English for the medium of teaching and recruiting international students. Regarding the use of English for internationalizing universities in Japan, Ryoko Tsuneyoshi conducted an important empirical study of cultural and structural issues stemming from "Englishization as internationalization" at Japanese universities (2005, 68). Overall, her study surmised that the use of English and a short-term study abroad program could attract international students from a wide variety of countries to Japan. Approximately half of the international students at her university came from Asian countries and the other half from Western countries. This finding was contrasted with the fact that degree-seeking international students came predominantly from Asian countries. The author explained this contrast in that, short-term programs in English widely drew potential international students from Western countries, who may not have Japanese language classes offered in institutions at home or a strong Japanese language capability in comparison to other Asian students. The short period of programs also extended the pool of international students to those who do not pursue degrees in Japan or cannot leave their home institutions for a long time.

Tsuneyoshi (2005) also found that their different levels of academic performance and cultural differences revealed some issues in taking courses taught in English. For example, international students' level of English influenced or hampered their achievement in Japanese language learning. In addition, those from Asian and Western European countries perceived teaching and learning style in English-mediated classes differently. While Asian students felt that classes were discussion-based, students from European and English-speaking countries felt that the classes did not involve enough discussion or lacked an American style of a comprehensive syllabus.

However, Japanese students did not feel equipped to handle courses taught in English, as well as the American-type of instruction, which employed "tight multiple evaluations and organized coursework" (Tsuneyoshi 2005, 83). In the context of Japanese culture, the author explained that such an academic culture could make Japanese students feel that they are not independent scholars as was expected at their age. Japanese students who experienced the competitive college entrance exam and years of preparation for it desired to have more of a social life during their undergraduate years and a relaxed environment in class, instead of tight instruction. Institutional support to be able to handle the level of English in class was also a necessary component.

Concerning faculty-related issues from English instruction, James Lassegard (2006) and Tsuneyoshi (2005) noted that it is difficult to recruit faculty to teach courses in English at Japanese universities. The authors attributed the reason to the extra workload that Japanese faculty need to take on for teaching in English in addition to their normal responsibilities as well as the minimal compensation. Japanese faculty also have additional work to address the different needs among Japanese and international students in class.

Tsuneyoshi continued that Japanese faculty members need to incorporate the Western or American style of instruction when teaching courses in English, which she referred to as the "Americanization" of teaching. This style includes "the preparation of a syllabus (e.g., readings, course descriptions, and multiple evaluation standards) that can be externally evaluated," and "discussions, field trips, and guest speakers" in class (2005, 81). She noted that "the conventional Japanese-style courses (e.g., whole-class, relaxed course evaluation and structure)" were challenged to meet international standards of instruction and evaluation in higher education, and that such courses could become very different from other regular courses at Japanese universities.

The issue related to staff, as discussed in Tsuneyoshi (2005), includes the finding that Japanese universities lack international education experts and staff to implement internationalization strategies on campus. In particular, the system of staff rotation at Japanese universities hinders the training of the staff to acquire the level of knowledge and English ability to work with international students. Tsuneyoshi pointed out that the perception of international educators and their needed presence in Japan are still lacking.

One of the major switches in the new Japanese government policy to recruit 300,000 international students after the one in the 1980s rested in the change of focus from the quantity to quality of international students (Ninomiya et al. 2009). Concerns about international student quality have been raised in Japan, such as their low level of Japanese language, absence in classes, longer time to complete graduate degrees, and especially media attention on their unauthorized labor and crimes (Lassegard 2006; McNeill 2009). According to a survey by Somusho (Lassegard 2006), the majority of Japanese faculty believed that the quality of international students depends on their increased Japanese ability and academic qualifications, rather than on the quality of faculty and the curriculum.

However, interestingly and importantly, Lassegard (2006) argues that these issues of international students in Japan, or their so-called quality, can be closely related to structural, cultural, and academic factors at Japanese universities, rather than international students' personal factors. In other words, changes needed to accommodate international students have not been made despite the increase of their number. For example, a lack of both stringent admission requirements for international students and foreign language support available on campus hampered their academic progress. Other influential factors included that international students may be asked to obtain doctoral degrees in a limited amount of time, especially in conjunction with government scholarships, and their need to complete a degree for jobs in their home countries, while Japanese students can leave without submitting a dissertation for other job opportunities (ibid.). While it is changing, the academic culture in Japan does not require a doctoral degree for faculty career, and many faculty members in Japan still do not hold doctoral degrees. Therefore, they may feel reluctant to confer doctoral degrees on international students or feel pressured to do so when international students are not qualified.

International students' need and academic culture in Japan can conflict in their obtaining doctoral degrees. Some professors in certain disciplines may also demand strict requirements for publications required for dissertation submission, which may delay international students' graduation.

More influential factors include Japanese faculty members' teaching and advising skills in working with international students. For example, international students, especially non-East Asian students with little Japanese ability, are likely to have difficulty in communicating and mentoring from faculty with little international experience (Lassegard 2006). Lassegard emphasized a need for faculty development to improve teaching and advising skills as well as English, and training sessions for both Japanese faculty and international students about intercultural communication. He added that the quality of courses taught in English could be improved by incorporating international students' evaluation.

This issue of international students, however their quality is defined, is also related to the low enrollment of high school graduates in Japanese higher education. As the population of high school graduates decreases in Japan due to the low birth rate, small private colleges, particularly outside the metropolitan areas, have struggled with the enrollment crisis. Their coping strategy to recruit international students, however, has led those universities to face the aforementioned problems, such as international students' classroom absence and working without proper documents/visas (McNeill 2009).

Discussion

The findings discussed above show that stakeholders on campus affected by the internationalization strategies at Korean and Japanese universities were generally critical of strategies focusing on the use of English and the Western model of instruction. As shown in the Korean case, students and faculty may accept internationalization as a desirable and positive initiative for students, as well as institutions. Nonetheless, they perceived it to be problematic as to how institutions have practiced and realized internationalization on campus.

Common issues related to using English for teaching, at both Korean and Japanese universities, included domestic students' struggles with English language ability, understanding the course content in English, and the different academic culture when the Western model of instruction was used. Korean students particularly expressed concerns that the use of English and its importance in higher education may disadvantage Korean students with low English capability, leading to an "English divide" or the issue of inequality in college entrance and performance at college. They also criticized the indiscriminant policy of a university to mandate that all disciplines teach courses in English.

The issues of recruiting qualified faculty to teach in English and their reluctance to teach such courses appeared as common in both countries. Japanese faculty experienced a challenge to incorporate the Western style of instruction. In addition, Korean faculty experienced a cultural clash between the financial incentives from teaching courses in English and the traditional concept of faculty. As the number of courses offered in English has become one of the main criteria for university evaluation, especially by media companies, universities appear to have no choice but to follow the trend to use English for their curricula. This gradual, but significant change suggests that external forces, such as government regulations and public views, influence the ways in which universities operate.

Moreover, by including a number of international faculty members in their public announcement criteria the Korean government has pushed universities to hire international faculty for its World Class University (WCU) Project. Recently Korean universities have also stipulated that newly hired faculty should be able to teach classes in English (MEST 2009b). Andres Bernasconi (2006) noted that the pace of organizational adaptation to a new environment at universities is correlated with the cultural makeup of its faculty. Universities with a large number of more recently appointed professors tend to adapt more quickly than those whose faculty members began their careers in the 1960s through 1980s. This means that the existing culture among faculty groups might work as a hampering factor for university innovation or adaptation.

The relatively slow progress in areas such as international faculty recruitment and internationalized curricular development at Korean universities in their internationalization efforts can be explained within this context. Some Korean professors may feel that changes such as treating student as clients, conducting course evaluations, and being paid based on performance are part of a new culture and reality that they find difficult to accept. The recent idea of financial incentives and performance-based salaries at Korean universities shows that while the old university culture romanticizing the role of professors may still exist, it may be receding as the new culture and approaches emerge.

From a cultural perspective, it was particularly interesting that both Korean and Japanese universities faced cultural dilemmas from using English as a medium for teaching courses. Korean professors experienced conflict between the financial compensation for teaching courses in English and the traditional notion of teachers in Korean culture. For Japanese students, the

American type of class structure, using multiple evaluations and detailed descriptions of what to do in a syllabus, made them feel unprepared and did not acknowledge them as independent scholars.

In addition, both Korean and Japanese universities share issues related to recruiting international students, the so-called quality of international students, especially related to their illegal labor, absence in classes, and visa overstays in both countries (Lassegard 2006; Yoo and Hwang 2009). Additionally, Japan and Korea have a common issue that the pool of high school graduates has decreased due to low birth rates. This phenomenon has driven small regional universities, often less prestigious ones, to attract international students, particularly from China, to fill their enrollment gaps. In turn, this strategy has led to the *Chinization* for internationalization and related issues discussed above. Both Japanese and Korean governments have responded by regulating visa issuance to Chinese students (Oh 2008). However, it should be noted that the dominant number of Chinese students is considered positively in Korea as an opportunity to promote cultural exchange and understanding between Korea and China and to bring financial benefits to the Korean economy (Hwang et al. 2009). In this regard, Lassegard's (2006) study is meaningful, as it emphasizes the importance of structural and academic support for international students by Japanese universities, as well as the improved quality of instruction in understanding and addressing the issue of international student quality. Other issues related to internationalization strategies, such as the dominance of English, separate space created for international students, an emphasis on appearance rather than on substance and the lack of specialized staff in international education have also been discussed.

Nevertheless, it is noteworthy that many Korean students overall regarded the internationalizing of the university system as positive and raised satisfactory examples of classes taught in English. They also mentioned the positive impact that international students may have on Korean students (see also Jon 2009). In particular, the positive examples of courses taught in English discussed in this chapter indicate that they can benefit students when the course content is considered as appropriate for using English as the medium of instruction, and good preparation is accompanied by faculty to incorporate an international dimension into the course. As another example, one student majoring in linguistics described a course titled, "Globalization of English," which included international students from various countries, whether their native languages were English or other ones. He explained that the course was satisfactory in helping to approach English as a nonnative speaker, as well as providing exposure to the different types of English spoken in the world, and for having gained confidence in English.

This study bears significance for reflecting voices from stakeholders directly involved in and influenced by internationalizing universities. However, it has the limitation that it lacks empirical data collected from universities in Japan; for example, interviews and field work. In future research, the equivalent level of data collection from both Japanese and Korean universities is desired for a further comparative study on internationalization.

Conclusion

In an article on the internationalization of universities in Asia, Mok (2007) raised an important question as to whether internationalization efforts have contributed to enriching students' learning and improving the quality of education. The findings in this study indicate that the current internationalization strategies, English-mediated courses and international student recruitment in Korea and Japan require addressing the related issues and finding appropriate measures to fit in the specific context of a country, institutions, individuals, and courses. Several successful examples of courses taught in English at a Korean university, as discussed in this chapter, demonstrate the potential to contextualize Western practices to the Korean context.

Furthermore, Mok emphasizes the importance of distinguishing "policy learning" and "policy copying" for Asian countries; otherwise, policy copying without "proper adaptation" and "careful contextualization" may lead to recolonization (2007, 438). In other words, internationalization strategies that Korean and Japanese universities have adopted from practices in Western European countries and the United States without contextualization—using English as the medium of teaching, adopting the American type of class structure and evaluation, and recruiting international students—may put them at risk of sacrificing their own traditions and identity in education and research in Korean and Japanese universities. These strategies should be accompanied by contemplating the right fit and contextualizing to their own contexts.

Bernd Wächter (2005) pointed out that non-English speaking countries, such as Japan and Korea in this chapter, are disadvantaged in their linguistic competitiveness. However, English has gained importance for communicating, distributing knowledge, and teaching in non-English speaking countries, as Futao Huang (2006) stated in a comparative study of internationalizing the curriculum. In addition, Korean and Japanese higher education is at the periphery of the global higher education system (Altbach 2006) as non-English speaking countries and the predominant outward-bound student mobility status. Therefore, adopting a dominant language globally, which is English, and the model of higher education from Western or American higher education may have been the most attractive and simple option for Korean and Japanese universities in an effort to internationalize campuses and also to increase their competitiveness.

However, as has been discussed in this chapter, these methods of internationalizing universities in Korea and Japan have been criticized for possible Westernization, Englishization, or Americanization, and have entailed the aforementioned issues discussed in this chapter. Therefore, internationalization strategies for Westernization without considering the specific context should be avoided, but internationalization for the particular context, Korean and Japanese higher education and their individual institutions in this case, is needed.

Notes

1. In January 2001, the Republic of Korea renamed its Ministry of Education as the Ministry of Education and Human Resource Development (MOE and HRD). Then the MOE and HRD is renamed the Ministry of Education, Science and Technology (MEST) by the revised *Government Organization Act* in February 2008 (MEST 2008d).
2. *Makkoli* is a Korean traditional alcohol drink that is less expensive than other alcohol drinks.
3. Seoul National University is considered the top university in Korea.

References

Altbach, Philip G. 2006. "Globalization and the University: Realities in an Unequal World." In *International Handbook of Higher Education*, ed. James J. F. Forest and Philip G. Altbach. Dordrecht, The Netherlands: Springer.
Bernasconi, Andres. 2006. "Breaking the Institutional Mold: Faculty in the Transformation of Chilean Higher Education from State to Market." In *The New Institutionalism in Education*, ed. Heinz-Dieter Meyer and Brian Rowan. Albany: State University of New York Press.
Byun, Kiyong, and Minjung Kim. 2010. "Shifting Patterns of the Government's Policies for the Internationalization of Korean Higher Education." *Journal of Studies in International Education*. doi:10.1177/1028315310375307. Available online at: http://jsi.sagepub.com.
Choi, Sung-Hae, and Woon-Hoe Kim. 2000. 교수 평가와 연봉제 [*Evaluation of Faculty's Performance and Performance-based Salary*]. Seoul: Sunhak-Sa.

Clark, Burton R. 1983. *The Higher Education System: Academic Organization in Cross-National Perspective.* Berkeley, CA: University of California Press.
Davis, Todd M. 2003. *Atlas of Student Mobility.* New York: IIE.
Huang, Futao. 2006. "Internationalization of Curricula in Higher Education Institutions in Comparative Perspectives: Case Studies of China, Japan and the Netherlands." *Higher Education* 51 (4): 521-539.
Hwang, Hyung-Joon, Duk-Young Yoo, and Min-Ki Shin. 2009. "중국인 유학생 6만명 시대 명암 (하) '中流' 흘러넘치는 대학가" ["The Era of 60,000 Chinese Students, Its Upside and Downside: (Last Story) College Town with Overflowing 'Chinese Trend'"]. *Donga Ilbo,* June 23, 2009. Available online at: http://www.donga.com.
Institute of International Education (IIE). 2009. *Record Numbers of International Students in U.S. Higher Education.* New York: IIE. Available online at: http://opendoors.iienetwork.org.
IIE. 2010. *Global Destinations for International Students at the Post-Secondary (Tertiary) Level, 2001 and 2009.* New York: IIE. Available online at: http://www.atlas.iienetwork.org.
Japan, Ministry of Education, Culture, Sports, Science and Technology (MEXT). 2004. *Outline of the Student Exchange System.* Tokyo: MEXT. Available online at: http://www.mext.go.jp.
Japan, MEXT. 2008. *Outline of The Student Exchange System: Study in Japan and Abroad.* Tokyo: MEXT. Available online at: http://www.mext.go.jp.
Jon, Jae-Eun. 2009. "Interculturality in Higher Education as Student Intercultural Learning and Development: A Case Study in South Korea." *Intercultural Education* 20 (9): 439-449.
Kim, Eun-Young. 2010. "Internationalization of Korean Higher Education." PhD diss., University of Illinois at Urbana-Champaign
Kim, Hee-Kyoon. 2008. "글로벌 KU 박차. 이기수 고려대 총장" ["Accelerating 'Global KU.' President Lee, Ki-Soo at Korea University"]. *Donga Ilbo,* August 12, 2008. Available online at: http://www.donga.com.
Kuwamura, Akira. 2009. "The Challenges of Increasing Capacity and Diversity in Japanese Higher Education through Proactive Recruitment Strategies." *Journal of Studies in International Education* 13 (2): 189-202.
Lassegard, James P. 2006. "International Student Quality and Japanese Higher Education Reform." *Journal of Studies in International Education* 10 (2): 119-140.
Lee, Young. 2009. "교육은 최고의 전략산업" ["Education is the Best Strategic Industry"]. Available online at: http://epic.kdi.re.kr.
McNeill, David. 2009. "Enrollment Crisis Threatens Japan's Private Colleges: Some Fill Empty Seats with Foreign Students, Creating New Problems." *Chronicle of Higher Education,* October 25. Available online at: http://chronicle.com.
Mok, Ka Ho. 2007. "Questing for Internationalization of Universities in Asia: Critical Reflections." *Journal of Studies in International Education* 11 (3-4): 433-454.

Ninomiya, Akira, Jane Knight, and Aya Watanabe. 2009. "The Past, Present, and Future of Internationalization in Japan." *Journal of Studies in International Education* 13 (2): 117-124.
Oh, Dae-Young. 2008. "일본대학의 국제화" ["Internationalization of Japanese Universities"]. 대학교육 [*T'aehak-Kyoyuk*] 153 (5/6). Available online at: http://magazine.kcue.or.kr.
Republic of Korea, Ministry of Education and Human Resource Development (MOE and HRD). 2003. *2003 국내외 유학생 통계* [*2003 Statistics on International Students in Korea and Korean Students Abroad*]. Seoul: MOE and HRD. Available online at: http://www.moe.go.kr.
Republic of Korea, MOE and HRD. 2004. 스터디 코리아 프로젝트: 외국인 유학생 유치 확대 종합방안 [*The Study Korea Project*]. Seoul: MOE and HRD. Available online at: http://www.moe.go.kr.
Republic of Korea, Ministry of Education, Science and Technology (MEST). 2008a. 국내외 유학생 통계 [*2008 Statistics on the Number of International Students in Korea*]. Seoul: MEST. Available online at: http://www.mest.go.kr.
Republic of Korea, MEST. 2008b. 스터디 코리아 *2008* [*2008 Statistics on the Number of Korean Students Studying Abroad*]. Seoul: MEST. Available online at: http://www.mest.go.kr.
Republic of Korea, MEST. 2008c. 스터디 코리아 발전 방향 [*Study Korea Project Development Strategies*]. Seoul: MEST. Available online at: http://www.mest.go.kr.
Republic of Korea, MEST. 2008d. *History*. Seoul: MEST. Available online at: http://english.mest.go.kr.
Republic of Korea, MEST. 2009a. 스터디 코리아 *2009* [*2009 Statistics on the Number of Korean Students Studying Abroad*]. Seoul: MEST. Available online at: http://www.mest.go.kr.
Republic of Korea, MEST. 2009b. 대학정보공시 계획 및 지침서 [*Plans and Guidelines for Publicizing University Information*]. Seoul: MEST.
Tsuneyoshi, Ryoko. 2005. "Internationalization Strategies in Japan." *Journal of Research in International Education* 4 (1): 65-86.
Wächter, Bernd. 2005. "Will European Higher Education Go English?" In *I Gotta Use Words When I Talk to You: English and International Education*, ed. Michael Woolf. European Association for International Education (EAIE) Occasional Paper No. 17. Amsterdam: EAIE.
Yoo, Duk-Young, and Hyoung-Joon Hwang. 2009. "중국인 유학생 6만명 시대 명암 (상) 무리한 유치 부작용" ["The Era of 60,000 Chinese Students, Its Upside and Downside: (First Story) Side-Effects of Recruitment Beyond Capacity"]. *Donga Ilbo*, June 22, 2009. Available online at: http://www.donga.com.
Yoo, Yong-Ha. 2007. "KAIST, 모든 강의 영어로…교수 20%만 정년보장" ["KAIST, All the Curriculum Taught in English…Tenure Guaranteed for Only 20% of Faculty"]. *Maeil Kyoungje*, October 1, 2007. Available online at: http://news.mk.co.kr.

Chapter 7

Higher Education Global Rankings System in East Asia

Peter Gregory Ghazarian

The first modern ranking of universities by *U.S. News & World Report* in 1983 set into motion a new trend in higher education. Despite initial criticism, ranking systems for higher education institutions (HEIs) have blossomed. Inspired by the Organization for Economic Cooperation and Development's (OECD) Programme for International Student Assessment (PISA), HEI rankings have expanded to become international assessments (Marginson 2009). The most notable of the international rankings are the Academic Ranking of World Universities (ARWU) by Shanghai Jiao Tong University's Institute of Higher Education and the London *Times Higher Education* (*THE*). These ranking systems rely on weighted indicators of an HEI's research, students, faculty, reputation, and rewards. The rankings produce their results based on the compilation of these indicators.

Although rankings are imperfect as measures of HEI quality, they have an important role in the marketization of higher education (Dill 2003; Slaughter and Rhoades 2004; Wedlin 2008). The rankings function as a higher education stock exchange and as competition intensifies between HEIs, their slight differences are accentuated. Rankings then inform consumers of HEIs, influence institutional marketing strategies, and prevent institutional complacency by pressuring HEIs to improve their standings (Buela-Casal et al. 2007). In doing so, rankings play into the global trend for greater accountability in higher education by providing comparative and publically available data on HEIs (Salmi 2009).

The transition from national to international ranking systems results, in part, from the increase in the transient population of students. Between 1999 and 2007, cross-border student mobility increased by 53 percent (UNESCO 2009). As student mobility increases, international rankings become much more relevant (Jobbins 2005). When cross-border students seek employment, unknown foreign HEIs can be referenced against more familiar (brand name) institutions in the rankings. This international comparability facilitates the future mobility of an HEI's graduates.

In a world of multinational corporations, domestic students are also influenced by the international prestige of the HEIs. The consequences of attending a particular institution extend beyond the domain of education. HEIs produce economic and status value for their students (Marginson 2009). Contributing to this production of value, international rankings place countries, individuals, and HEIs within a global hierarchy. This view of higher education has led to the popular use of terms such as "world class" and "world-class universities" (Buela-Casal et al. 2007).

The concept of a world-class university has a relatively long, but unclear history. Although the term remains quite popular, it lacks a clear definition. Specifically, even though the concept predates international rankings, the rankings increasingly define what it means to be world class (Deem et al. 2008). In fact, the creators of the ARWU admit that a significant part of their motivation in setting up their system of ranking was to measure the gap between local Chinese HEIs and top-ranking "world-class" HEIs (Liu and Cheng 2005). Based on the results of the early ARWU and *THE* rankings, the ranking methodologies seem to equate "world class" with the characteristics common to the traditionally elite HEIs in the United States and United Kingdom: large, comprehensive, English-speaking, research-intensive and science-focused (Altbach 2006).

Thus, rankings as a measure of quality in higher education are more political than technical; certain interests are met at the expense of others (Skolnik 2010). This inherent bias underlies much of the criticism of ranking systems. Yet, with no real competition and by merit of broad media exposure, HEI rankings have come to exert great influence over public perceptions of HEI prestige. In other words, "built-in bias...does not rob rankings of their power" and their ability to capture public attention creates pressure on the institutions they evaluate (Marginson and van der Wende 2007, 309). Public acceptance of HEI rankings, in turn, forces the hand of institutions to accept the rankings and their measurements of HEI quality.

Nevertheless, ranking systems offer benefits as well as drawbacks for HEIs. The rankings create a system that pressures HEIs in a particular direction. Institutions that wish to do well must focus resources on the indicators specified by the ranking systems. Rather than allowing HEIs to pick and choose which statistics to publish in glossy brochures, the rankings call attention to uniform indicators. As a result, HEIs may begin to focus specifically on that which is measured to determine their rank. Through this pressure, rankings exert influence beyond their intended audience of higher education consumers and start to have a sway over higher education policy.

The HEI-government relationship is no longer as simple as it may have been in the past. For public officials with little time and the need for a lot of information, rankings serve as a convenient lens through which to evaluate HEIs (Dill and Soo 2005; Marginson and van der Wende 2007). This can reframe the way in which a government concerns itself with higher education by introducing a third-party evaluator of HEIs. As a result, the rankings complicate the relationships between HEIs and governments in East Asia by idealizing a particular image of higher education (Deem et al. 2008) that may not be in tune with the ideal at every HEI. There can be dissonance between the reality of HEI organizational structure and culture as compared to what policymakers would like to see. Thus, the rankings can create pressure on HEIs through both higher education consumers and public policy.

The rankings offer the possibility of a level playing field for HEIs. New or relatively unheard of HEIs can establish themselves by improving defined aspects of their institutions measured by the indicators. This system could facilitate a shift away from "the old elite" (Hazelkorn 2008) by providing clear parameters for HEIs to target. Instead of resisting rankings, HEIs have transformed into a marketing tool, and ultimately a driver for institutional reform (West 2009). Although the indicators may not be representative of HEI quality, an institution can reap the benefits of improved rank by focusing on improving them.

Therein lies the attraction of these international ranking systems to HEIs in East Asia; they are an opportunity to establish a global reputation. However, seeking that recognition comes at a significant cost. By focusing on particular indicators, HEIs may neglect other aspects of their institutions in order to conform to an international standard. Even within that standard, HEIs are confronted with an opportunity cost when allocating resources to improve ranking indicators. Yet the nature of this cost and the relative importance of the indicators remain unclear.

This chapter then seeks to address three major points: (1) determine the interaction between the ranking indicators of East Asian HEIs, (2) determine the relative importance of indicators as predictors for the overall rank of HEIs in the region, and (3) provide suggestions as to how East Asian HEIs could implement strategies to improve their standings in the rankings.

Overview of the International Higher Education Rankings

The ARWU and *THE* attempt to bring coherency to the national ranking systems that preceded them. A lack of agreement on acceptable indicators led to the establishment of unrelated systems around the world (Usher and Savino 2007). The ARWU and *THE* seek to establish international comparability between HEIs by standardizing the measures by which HEIs are judged.

The indicators classify and measure six elements of higher education quality. As organized by Alex Usher and Massimo Savino (2007), these include:

1. Characteristics of accepted students—secondary school performance, standardized examination scores, international and ethnic diversity of the student body, institutional selectivity;
2. Learning inputs in terms of resources and staff—faculty/student ratio, staff qualifications, scholarship availability, total expenditure;
3. Learning outputs—graduation rates, retention rates;
4. Final outcomes in the form of alumni accomplishments—employment outcomes;
5. Research—number of citations and publications, research rewards; and
6. Reputation—peer appraisal, employer appraisal.

Differences across national contexts prevent many indicators from being used in international rankings. The process of broadening indicators to international comparability has occurred differently for each international ranking system.

The ARWU and *THE* share research-intensive universities as the ideal model for their rankings because of their international recognition among HEIs (Marginson and van der Wende 2007). Yet the amount of value each of these ranking systems ascribes to particular aspects of that model differs considerably. The ARWU focuses extensively on research output because of the international comparability and verifiability of the data (Liu and Cheng 2005). *THE* rankings rely, to a large degree, on employer opinions and peer appraisal. The process of compiling an indicator of reputation involves collecting voluntarily submitted survey data from academics, academic administrators, and employers. The exact breakdown of these ranking systems' indicators and their weights are listed in Table 7.1.

While research makes up 60 percent of the ARWU rankings, it is a mere 20 percent in *THE*. Meanwhile, *THE* assigns 50 percent of its weight

Table 7.1 Indicators and Weights for the ARWU and *THE*

ARWU Indicators	Weight	*THE* Indicators	Weight
Alumni Nobel prizes and Fields medals	10%	Peer Review of HEI Reputation	40%
Faculty Nobel prizes and Fields medals	20%	International Reputation among Recruiters	10%
Highly cited Researchers	20%	Citations in Thomson's Scientific Database (2004-2006) or Scopus (2007-2009) per Faculty Member	20%
Papers published in Nature and Science	20%	Student-to-faculty Ratio	20%
Papers Indexed in the Science Citation Index-expanded and the Social Science Citation Index	20%	Number of International Students	5%
Per-capita Performance	10%	Number of International Faculty	5%

to survey data from "peer review" and employer perceptions of HEI reputation. These weights contribute to the variety in the final rankings each system produces.

ARWU's heavy concentration on research indicators comes at the cost of not considering other aspects of higher education quality. Meanwhile, *THE* assumes that impartial and informed employers and academics can provide meaningful information about HEI quality (Usher and Savino 2007). These issues only begin to touch on answering the criticism of the ranking systems and provide insight into the nature of the rankings.

With the selection of indicators and the assignment of their respective weights, bias enters the equation. This bias may reflect the status quo of a particular cultural view of HEIs or simply the idiosyncratic views of the ranking compilers. For instance, in order to earn public acceptance, newly founded ranking systems might work with indicators to ensure that traditionally prestigious HEIs rank well. With no natural default for what ought to be measured, rankings can and do reflect particular perspectives on higher education quality.

Reactions to the Rankings

Initially, HEIs resisted the ranking systems. Examples of such resistance were quite common throughout the world. In the 1990s, Japanese

HEIs resisted diversification from the single indicator of standardized test score selectivity; the HEIs refused to release information that would make other indicators a viable option (Yonezawa et al. 2002). National newspapers in the country wanted to build up ranking systems based on measurements of faculty, students, and learning at the HEIs. However the HEI's outright refusal to share information prevented the creation of the more sophisticated rankings.

The Japanese HEIs were not alone in their resistance to scrutiny. In China, HEIs also attempted to obstruct the publication of rankings. A number of HEIs actively sought government intervention to stop the perceived threat of budding national ranking systems (Wang 2009). The institutions directly appealed to the government to censure the rankings on the grounds that it could lead to the defamation of their universities. In both of these cases, HEIs actively resisted external evaluation.

In other contexts, early rankings encountered a different kind of resistance. In the United Kingdom and United States, the opacity of early methodologies and their lack of coherency led academics to dismiss the rankings. Rachel Bowden clearly expresses this attitude, stating that:

> until [rankings provide personalized program-by-program results], league tables really ought to be regarded purely as a source of "infotainment"; that is, as they stand, although they do supply us with a certain amount of "information" (albeit limited) about universities, they also provide those both within and outside of higher education with an unquestionable amount of "entertainment." (2000, 58)

Academics made the easy mistake of assuming that because the rankings were scientifically unsound that they were harmless. Rather than argue against the publication of the early rankings, academics more often simply ignored them.

Such resistance and avoidance, however, had little effect over public opinion of the rankings. The combination of increasingly competitive admissions and raising tuition fees fueled public demand for information on HEIs. The lack of any strong, publicized, and organized resistance over time to rankings secured them a sense of public credibility (Marginson and van der Wende 2007).

Criticism of the Rankings

The rise of rankings of HEIs has been accompanied by a considerable amount of criticism on the part of academics. Even the *THE* website concedes it is "rather crude to reduce universities to a single number" (*THE* 2010). The act of ranking HEIs depends on potentially meaningless differences. That the different numerical values assigned to universities must in most cases be statistically insignificant raises serious questions about the validity of any system attempting to "rank" HEIs (Buela-Casal et al. 2007).

Criticisms of HEI ranking systems can be classified into "three categories of concern," consisting of "technical and methodological process... usefulness of the results as consumer information [and] comparability of complex institutions with different goals and missions" (Hazelkorn 2007, 90-91). Additionally, it is important to consider a fourth, emerging concern in the literature: the alarm over the consequences of ranking systems on HEIs and higher education governance.

Technical and Methodological Concerns

Criticism of technical and methodological process focuses on the choice of indicators, the assignment of their weights, and methodological opacity. Critics warn that compilers wield too much control over the results when establishing a methodology for a ranking system. A common criticism focuses on whether the weights assigned to particular indicators are justified or are assigned arbitrarily (Buela-Casal et al. 2007; Usher and Savino 2007). The weighting of indicators remains a delicate issue, as even slight changes to indicator weights could alter the ranking results. Weights provide an easy route by which the bias of ranking compilers can significantly influence HEI showings.

Compilers of the rankings possess similar power over the choice of indicators included in the rankings. Critics were concerned over the possible decision to include weak or biased indicators (Marginson 2009). For instance, there are more Nobel Laureates and Fields medals in the United States and United Kingdom than in all other countries combined (*BBC News* 2010). Thus, the inclusion of Nobel prizes and Fields medals within the ARWU might be considered a biased indicator. The process of assigning a weight to indicators and then choosing which indicators to measure reveals how the views of the compilers impose upon the final results of the ranking systems.

Other technical criticism focuses on the absence of potentially significant indicators. Despite their methodological differences, the international rankings tend to produce a similar list of the very top HEIs. Usher and Savino (2007) suggest the possibility of a "lurking indicator" that would explain for so much variation beyond ninth place in various rankings. These critics argue that the differences in the rankings past the ninth place are the result of an essential, but missing indicator. They suggest that if such an indicator could be isolated and included within the rankings, it would reconcile the differences between their results.

Another problem emerges out of the possible interaction between rank and indicators over time. Researchers have also called attention to the cyclical nature of ranking systems that attempt to measure HEI reputation. Cassandra M. Guarino et al. (2005) argue that if reputation is included as an indicator (as in *THE*), the rankings will only perpetuate the dominance of a select number of schools at the top by building upon the very reputations they are intended to measure. These criticisms highlight methodological weaknesses in the ranking systems that still may need to be addressed.

Concerns also emerge over lapses in the quality of data collection. The processes that make up the collection of original survey data are of particular interest. Simon Marginson (2009) points out that the 1 percent response rate by experts contacted to provide an opinion of HEIs for the *THE* peer review indicator raises serious methodological concerns. The sample of survey respondents is highly unlikely to be representative of the entire academic community. Consequently, the reputation data compiled for the indicator would probably not reflect the actual views of the academic community.

Concerns with Rankings as Consumer Information

Some critics move beyond the process by which rankings are compiled and attack the stated goal of ranking systems as a means of informing consumers of higher education. For instance, the emphasis on quality of research over quality of teaching in rankings (Buela-Casal et al. 2007) indicates that rankings may not be the best source of information on HEIs for those planning to attend undergraduate programs. The exact nature of the relationship between quality in research and quality in teaching remains a topic of debate. Mick Healey (2005) suggests that linking quality research to results in student learning requires certain abilities on the part of a lecturer. That is to say that, simply because a lecturer performs well as a researcher, does not necessarily mean she/he is an effective teacher. Thus, critics argue that indicators directly measuring teaching quality and the ability to translate faculty research into learning for students would be more suitable for informing consumers of higher education. Such an approach would focus on the services that an HEI provides to the student rather than on the production of research.

Further criticism emerges from the disconnection between the perspectives of ranking compilers and the consumers of rankings. Leon Cremomini et al. (2008) argue that the rankings have limited usefulness to student-consumers because of differences in attitudes and values. A university that ranks well primarily as a result of its strong business program may be meaningless to a future student of the natural sciences. Similarly, cross-border students may find that schools that rank high lack the cultural readiness to successfully host students from other cultures and cannot provide them with the same level of opportunity provided to domestic students (Agnew and VanBalkom 2009).

Difficulties in Comparing HEIs

Not all HEIs operate around the same organizational structure and therefore cannot easily be compared. According to the cultures they serve, institutions often differ in their approach and organization. Alternative models to the traditional university include, but are not limited to, small and specialized HEIs, polytechnic institutes, and liberal arts colleges (Kyvik 2004). These alternative approaches to higher education are not without merit. Thus, many critics of higher education rankings argue that these HEIs should not be penalized for their diversity of approaches. However in forcing all HEIs into a comparable set of indicators drawn from one idealized model of higher education, international rankings are in essence penalizing certain HEIs.

Skewed Perceptions of Higher Education

A final set of concerns that merit consideration deal with the unintended consequences of rankings. The political force of rankings extends far beyond higher education consumers. In many cases, the rankings are a force for change in higher education. This influence emerges as international rankings expand beyond their original intentions, and acquire more meaning than the indicators used actually represent (Higher Education Funding Council of England [HEFCE] 2008). This can have serious consequences for HEIs, because of the subsequent transformation of their goals, changes in the way in which they are managed, and the impact on those institutions that fail to perform according to those indicators outlined by the rankings.

Changes to the goals of HEIs have significant impact on the academic community and its relationship to greater society. The competitive, hierarchical nature of rankings interferes with the role of HEIs as the source of "open source knowledge production" in the knowledge economy (Marginson 2009, 11). Pitting HEIs against one another in a zero-sum game has the possibility to disrupt the efficient allocation of limited resources, actually impairing HEI productivity. If HEIs focus too heavily on increasing the volume of publications and per capita output, difficult but important long-term studies may be ignored in favor of projects seen to have a quicker return. In their increasing concern for status, HEIs risk drifting away from their primary research and teaching goals.

Meanwhile, important regional and local institutions often suffer as a result of international rankings. The rankings can draw attention to national champions engaged in the "world-class" competition and consequently drain resources away from the excluded institutes. Ellen Hazelkorn draws attention to the fact that unranked HEIs may be "ignored, marginalized or by-passed," (2009, 19) ultimately suffering as a result of the publication of rankings. By focusing excessively on the excellence of particular institutions, the rankings draw attention away from an effort to build a strong system of higher education. In funneling resources to those HEIs at the top, the rankings could ultimately be to the detriment of education for greater society. Regardless, the onslaught of criticism of ranking systems has done much to shape their reform. Even so, compilers often have not been able to address the root of all these concerns.

Changing Practices

In response to this growing policy influence, a number of academics began to focus on ranking systems and their methodologies. The increasing involvement of the academic community has served as one of the driving factors behind their reform. From the Warsaw International Meeting on Ranking in 2002 to the Institute for Higher Education Policy and UNESCO's European Centre for Higher Education Washington, DC 2004 Meeting, scholars devoted to ranking systems made great strides in improving the systems' methodological rigor and establishing greater transparency (Merisotis and Sadlak 2005). A push toward clear methodological processes followed these conferences. For instance, previously opaque and unknown methodological processes gave way to publicly available information on ranking methodologies. Both the ARWU and *THE* websites clearly define the indicators used, their relative weight, and the processes by which they are collected.

A second push for the improvement of ranking systems has concentrated on their divorce from private interests. Responsibility for compiling the rankings has moved away from mass media publications toward independent, nonprofit research centers. This shift reflects the growing significance of rankings as an instrument of HEI evaluation (Buela-Casal et al. 2007) and an attempt to establish their credibility. Though the fundamental issue of design bias remains, the changes have addressed concerns over methodology. Rankings have opened the inner workings of their methodologies up to the public and have placed control over rankings into the hands of independent organizations.

In the Context of East Asian Higher Education

As in other realms of public policy, having a flawed account of HEI quality is ultimately seen as better than having nothing at all (Sadlak et al. 2008). Flawed policy instruments can be refined and perfected over time. As Hongcai Wang (2009) describes in the case of China, ranking systems have the potential to hold HEIs accountable to society by forcing them to be evaluated against their peers. The rankings allow consumers, policymakers, and academics to perceive higher education beyond just word of mouth and personal experience. Although the systems are not perfect, they are an improvement in the sense that they synthesize information on an issue of public concern.

In East Asia, ranking systems continued publication has earned the public's attention and has given rankings influence over national policymakers and HEIs. In spite of the early resistance of HEIs to the emergence of the ranking system, their popularity with parents and students has pressured academia to accept them (Van Dyke 2005). As the rankings compile and report data back to the public, the systems begin to shape public opinion. This process often translates into policy influence as public perceptions of HEIs and HEI policy extend beyond students and parents and into the policymaking arena (Sadlak et al. 2008).

From the perspective of East Asian governments, the rankings exert pressure on higher education policy (Deem et al. 2008). This can result in direct pressure from governments on HEIs. As one Japanese HEI leader explains, "The government wants a first class university for international prestige.... Rankings are becoming important to present Japan attractively and getting good students and good workers as the population declines. That's the government's motivation" (Hazelkorn 2009, 12). Higher education policy fits within the broader framework of public policy plans for the future of a country. Governments cannot afford a weak showing, as it would bode poorly for national reputation, elected policymakers, and economic forecast.

As a result of downward pressure, East Asian HEIs have begun transforming higher education at the institutional level. That effort has included developing English language international programs and pressing for changes to the traditional role of the professor. In Japan, these rankings-driven initiatives have taken the form of financial incentives to professors for research and an emphasis on internationalizing higher education in terms of increasing the quantity of international students and providing more programs available in English (Hazelkorn 2009). This practice seems similar to the kinds of initiatives being pursued in both South Korea and Taiwan as indicated by Chapters 2 and 5.

As East Asian economies establish themselves as leaders in the new world order, their governments will seek to establish a system of higher education capable of supporting continued economic growth. Competition over highly cited researchers and the best young talent complements preexisting international competition over access to natural resources (Marginson and van der Wende 2007; Hazelkorn 2009). For countries already actively engaged in competition for access to global markets, rankings serve to introduce competition into the realm of academic human resources. Within the higher education market, rankings create a strong incentive to attract high quality students and researchers in order to build up a country's system of higher education (Gaul 2005). They provide an arena where countries can compare their HEIs and understand some of their strengths and weaknesses relative to one another.

A Question of Indicators

Certain indicators are of greater relative importance for ranking within certain regions. This means that in East Asia, certain indicators may correlate more strongly with international rank. Indicators might also have associations with other indicators, suggesting a different degree of relative importance and the possibility of interplay. *THE* indicators could associate with ARWU rank, suggesting the possible importance of indicators beyond the ranking system from which they originate. This study will consider the relationship of indicators across the ARWU and *THE* ranking systems in order to better understand their importance to HEI rank. In analyzing the ranking data, it will determine the relative predicative value of indicators for overall ranking of HEIs in East Asia. The ultimate goal of the study is to determine the relative importance of indicators for HEIs in the region.

Methods

Using publically available data for the indicators from the ARWU and *THE* rankings, this study assesses what the rankings reveal about higher education in East Asia. Each year's ARWU and *THE* data set between 2007 and 2009 are analyzed for trends and patterns. All 12 indicators from ARWU and *THE* rankings are considered. Indicators 1 through 6 are from the ARWU and 7 through 12 are from *THE*. They are defined as:

1. Alumni—the total number of alumni of an institution who have won Noble prizes and Fields medals.
2. Staff—the total number of the staff of an institution that have won Nobel prizes in physics, chemistry, medicine, economics, and Fields medal in mathematics.
3. HiCi—the number of highly cited researchers in 21 subject categories according to Thomson ISI.
4. N&S—the number of papers published in nature and science within the five years preceding the year of ranking.
5. PUB—the total number of papers indexed in the Science Citation Index-Expanded (SCI-expanded) and the Social Science Citation Index (SSCI) in the year directly preceding the year of ranking.
6. PCP—the weighted scores of the first five ARWU indicators divided by the number of full-time academic staff.
7. PeeRev—the composite score for reputation drawn from a voluntary response peer-review survey submitted to academics.
8. EmplyrScr—the score for reputation drawn from voluntary response surveys submitted to major employers of graduates.
9. SSRatio—the ratio of students to staff.
10. CitePrStf—the total number of citations for papers published at an HEI divided by the number of full-time staff.
11. Intstaff—the number of international staff as a proportion of total staff.
12. Intstu—the number of international students as a proportion of the student body.

The study correlates these indicators to one another and to ARWU rank. These correlations reveal how East Asian HEIs deviate from the theoretical "norm established by ARWU. The analysis limits its scope to the ARWU because of the ranking's prominence in the East Asian region and the external verifiability of ARWU data, which are publically available from third-party sources.

The ARWU does not calculate all HEI total scores; only those between 1 and 200 are listed with an ARWU total score. Therefore, the total score for these HEIs have been calculated according to the formula provided within the ARWU methodology. Given the incompatibility of data between years, the analysis does not aggregate data across years. Comparing results by year provides insight into trends in the relationships between indicators and rank.

For each year, the total number of East Asian HEIs present on both the ARWU and *THE* rankings fluctuates: 24 in 2007, 23 in 2008, and 26 in 2009. For simple regressions on ARWU indicators and ARWU total score, data for all East Asian HEIs on the ARWU rankings were used, numbering 66 in 2007, 68 in 2008, and 70 in 2009. There were no cases in which East Asian HEIs on the *THE* were not also ranked in the ARWU.

Researcher Perspective

Problems can be approached from multiple perspectives, each offering advantages as well as disadvantages for research (Evred and Louis 1981). This study of East Asian HEIs comes from an outsider perspective. Lacking firsthand knowledge, the researcher is dependent upon indicator data and published materials on East Asian HEIs. As the stated goals of organizations often do not align entirely with their day-to-day practices, the reality of practice within HEIs can differ considerably from published matter. While the outsider perspective creates some limitations, it also provides the study with certain strengths.

The most significant weakness of the outsider perspective is the consequent decontextualization of the study from East Asian HEIs. Insider researchers often share worldviews with their subjects (Collins 1986; Palmer 2006). Uninformed by insider knowledge of the organizational cultures and structures of East Asian HEIs, this study can only provide general observations based upon the findings. The recommendations are therefore divorced from the contexts of individual HEIs. On one hand, a different researcher perspective can provide greater insight into an issue (Agar 1996; Palmer 2006). On the other hand, the suggestions of this study could be seen as situational irrelevant, overly idealistic, or practically impossible depending upon the particular context of a given HEI.

Yet, this outsider perspective also lends certain strengths to the study. As a result of its outsider view of East Asian HEIs, the study is more likely to provide neutral, generalizable findings. Within this study, the researcher remains uninvolved in the internal organizational politics of the HEIs in question and therefore the study can be conducted free from many potential biases. Concern for local interest groups does not play a role in the analysis of data and their interpretation into findings. As a result, the study grounds itself more firmly in objective and verifiable data.

Insider research and outsider research serve to complement one another (Sayer 1992). Taking this into consideration, future insider studies of rankings and changes to East Asian HEI organization and strategy would prove invaluable. Insider cultural knowledge can improve the overall results of research (Foley et al. 2001). An insider perspective would help to clarify how the general findings of this study could be effectively translated into practical action at the organizational level. As a foundation for such work, this study provides factually rooted insight into the state of HEI rankings and relative importance of indicators within the East Asian region.

Design of Analysis

The analysis is designed to clarify the presence, absence, and relative strength of any relationships between the indictors and ARWU rankings. As a preliminary analysis, the study considers correlation matrices for indicators from both the ARWU and *THE*. These matrices summarize the strength of linear relationships between each pair of indicators. A correlation matrix for each of the years reveals the presence or absence of associations and how (or whether) associations between indicators have changed over the years. The matrices provide insight into the relationships between indicators.

As a first step in the primary analysis, the study considers R-squares from individual simple regressions and quadratic regressions for each indicator and the ARWU total score. The study generates these R-squares for each indicator by year. Comparing these values to one another reveals the relative importance of indicators associated with the ARWU total score. They also depict how the importance of indicators fluctuates over time.

The second step of the primary analysis is recursive partitioning of ARWU and *THE* indicators relative to ARWU total score. This recursive partitioning only includes those indicators found to correlate significantly with ARWU total score in the preceding individual regressions. The recursive partitioning groups data by the indicator value that best predicts ARWU total score (and thus rank). Each subsequent partition is impacted by those preceding it, partitioning a preexisting group into the next best-predicted groups. This process also isolates the relative predictive value of the three most influential indicators by year.

Indicator to Indicator Correlations

Within each year, ARWU indicators correlate strongly with other ARWU indicators. Of particular strength are the correlations between publications in nature and science with number of highly cited researchers (.7380 to.7860), number of publications in nature and science with alumni awarded Nobel prizes or Fields medals (.7723 to .7825), and Nature and Science with per capita performance (.7017 to .7318).

There are two relatively weak correlations between ARWU indicators. The first is the number of publications in the SCI-expanded and SSCI with highly cited researchers (.3380 to .4212). The second consists of the number of publications with faculty awarded Nobel prizes and Fields medals (.3780 to .4437).

Strength of correlations for *THE* indicators varies considerably. Some *THE* indicators correlate strongly with ARWU indicators. *THE's* citations per staff member maintain a strong positive relationship with ARWU's per capita performance (.5961 to .8174). Also of note are student to staff ratio with nature and science publications (.4860 to .5333) and student to staff ratio with per capita performance (.4965 to .6205). Interestingly, an inverse relationship between ARWU indicators and number of international staff strengthens over time. For example, the correlation between number of international staff and number of publications in the SCI-expanded and SSCI is -.2389 in 2007, -.3827 in 2008, and -.4444 in 2009. In 2008 and 2009, number of international staff also correlates negatively with publications in nature and science (-.4154 to -.4570). The relative consistency of negative correlations with international staff is particularly striking.

THE indicators do not correlate strongly with one another, although there are a few exceptions. Interestingly, there is a dramatic jump in correlation between peer review scores and employer review scores from .4169 in 2007 to .8322 in 2008 and .7296 in 2009. Another exception is the consistently strong relationship between numbers of international staff and international students (.7723 to .8456). Outside of these two sets of indicators, correlation between *THE* indicators appears relatively weak.

Indicator and ARWU Total Score Regressions

Given that the ARWU total score is directly derived from the indicators, it is unsurprising that all of these correlations are statistically significant for both linear and quadratic regressions (ANOVA $p < .0001$). All R-square values reported are from the quadratic regressions. The relative strength of correlation between ARWU indicators and ARWU total scores is very consistent across the three years. The relative strength of ARWU indicators' correlation with ARWU total score for all years is outline in Table 7.2.

The consistent strength of correlation between publications in nature and science and ARWU total score is strikingly high (.8533 to .8730), revealing just how important nature and science are to rank in East Asia.

Table 7.2 R-Squares for Indicators and ARWU Total Score

Rank	Indicator	2007	2008	2009
1	Papers published in Nature and Science	.8730	.8700	.8533
2/3	Papers indexed in SCI-expanded and SSCI	.8313	.8177	.7756
2/3	Highly cited researchers	.8210	.8101	.7938
4	Alumni Nobel prizes and Fields medals	.7327	.7249	.7620
5	Per capita performance	.7291	.6544	.6960
6	Staff Nobel prizes and Fields medals	.4924	.5277	.5297

Also noteworthy are the gaps between the top indicator, the second/third indicators, the fourth and fifth indicators, and the last indicator. These gaps suggest tiers of importance for indicators, with research-related indicators dominating the most important top positions. Of least importance are staff Nobel prizes and Fields medals. While other ARWU indicators correlate with ARWU total score with an R-squared of .7 or more, staff Nobel prizes and Fields medals correlates to a much weaker degree (.4924 to .5297). This suggests that the number of staff Nobel prizes and Fields medals is of relatively little significance within the region.

Of the *THE* indicators, only two significantly correlate with ARWU total score. These indicators are student-to-staff ratio and citations per staff. Of the two, student-to-staff ratio is the more consistent, with a statistically significant linear and quadratic regression for each of the years. Citations per staff has only a suggestive correlation in 2007 (ANOVA p=.1011), but significant correlations in 2008 (ANOVA p=.0103) and 2009 (ANOVA p=.0453). Interestingly, the number of international staff has an inverse relationship with ARWU total score in every year, although the p-value for this relationship is only suggestive (ANOVA p=.0939). The number of international students also has a suggestive inverse relationship with ARWU total score in 2008 and 2009. These findings suggest that there tends to be a larger presence of internationals at the East Asian HEIs with lower rankings.

Recursive Partitioning Analysis

Research-focused ARWU indicators emerged as the source of all partitions in all years, with no *THE* indicators playing a role:

> In 2007, the first through third partitions, respectively, were (1) number of highly cited researchers, (2) papers in the SCI-expanded and SSCI, and (3) per capita performance.

In 2008, the partitions were (1) number of publications in nature and science, (2) papers in the SCI-expanded and SSCI, and (3) number of highly cited researchers.

In 2009, the partitions consisted of (1) number of publications in nature and science, (2) papers in the SCI-expanded and SSCI, and (3) per capita performance.

These findings seem to echo results from the quadratic regressions, albeit the partitioning lends greater weight to per capita performance. Number of publications in nature and science is the most predictive indicator for 2008 and 2009. These findings further emphasize the importance of this indicator. Additionally, the consistence of per capita performance as the third most predictive indicator suggests that the indicator may be of greater predictive value when considered in conjunction with other indicators. Therefore, while per capita performance may not have as strong of a relationship with ARWU total score, it has a predictive value for other important indicators, such as number of publications in nature and science.

Discussion

In East Asia, HEIs' ARWU rankings depend heavily upon publication-focused indicators. This result is hardly shocking, given the 60 percent weight assigned to research indicators. The importance of research indicators seems to be strengthened by the weak showing for Nobel prizes and Fields medals across the region. The analysis provides insight into the nature of research that results in higher rankings. Specifically, it draws attention to the possibility of different relationships between research and rank, the significance of student-to-staff ratio, and the influence of internationals on HEI ranks in East Asia.

The top East Asian HEIs are primarily associated with higher numbers of publication in nature and science. The importance of the indicator may suggest that having articles accepted into such prestigious journals reflects a certain capacity for high-quality research. Publications in nature and science correlate strongly with the number of highly cited researchers and publications in SCI-expanded and SSCI. This trend further supports the idea that nature and science publications serve as a mark of research capacity at East Asian HEIs. Fostering and maintaining such a capacity is very important for continued ranking success.

The relationship between the other two most predictive indicators, number of highly cited researchers and number of publications in SCI-expanded and SSCI, is less clear. Though both of these indicators correlate strongly with ARWU total score, correlation between the two indicators is among the weakest between ARWU indicators. This weak correlation suggests that the publication of acclaimed research work and maintaining a high level of research volume at an HEI are not necessarily related. One possible explanation could be different organizational approaches to research at East Asian HEIs.

Some East Asian HEIs may be specialized within certain fields of research, reflected by larger numbers of highly cited researchers within those areas of expertise. Such specialization would not always generate greater quantity of research, but could lead to large numbers of citations. Alternatively, some East Asian HEIs may excel as a result of their large research capacity. In other words, while their work may not receive the same amount of attention as the aforementioned specialized HEIs, research work is produced in greater volume. If true, East Asian HEIs have alternate routes toward higher rankings: specializing within a certain field or a building up high volume output of publications.

Research-focused ARWU indicators also correlate strongly with student-to-staff ratio, a *THE* indicator. The finding suggests that fewer students per staff member at an East Asian HEI serve as a strong predictor for the more publications in nature and science and improved higher per capita performance. This result speaks to the possible importance of a low staff to student ratio. Multiple explanations exist for this outcome. East Asian HEIs with strong research programs may simply be more selective and admit fewer students. In such a case, research excellence could exist independently of student numbers relative to staff numbers. The ratio would just incidentally be lower at such HEIs. Alternatively, staff at HEIs with fewer students per staff member might be able to devote more attention to research. This could also explain the strong correlation.

The nature of the relationships of *THE* indicators with the number of international staff and number of international students with publication-focused indicators raises a number of important questions. The presence of an inverse relationship between the number of international staff and publications could be the result of a number of phenomena. It is possible that East Asian HEIs originally weaker in terms of research are recruiting international staff and students as a "quick-fix" to improve *THE* rankings. Rather than develop research programs or develop an infrastructure to promote greater research output, such institutions might simply hire foreign faculty and recruit foreign students. Three potential problems emerge when taking such an approach.

First, a lack of selectivity in hiring and admitting international students and faculty would drain resources and fail to contribute meaningfully toward improving an HEI's rank. Although the number of international students and faculty at the institution would go up, they would not be likely to contribute meaningfully to research output. Second, organizational inability to cope with and support talented international faculty and students could ultimately mean that they too simply become a drain on HEI resources. Third, an explanation for the negative predictive value of international students and faculty on publications may be that East Asian HEIs are redirecting resources away from research by recruiting international staff and students. As numbers of international students and faculty rise, the amount and quality of research may also drop. The strengthening inverse relationship between research-focused indicators and *THE* measures of international staff and students at East Asian HEIs suggests that this issue may persist or even worsen in the future of East Asian higher education.

Thus, the findings reveal that improving indicators and raising HEI ranking can be a difficult process. In order to move up the ranks, HEIs may need to carefully consider an overall strategy. In terms of research, this strategy could include focusing on high quality work by specializing within one field or providing incentives to staff members in order to increase the volume of research publication. The findings also suggest that striving to attain a low student-to-staff ratio may lead to benefits for HEI research.

East Asian HEIs must seriously consider the role that international staff and students will play at the institute and weigh the potential costs against the benefits. If an HEI has the will and resources to push for the organizational change necessary to establish an inclusive and supporting environment for international students and faculty, such a strategy may be a worthwhile pursuit. However simply recruiting and accepting international students and faculty at a standard relatively lower than those for domestic staff and students may simply be a waste of resources.

Future research would benefit from an insider perspective on the issue of rankings at East Asian HEIs. Such insider research should investigate the role of international students and faculty at East Asian HEIs, the role of interest groups and institutional politics in attempting ranking-related reforms, and the institutional repercussions of international recruitment programs. Such research would allow for a fuller picture of the changes occurring at East Asian HEIs and the barriers they face in the attempt to improve higher education in the region.

Conclusion

ARWU and *THE* indicators provide direct and indirect pressures on East Asian HEIs. Hazelkorn (2009) reports that HEI leaders and senior administrators around the world have a strong desire to rank high, believe that the rankings have influence beyond their intention (a student-consumer audience), and despite criticizing them, ultimately feel that they benefit their HEI. Roland Proulx (2007) has found that HEIs around the world consider ARWU and *THE* indicators in their strategic plans and branding processes. These pressures facilitate initiatives to "internationalize" away from past models of higher education in East Asia. *THE* indicators directly encourage recruitment of both international faculty and students and that pressure is complemented by the emphasis that ARWU and *THE* place on faculty and alumni gaining recognition in mainly English-language journals. Yet the findings suggest that efforts to internationalize East Asian HEIs may not be bringing about the intended results.

Although many governments and HEIs in East Asia place high value on recruiting international students and faculty, a stronger focus on improving research quality may provide greater benefit. Moving forward, East Asian HEIs need to begin thinking seriously about implementing institutional strategies for improving their showings. In fact, many HEIs even set up teams or individuals who assume the responsibility of overseeing the university's performance within the relevant indicators and keeping track of how their own HEI measures up against its peer institutions (Hazelkorn 2007).

Creating an organizational apparatus at East Asian HEIs responsible for monitoring the indicators included in the ranking systems would not only allow for improvement in HEI rank, but could also serve as an institutional quality control mechanism. Collecting and analyzing data on indicators at the institutional level at a regular interval would help East Asian HEIs to understand quality within their specific context. That understanding could allow for institutional improvement, so long as the body responsible for collecting and analyzing the data also had the clout necessary to push for organizational change.

International rankings provide East Asian HEIs with an avenue for shaking up traditional prestige paradigms in higher education. In their pursuit of higher rankings, are East Asian HEIs and their host governments actually focusing on the right indicators? The attempt to quickly improve showing on the rankings could ultimately mean lower results in the long term. In order to develop an effective strategy for improving rankings, HEIs and governments must pay careful attention to the indicators. After understanding how the indicators relate to rank, HEIs and governments can begin to shape policies to effectively improve their rankings, and reputations, over time.

References

Agar, Michael H. 1996. *The Professional Stranger: An Informal Introduction to Ethnography.* San Diego: Academic Press.

Agnew, Melanie, and W. Duffie VanBalkom. 2009. "Internationalization of the University: Factors Impacting Cultural Readiness for Organizational Change." *Intercultural Education* 20 (5): 451-462.

Altbach, Philip G. 2006. "The Dilemmas of Ranking." *International Higher Education* 42 (4): 2-3.

BBC News. 2010. "BBC News—Which Country has the Best Brains?" *BBC News*, October 9, 2010. Available online at: http://www.bbc.co.uk.

Bowden, Rachel. 2000. "Fantasy Higher Education: University and College League Tables." *Quality in Higher Education* 6 (1): 41-60.

Buela-Casal, Gualberto, Olga Gutiérrez-Martínez, María-Paz Bermúda-Sánchez, and Oscar Vadillo-Muñoz. 2007. "Comparative Study of International Academic Rankings of Universities." *Scientometrics* 71 (3): 349-365.

Collins, Patricia Hill. 1986. "Learning from the Outsider within: The Sociological Significance of Black Feminist Thought." *Social Problems* 33 (6): S14-S32.

Cremomini, Leon, Don Westerheijden, and Jürgen Enders. 2008. "Disseminating the Right Information to the Right Audience: Cultural Determinants in the Use (and Misuse) of Rankings." *Higher Education* 55 (3): 373-385.

Deem, Rosemary, Ka Ho Mok, and Lisa Lucas. 2008. "Transforming Higher Education in Whose Image? Exploring the Concept of the 'World-Class' University in Europe and Asia." *Higher Education Policy* 21 (1): 83-97.

Dill, David D. 2003. "Allowing the Market to Rule: the Case of the United States." *Higher Education Quarterly* 57 (2): 107-210.

Dill, David D., and Marja Soo. 2005. "Academic Quality, League Tables, and Public Policy: a Cross-national Analysis of University Ranking Systems." *Higher Education* 49 (4): 495-533.

Evred, Roger, and Meryl Reis Louis. 1981. "Alternative Perspectives in the Organizational Sciences." *Academy of Management Review* 6 (3): 385-395.

Foley, Douglas A., Bradley A. Levinson, and Janise Hurtig. 2001. "Anthropology Goes Inside: The New Educational Ethnography of Ethnicity and Gender." In *Review of Research in Education*, ed. Walter G. Secada. Washington, DC: American Educational Research Association.

Gaul, Jens-Peter. 2005. "Assessment, Control, and Autonomy: Macroscopic Perspectives." *Higher Education in Europe* 30 (2): 167-171.

Guarino, Cassandra M., Gregory K. Ridgeway, Marc Chun, and Richard Buddin. 2005. "Latent Variable Analysis: A New Approach to University Ranking." *Higher Education in Europe* 30 (2): 148-165.

Hazelkorn, Ellen. 2007. "The Impact of League Tables and Ranking Systems on Higher Education Decision Making." *Higher Education Management and Policy* 19 (2): 1-24.

Hazelkorn, Ellen. 2008. "Learning to Live with League Tables and Ranking: the Experience of Institutional Leaders." *Higher Education Policy* 21 (2): 193-215.
Hazelkorn, Ellen. 2009. "Rankings and the Battle for World-class Excellence: Institutional Strategies and Policy Choices." *Higher Education Management and Policy* 21 (1): 1-22.
Healey, Mick. 2005. "Linking Research and Teaching to Benefit Student Learning." *Journal of Geography in Higher Education* 29 (2): 183-201.
Higher Education Funding Council of England (HEFCE). 2008. *Counting What is Measured or Measuring What Counts? League Tables and Their Impact on Higher Education Institutions in England*. Bristol, UK: Higher Education Funding Council for England.
Jobbins, David. 2005. "Moving to a Global Stage: a Media View." *Higher Education in Europe* 30 (2): 137-145.
Kyvik, Svein. 2004. "Structural Changes in Higher Education Systems in Western Europe." *Higher Education in Europe* 24 (3): 393-409.
Liu, Nian Cai, and Ying Cheng. 2005. "The Academic Ranking of World Universities." *Higher Education in Europe* 30 (2): 127-136.
Marginson, Simon. 2009. "The Knowledge Economy and Higher Education: a System for Regulating the Value of Knowledge." *Higher Education Management and Policy* 21 (1): 1-15.
Marginson, Simon, and Marjik van der Wende. 2007. "To Rank or be Ranked: The Impact of Global Rankings on Higher Education." *Journal of Studies in Higher Education* 11 (3&4): 306-329.
Merisotis, Jamie, and Jan Sadlak. 2005. "Higher Education Rankings: Evolution, Acceptance, and Dialogue." *Higher Education in Europe* 30 (2): 97-101.
Palmer, John D. 2006. "Negotiating the Indistinct: Reflections of a Korean Adopted American Working with Korean Born, Korean Americans." *Qualitative Research* 6 (4): 473-495.
Proulx, Roland. 2007. "Higher Education Ranking and League Tables: Lessons Learned from Benchmarking." *Higher Education in Europe* 32 (1): 71-82.
Sadlak, Jan, Jamie Merisotis, and Nian Cai Liu. 2008. "University Rankings: Seeking Prestige, Raising Visibility and Embedding Quality-Editors' Views." *Higher Education in Europe* 33 (2&3): 195-199.
Salmi, Jamil. 2009. "The Growing Accountability Agenda: Progress or Mixed Blessing?" *Higher Education Management and Policy* 21 (1): 1-21.
Sayer, Andrew. 1992. *Method in Social Science: A Realist Approach*. London: Routledge.
Skolnik, Michael L. 2010. "Quality Assurance in Higher Education as a Political Process." *Higher Education Management and Policy* 21 (1): 101-122.
Slaughter, Sheila and Gary Rhoades. 2004. *Academic Capitalism and the New Economy*. Baltimore: Johns Hopkins University Press.
Times Higher Education (THE). 2010. *Robust, Transparent, and Yours*. London: THE. Available online at: http://www.timeshighereducation.co.uk.
UNESCO. 2009. *Global Education Digest 2009: Comparing Education Statistics Across the World*. Montreal: UNESCO Institute for Statistics.

Usher, Alex, and Massimo Savino. 2007. "A Global Survey of University Ranking and League Tables." *Higher Education in Europe* 32 (1): 5-15.

Van Dyke, Nina. 2005. "Twenty Years of University Reports Cards." *Higher Education in Europe* 30 (2): 103-125.

Wang, Hongcai. 2009. "University Rankings: Status Quo, Dilemmas, and Prospects." *Chinese Education and Society* 41 (1): 42-55.

Wedlin, Linda. 2008. "University Marketization: the Process and Its Limits." In *The University in the Market*, ed. Lars Engwall and Denis Weaire. London: Portland Press.

West, Peter W. A. 2009. "A Faustian Bargain? Institutional Responses to National and International rankings." *Institutional Management in Higher Education* 21 (1): 1-10.

Yonezawa, Akiyoshi, Izumi Nakatsui, and Tetsuo Kobayashi. 2002. "University Rankings in Japan." *Higher Education in Europe* 27 (4): 373-382.

Chapter 8

Internationalization of Higher Education in East Asia: Issues, Implications, and Inquiries

Mary Shepard Wong and Shuang Frances Wu[1]

Internationalization has emerged as one of the top priorities for higher education institutions around the world, and East Asia is no exception, as is evidenced by the studies in this volume. However, higher education institutions often fail to clearly articulate the rationale and conceptualization of their internationalization policies. Thus internationalization efforts frequently result in change that is only superficial or isolated rather than deep and pervasive. As noted in the introduction and several chapters in this volume, in the case of East Asian universities, internationalization efforts may even run counter to institutional identity, which may force higher education institutions to sacrifice quality and integrity for the perception of meeting globalization demands through rudimentary internationalization policies.

The authors in this volume explore issues of internationalization of higher education in South Korea, Japan, Taiwan, Hong Kong, Singapore, and Mainland China. They apply, contest, and construct educational theories in their analyses of the tensions and dilemmas caused by the influence of globalization on higher education. They document how governments and higher education administrators in East Asia interpret and implement internationalization in ways shaped by the West, especially the United States. They also note how local ways of internationalization are emerging, which provide more contextualized, less U.S.-centric understandings of the process of internationalization in East Asia. The authors describe how the marketization of education has reduced internationalization initiatives to "the competitive rush for international students and their money" in some cases (see Chapter 1), yet they also note hints of a social justice rationale for internationalization in other cases (see Chapter 5).

In this final chapter we revisit two broad issues, often interrelated and intertwined, that were raised in the studies of this volume: (1) contextualization versus Westernization in East Asian higher education institutions' internationalization efforts, and (2) the consequences on higher education constituents, both positive and negative, that accompany their attempts to become world-class universities. We then propose the following policy implications for East Asian higher education institutions: curriculum internationalization as the core, faculty engagement as the vehicle, and global competency development as the goal. Following this, we describe and apply analytical frameworks that enable institutions to: identify their rationales for internationalization, assess the outcomes of their internationalization efforts, and analyze change at the institutional level as the result of such efforts. We conclude with questions to direct future research.

Contextualization versus Westernization

In several chapters of this volume, the authors discuss the importance of contextualization in internationalization and thus the need for strategies that do not simply imitate the West but that serve the unique needs of their region (see Chapters 2, 3, 5, and 6). Several concerns arose among East Asian higher education constituents: faculty and student dilemmas as a result of the increasing prestige of the English language in academia; Western, and in particular, U.S. models, as the ultimate standards for internalization; and international partnerships exclusively with core nations, such as the United States.

Faculty and Student Dilemmas Due to the Increasing Prestige of English

In South Korea, Japan, and Taiwan, faculty and students alike criticized the increasing use of English as the medium of instruction in higher education (see Chapters 2, 5, and 6). Faculty noted the negative effect that this push has had on the quality of teaching and learning, as using a foreign language adds to the challenge in the teaching and learning process. Newly hired faculty members are expected to teach courses in English, which creates undue pressure on them. Students also noted that those with limited English proficiency were disadvantaged because of this trend.

In contrast, the case for Hong Kong and Singapore did not find the use of English as the medium of instruction problematic (see Chapter 1). Instead, David Chan noted that the governments of Hong Kong and Singapore embraced this perceived "advantage" and contended that the use of English "raised the cosmopolitan character" and thus positioned these two regions "to go further ahead in their internationalization of higher education."

It is clear from the above examples of South Korea, Japan, Taiwan, Hong Kong, and Singapore, that language is not value free and can serve to either promote or impede internationalization, depending on the context. The selection of any language as a medium of instruction benefits some over others, and issues of access, equity, and quality must not be ignored or sacrificed for a mere Western façade of internationalization.

Several studies in this volume also found the pressure to publish in English language journals posed challenges for faculty members in East Asia (see Chapters 2, 5, and 6). These faculty members are required to not only excel in their respective disciplines, but also be able to write academic papers in English. Language difficulty aside, the Eurocentric nature of many English journals makes it difficult for East Asian faculty's research to be considered. This reality positions faculty members in East Asia at a disadvantage.

Western Models as the Ultimate Standards

Higher education institutions in East Asia, consciously or subconsciously, equate internationalization to Westernization, and in particular, Americanization. This is reflected in universities emulating Western instructional styles, adopting a customer-orientation common in Western education, and using increasing international student enrollment as a prominent internationalization strategy (see Chapters 5 and 6). Although the above may have merits, they are often implemented without thoughtful consideration of the local context.

In emulating Western instructional styles, the cultural backgrounds of faculty and students could be neglected. Asian cultures often regard the teacher-student relationship as a hierarchical one. The teacher is highly esteemed and considered the center of the classroom, while the student is to be instructed (Schneider and Lee 1990). The Western model that emphasizes a learner-centered instructional style can conflict with Asian faculty's and students' values and practices and create dilemmas for both groups. Faculty members, in some East Asian universities, feel a paradigm shift in education from an intellectual pursuit to making it a viable commercial product is difficult, if not impossible. For example, in the case of South Korea, some professors resist such Western educational practices as treating student as clients, conducting course evaluations, and merit-based salaries (see Chapter 6).

Increasing international student enrollment is one of the most widely utilized internationalization strategies in the United States. Its popularity also lies in its ability to bring in revenue for the institution. Many institutions in East Asia follow this model of internationalization and heavily invest in recruiting international students. However, like many U.S. institutions, East Asian institutions often fail to incorporate international students into the fabric of the campus (see Chapters 2, 5, and 6). One example is the separate housing facilities for international students away from domestic students, which creates physical distance and therefore, social isolation. Another example is the lack of local language requirement for international students.

Partnerships with Core Nations in the West

Anthony Welch and Rui Yang (see Chapter 3) note the ethnocentric focus of the experience of "White, wealthy, Western" countries in higher education internationalization, and contend that a Chinese perspective with a Confucian, Buddhist, Taoist, Islamic, Communist mix might add some balance to this discourse. Their study on the regional Xinjiang University adds complex and fresh insights to this discussion. It is ironic that this culturally rich, religiously diverse, strategically located "pearl" institution in the birthplace of globalization, the Silk Road, seeks to internationalize by searching for partnerships primarily with the U.S. instead of creating more alliances with local regions in Central Asia. Starstruck with Western education, institutions like Xinjiang University may overlook the cultural, geographic, and historical assets they have at their doorstep. Perhaps they could learn from the South Korean example (see Chapter 5) and seek out alliances closer to home and recognize the potential they have to be leaders in internationalization in their own regions.

To some extent, this concern is echoed through the investigation of summer programs in which South Korean institutions recruited professors from "highly recognizable schools in the United States [and] Europe." It is encouraging, however, that South Korea seeks to establish more localized partnerships with "some parts of East Asia" as well (see Chapter 5).

In contrast to the concern for exclusive partnerships with core nations in the West, Chan (Chapter 1), in supporting the Western alignment argument, suggested that as former colonized regions, Hong Kong and Singapore could use their connection with the West to their advantage. In the case of Singapore, institutions benefit from their connection with the "name brand" of prestigious universities in the West by inviting them to offer "offshore" programs. Partnerships with not only the West, but also nations and regions in other parts of the world, including neighboring East Asian countries, are necessary, in order for institutions in East Asia to be truly internationalized.

"World-Class" Status, Rankings, and Internationalization

Globalization has propelled East Asian higher education institutions to strive for the "world-class" university status. Indeed, the drive behind internationalization efforts in East Asian higher education institutions is the desire to become "world class." Furthermore, in part because the definition of a world-class university lacks clarity, many higher education stakeholders look to international rankings to determine the relative success and prestige of institutions.

International Higher Education Rankings

East Asian societies traditionally are hierarchical. Rankings therefore have unique appeal and significance to East Asian higher education constituencies. Even prior to the advent of globalization of market economy and internationalization of higher education, the concept of tiers was prevalent among East Asian higher education institutions, such as those in China. For example, the 107 key universities in China represent higher academic prestige, resembling the characteristics and functions of research universities in the West (Ma 1999). East Asian higher education institutions' desire to become world class causes them to focus resources on improving international rankings. At the same time, international ranking systems fuel the desire to become world class (see Chapter 7).

Higher education institutions have resisted global rankings for the protection of their status. Academics, in particular, have dismissed global rankings based on the grounds of unsound methodologies (see Chapter 7). Despite such resistance, the benefits of global rankings are being recognized by higher education constituents. Rankings create a mechanism of accountability for institutions, and at the same time provide a vehicle for institutions to increase their visibility. Rankings also provide information to potential students about academic quality, although the results may be sometimes oversimplified and subjective.

Compromises to Become the "World-Class" University

International ranking systems value certain characteristics that are common to elite U.S. institutions. For example, large, comprehensive institutions that use English as the medium of instruction and are research-intensive and science-heavy receive a higher ranking. In addition, the rankings give preference to publication in English journals (see Chapter 7). All the above present challenges to higher education institutions in East Asia, especially those that have smaller enrollment and fewer resources. Furthermore, it is not without sacrifices that institutions seek to become world class. For example, universities in East Asia may hire foreign faculty and admit international students on less stringent requirements or may not require proficiency in the local language as a graduation requirement for international students (see Chapter 5).

Moreover, the impact that seeking world-class status can have on ethnic minority universities and its students is noteworthy. One could argue that globalization brings about unprecedented educational and career opportunities to ethnic minorities. However, issues of educational access and equity for these populations become more visible as the result of globalization. Take, for an example, the case of Yanbian University (Chapter 4) in the Yanbian Ethnic Korean Autonomous Region in northeastern China. Yanbian University increased enrollment of the majority Han students in an effort to boost the academic quality needed to gain recognition as a world-class university. This competes with the mission of the university, which is to serve ethnic Koreans. Through studies in this volume, an important conclusion is that the world-class East Asian university or an ethnic minority's university does not mean one that conforms to the standards of an elite university in the United States.

Implications

Although initiatives such as international partnerships and increasing international student enrollment may move institutions toward internationalization, curriculum internationalization cannot be neglected in order for internationalization to meaningfully impact student learning. Indeed, Maurice Harari (1992) calls curriculum the heart of internationalization (see also Green and Olson 2008). The suggestion by John D. Palmer and

Young Ha Cho (Chapter 5) for international students in South Korea to fulfill the Korean language graduation requirement is an example of curriculum internationalization that significantly impacts student learning.

Successful internationalization requires strong support from the administration; however faculty members ultimately need to drive the process (Green and Olson 2008). Amy Roberts and Gregory S. Ching (Chapter 2) argue the chief vehicle for developing and sustaining the National Cheng-Chi University (NCCU) as a world-class institution is the engagement of faculty within both local and global dimensions. All faculty members, domestic and foreign, need to engage in the internationalization efforts. Foreign faculty need to have the same roles and privileges of domestic faculty (see Chapter 5). Areas that institutions need to actively address in order to promote engagement and collaboration among all faculty include isolation of foreign faculty, tensions between domestic and foreign faculty, and issues that arise due to the dominant status of English (see Chapters 5 and 6).

Investment in faculty is vital to faculty engagement. What can be done to make faculty investment a higher priority is a question that each institution needs to address. In times of economic uncertainty, encouraging and supporting faculty to find external funding, and rewarding international collaboration are but two suggestions, but ultimately the institutions must commit to offer both financial and human resources to create and sustain the needed faculty engagement.

Global Competency Development as the Goal

In order to move internationalization from mere rhetoric to reality, it is essential for institutions in East Asia to look beyond the institution as the unit of analysis, and to consider the individual student. Since the list of global competencies is extensive and differs across disciplines, the American Council of Education (ACE) recommends that institutions of higher education generate an all-faculty discussion around which competencies are viewed as most relevant and important to a given institution, focusing on just one or two in the areas of knowledge, attitudes, and skills (Green and Olson 2008).

Once an institution has determined one or two overarching global competencies for all students in each of these areas, individual departments can articulate more specific global competencies for their students. Faculty can then revise syllabi so that their learning outcomes flow from the university outcomes and are supported by relevant course activities and projects and assessed directly in measurable ways.

Staff can also consider how co-curricular activities can address the outcomes they find most relevant to their areas. ACE notes that not every competency needs to be addressed in every curricular or co-curricular activity, but that a well-integrated approach will ensure a synergy (Green and Olson 2008). Assessment should take place on the course, program, and institutional level with alignment explicitly stated. Institutions can add this internationalization aspect to the campus-wide assessment they already have in place, or begin to develop it as part of a strategic plan.

International programs and internationalized curriculum are only as good as the changes they generate in students. If students are involved in international programs and yet if their knowledge of other nations has not been increased, their awareness of multiple perspectives has not been heightened, and their skills of interacting with people from diverse cultures have not been improved, then internationalization has been reduced to rhetoric used to promote the institution. For meaningful internationalization to take place, the change must be demonstrated and assessed in the knowledge, attitudes, and actions of the participants.

One definition of global competence is "the multiple abilities that allow one to interact effectively and appropriately across cultures" (Fantini et al. 2001, 8). Although specific global competencies are difficult to articulate, reaching consensus on a set of competencies and their measures is key in identifying to what extent internationalization has been successful. Thus the crucial question to ask is: What differences will internationalization make in what students will know, feel, and do and how they interact with others in the world? Put another way, what knowledge, attitudes and skills are needed for students to engage meaningfully in the global community? These three aspects, relating to the head, heart, and hand, are essential in assessing global competencies (Slimbach 2004).

An important dimension in evaluating internationalization is to analyze and assess the individual, as international programs and internationalized curriculum are only as good as the changes they generate in people. Perhaps the data provided in some of the studies in this volume could be used as a baseline to compare to those in the future to see if there is change in student and faculty global competence, providing both a macro (institutional or national) and micro (student) level analysis as well as a longitudinal one.

Analytical Frameworks

Frameworks to Rationalize Internationalization

Articulating a clear rationale for internationalization is vital because the rationale shapes and sustains internationalization. Although different stakeholders may agree that it is important to have a "world-class" university that produces internationally knowledgeable and globally competent graduates, they may not see eye to eye on the reasons why. For example, administrators may feel the pressure to increase the ranking of their university and thus view national competitiveness as the chief rationale, while academics may believe that scholarly and social change rationales should take priority. Some of these different rationales may be in conflict at times, such as generating revenue versus enhancing international research, causing stakeholders to disagree as to where resources should be allocated to improve internationalization. Other rationales can also be mutually reinforcing such as enhancing intercultural skills and preparing students for a global workforce. Arriving at a consensus of the chief rationale for internationalization and finding ways that different rationales can be mutually reinforcing is crucial for successful internationalization.

The literature classifies rationales for internationalization in four broad categories: academic, economic, social, and national security (Green and Olson 2008). An academic rationale for internationalization contends that internationalization strengthens liberal arts education and enhances the quality of teaching and research. It is supported by the belief that faculty members need to be knowledgeable about scholarship in other countries and that they need to be sure their courses are relevant to students from a diverse population. Moreover, this view maintains that faculty members need to be aware of the changes globalization has made in their fields and prepare students to teach, research, or work in a variety of cultural settings.

Economic and entrepreneurial rationales for internationalization maintain that the primary benefit of internationalization is that it prepares students for careers, generates income for the institution, and contributes to local economic development and competitiveness. A social rationale assumes the value of internationalization lies in the contribution to the common good that can result by internationalization, such as enhancing students' ability to live in an increasingly multicultural environment; contributing to the development, excellence, and relevance of institutions in other countries; and improving international and intercultural understanding. The final category, national security and foreign policy rationales view the purpose of internationalization as providing experts required to support national foreign policy and diplomacy and creating goodwill and support for one's country in other countries.

Clearly, there was evidence of all four of these rationales for internationalization in the data and analysis provided in this volume. However, East Asian higher education institutions may need to further explore ways that different rationales can be mutually reinforcing so that a synergy can be created to maximize the effects of internationalization efforts as assessed with the following frameworks.

Frameworks to Assess Internationalization

We adopt the definition of internationalization as "the process of integrating an international/intercultural dimension into the teaching, research, and service functions of the institution" (Knight 1994, 3). It has been noted by Madeleine F. Green and Christa Olson (2008) that there is neither one best way to internationalize higher education nor is there one point at which an institution can declare itself fully internationalized. However, even though internationalization will look different at different institutions, there are common measures that would identify where an institution of higher education is located along a continuum.

Performance Indicators

When evaluating the success of internationalization at a higher education institution, one must look at much more than the number of students who study abroad or the foreign students it attracts. Several frameworks to identify and assess internationalization have been developed, such as those referenced in this volume. For example, Roberts and Ching (Chapter 2) noted that in Taiwan the following performance indicators are analyzed when assessing internationalization: (1) institutional commitment, (2) strategic planning, (3) funding, (4) institutional policy and guidelines, (5) organizational infrastructure and resources, (6) academic offerings and curriculum, (7) Internet presence, (8) faculty and faculty development, (9) international students and scholars, (10) study abroad, (11) campus life, and (12) performance evaluation and accountability.

Multiple Analytical Frameworks Used to Analyze Internationalization

In a case study conducted at the University of Minnesota, Twin Cities, Brenda Ellingboe (1998) drew from four bodies of literature: intercultural competence, organizational change, international education, and curriculum to analyze internationalization efforts. Ellingboe's study illustrates the usefulness of applying multiple analytical frameworks to understand the complexity and multitude of factors involved in internationalization of higher education institutions. The multiple models allowed her to note similarities and differences in data across five colleges at one university and therefore make comparisons and contrasts. This study, like several in this volume, illustrates that using multiple analytical frameworks can add depth to analysis. Hans de Wit (2002) notes six different organizational models for analyzing internationalization in higher education, four of which focus on prescriptive and descriptive aspects and two of which take a process approach.

Typology of Change

A typology that we found useful addresses the depth and pervasiveness of the changes in internationalization being sought in an institution, ranging

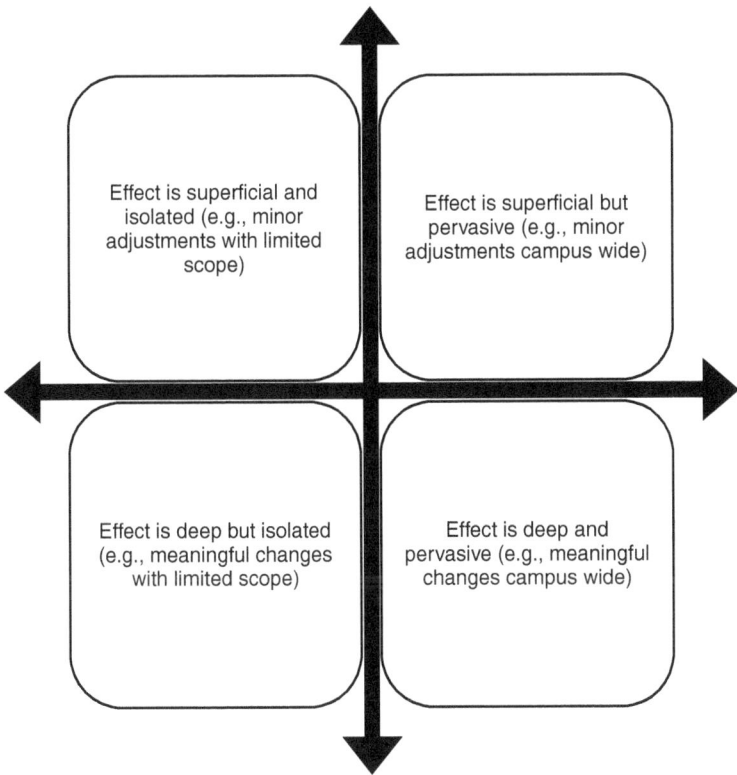

Figure 8.1 Typology of Change
Source: Adapted from Eckel, Green and Hill (1998).
Note: Vertical =Depth; Horizontal=Pervasiveness

from "tinkering" to transformational change (Eckel et al. 1998). This typology of change has two dimensions, breadth and depth, with four variations outlined in Figure 8.1. As one moves down the vertical axis there is greater depth of change, and as one moves to the right on the horizontal axis, the pervasiveness of change increases. Any typology risks oversimplification and cannot account for the complexity of the process. This framework is provided to consider the nature of change but it is important to keep in mind that change is often resisted, slow, not linear, and never predictable.

Superficial and Isolated Change

Adjustments, or mere "tinkering" is found in quadrant one on the top left where there is a minimum of depth and breadth of change toward internationalization. These changes typically are just "more of the same thing" such as recruiting more international students while not making changes needed to the campus to fully integrate them. For example, in this volume it was noted that foreign students did not feel a part of the institution and suggested that more needed to be done to ensure they were fully integrated to campus life and culture (see Chapters 5 and 6). Thus a change of simply recruiting more foreign students without ensuring their integration produces a change that is superficial and does not affect a broad spectrum of people, programs, or policies, and thus does not result in substantial internationalization.

Superficial but Pervasive Change

Quadrant two, on the top right, is far-reaching change, affecting a large number of people but because this type of change is not deep, the effect is not significant. It may affect all students but only in a superficial way so it would not be enough to produce a lasting or deep impact. For example, in the South Korean context, requiring all Korean students to take a few courses in English, or all foreign students to take just one or two Korean language courses is pervasive but not deep, as this would not produce a sufficient proficiency level in the language for students to communicate effectively and thus would not be sufficient for them to overcome the linguistic barriers described in the study.

Deep but Isolated Change

Isolated change is found in quadrant three on the bottom left, which is deep change but limited in scope. This typically takes place when one program or department produces a significant change that affects the core of a program or department, but because it is not implemented across the campus, its impact is narrow. If the unit of analysis is the institution, this limited change is not enough to make a large impact. An example discussed in this volume, is when an institution offers an international program that is isolated to one part of campus or one department but that does not permeate the university as a whole such as a summer program that is conducted in just one department (see Chapters 5 and 6).

Deep and Pervasive Change

The bottom right, or quadrant four, is transformational change which is both pervasive and deep, resulting in a synergy of connected changes or a cascading effect that impacts the institution at its core. Green and Olson state "[t]ransformational change is intentional, requiring leadership, strategy, and time. It is a long term under taking that involves many people, usually over the course of at least five to 10 years" (2008, 22). There were not clear examples of comprehensive or transformational change in internationalization in the studies in this volume, but there were indications that it could emerge.

Chan's (Chapter 1) analysis of higher education in Hong Kong and Singapore provides an example of a macro analysis beyond the institutional level to the national level. The analytical framework provided here could be applied at national level to examine the depth and breadth of change. In the case of Hong Kong, transformational change is just emerging. While assessing internationalization on the national and institutional level is important, it is crucial to move beyond using the institution as unit of analysis and examine the individual student. This would allow the institution to look at not only output (e.g., number of foreign students and faculty) but also outcomes (e.g., student and faculty growth in global competencies).

Further Inquiries

We conclude this chapter with a list of questions we hope will continue and extend the discussion of internationalization of higher education in East Asia. We ask readers general questions on internationalization of higher education in East Asia, specific questions related to the studies in this volume, and finally probing questions about the future of the nations and regions addressed in the volume before concluding with some final thoughts.

General Questions on Internationalization of Higher Education in East Asia

1. How does internationalization of higher education in East Asia differ from that of the West?
2. What can the nations/regions of East Asia learn from each other in terms of internationalization?
3. What are the rationales of internationalization for various East Asian higher education institutions and how do the differing rationales affect internationalization efforts?
4. What are the goals of internationalization of higher education in East Asia?
5. What types of internationalization efforts in East Asian higher education have resulted in change that is both deep and pervasive?
6. To what extent does internationalization of higher education in East Asia result in the development of globally competent faculty and students?
7. Who serves to gain and who serves to lose in the current changes being sought in the name of internationalization of higher education in East Asia?

Specific Questions Related to Studies in This Volume

1. What unique contribution does each study in this volume make to our understanding of internationalization of higher education in East Asia?
2. What insights do these chapters offer in terms of globalization and internationalization theory?
3. What language policy implications can be drawn from these studies, and what impact would these have on access, equity, and quality of education?
4. What research questions still need to be investigated and what type of studies might address them?
5. What do these studies have to say on the issues of contextualization, rankings, and access and how these relate to internationalization efforts in East Asia?
6. What evidence was found for faculty as change agents, changes in curriculum, and global competence development?
7. What benefits can be found in seeking local rather than Western partnerships when internationalizing higher education in East Asia?

Probing Questions Related to Specific Regions or Countries

1. What unique contribution does South Korea have to make to internationalization of higher education in East Asia and in what ways can it become a leader of internationalization in the region?
2. What key challenges does Taiwan face in term of internationalization of higher education and what are some best practices?
3. How do issues of identity, access, and equity impact the internationalization efforts of China in terms of ethnic minority populations?
4. What are the implications of the changes in education in Hong Kong and Singapore to a more corporate, managerial, entrepreneurial model in their efforts to internationalize?
5. In what ways has Japan stood out in its efforts to internationalize higher education and what key challenges does it face?
6. How does the drive to become "world class" and achieve top rankings affect internationalization of higher education in each of the countries in East Asia?
7. What languages will become more prevalent to contest the dominance of English as both the medium of instruction in institutions of higher education and the language of the top academic journals?

Final Thoughts

Through this chapter, we sought to stimulate those involved in internationalization in colleges and universities in East Asia to think deeply and differently regarding the fundamental purpose and ultimate goals of internationalization. We posited that assessment must go beyond the number of programs and international students and consider whether and to what extent students' values and behaviors are positively transformed as the result of their international and intercultural experience. Finally, we hope to engage students, faculty, staff, and administrators on East Asian university campuses in discussions on how to cultivate a culture that embraces and supports internationalization.

We believe that successful internationalization initiatives in higher education require a strong, clear, and comprehensive vision from the leadership as well as input and support from the administration and faculty. Vital to the success is a comprehensive plan that is embraced by key constituents and includes an appropriate and feasible assessment plan to monitor and adapt efforts to meet the needs of a changing world. Several challenges can affect the success of these initiatives, but much can be learned from case studies of internationalization such as those in this volume.

More investigations conducted at different types of institutions are needed to better understand internationalization of higher education in East Asia. Studies that look at internationalization initiatives at higher education institutions that are large and small, private and public, secular and faith-based, national and international for example, would do much to help us better understand how context affects internationalization efforts in East Asia and beyond.

NOTE

1. The authors of this chapter continue the "insider/outsider" collaboration present in several of the chapters of this anthology. Wong is an Caucasian American who has taught in China, completed a masters in Chinese, and teaches in East and Southeast Asia annually as a professor in TESOL. Wu, a native of China, completed her undergraduate in China before pursuing master's and doctoral studies in the United States. Both authors teach and research issues related to internationalization of higher education at Azusa Pacific University in Southern California.

REFERENCES

de Wit, Hans. 2002. *Internationalization of Higher Education in the United States of America and Europe: A Historical, Comparative, and Conceptual Analysis.* Westport, CT: Greenwood Press.

Eckel, Peter, Barbara Hill, and Madeleine F. Green. 1998. *On Change. En Route to Transformation.* Washington, DC: American Council on Education.

Ellingboe, Brenda J. 1998. "Divisional Strategies to Internationalize a Campus Portrait: Results, Resistance, and Recommendations from a Case Study at US University." In *Reforming the Higher Education Curriculum: Internationalizing the Campus*, ed. Josef A. Mestenhauser and Brenda J. Ellingboe. Washington, DC: Oryx Press.

Fantini, Alvino. E, Fernando Arias-Galacia, and Daniel Guay. 2001. "Globalization and 21st Century Competencies: Challenges for North American Higher Education." Consortium for North American Higher Education Collaboration Working Paper Series on Higher Education in Mexico, Canada and the United States (Working Paper No. 11), Boulder, CO: Western Interstate Commission on Higher Education.

Green, Madeleine F., and Christa Olson. 2008. *Internationalizing the Campus: A User's Guide*. Washington, DC: American Council on Education.

Harari, Maurice. 1992. "Internationalization of the Curriculum." In *Bridges to the Future: Strategies for Internationalization Higher Education*, ed. Charles B. Klasek, Brian J. Garavalia, and Kathy J. Kellerman. Pullman, WA: Association of International Education Administrators.

Knight, Jane. 1994. *Internationalisation: Elements and Checkpoints*. Ottawa: Canadian Bureau of International Education.

Ma, Jin-Chuan. 1999. "Fund Allocations for Information Resources in China's Key Universities." *College & Research Libraries* 60 (2): 174-178.

Schneider, Barbara, and Yongsook Lee. 1990. "A Model for Academic Success: The School and Home Environment of East Asian Students." *Anthropology & Education Quarterly* 21 (4): 358-377.

Slimbach, Richard. 2004. *Transcultural Journeys*. Monrovia, CA: World Wise Books.

Contributors

David Kinkeung Chan is an associate professor in the Department of Asian and International Studies, and concurrently as the convenor, Comparative Education Policy Research Unit at the Department of Public and Social Administration, City University of Hong Kong. His expertise is in sociology of education, with research interests on comparative education policies and reforms in Asian societies. He has edited volumes with book chapters, and has contributed many articles in internationally and regionally peer referred journals, such as: *Comparative Education, International Journal of Educational Management, International Journal of Education Reform, Journal of Contemporary China, Globalization, Education and Societies, Higher Education Policy, Policy Futures in Education, Asia Pacific Journal of Education*, among others.

Gregory S. Ching is an assistant professor in the Department of Applied Foreign Languages at Lunghwa University of Science and Technology, Republic of China (Taiwan). He is the recipient of the Taiwan Scholarship for three consecutive years (2007-2009); a scholarship given to outstanding international PhD students studying in Taiwan. His current research interest includes, but not limited to, the following: internationalization of higher education, student engagement, cross-cultural adaptability, work ethics, and bibliometrics.

Young Ha Cho is an assistant professor at the Graduate School of Education in Kyung Hee University-Seoul Campus. Before his current professorship, Cho was an associate research fellow for the Korean Educational Development Institute, the national educational policy research institute in South Korea, and joined in higher education level-policy projects. He also served as senior researcher of Korean Council for University Education in 2005. His scholarly interests have mainly been in organizational behavior studies from open system perspective. Cho also attempts to reflect social values in his research concerns, such as social capital and civic values, in order to understand educational organizations within richer social contexts. The current issue that his research takes note of is social engagement of higher education.

Peter Gregory Ghazarian is a doctoral candidate at Boston University's School of Education and a senior lecturer at Northeastern University. His research interests encompass economics, public policy, and assessment in education. His work focuses on regional integration, the international flow of human capital and the role of education in post-industrial economies.

W. James Jacob is director of the Institute for International Studies in Education at the University of Pittsburgh's School of Education, and is the former assistant director of the Center for International and Development Education at UCLA. His research focuses on program design, implementation, and evaluation; HIV/AIDS multisectoral capacity building and prevention; and higher education organizational analysis with geographic emphases in Africa, East and Southeast Asia, and the Pacific Islands.

Jae-Eun Jon is research professor of the Higher Education Policy Research Institute at the Korea University, Seoul, Korea, and postdoctoral associate of the Department of Organizational Leadership, Policy, and Development at the University of Minnesota-Twin Cities. She received a PhD from the Comparative and International Development Education Program in the Educational Policy and Administration Department at the University of Minnesota. Her research interests include the internationalization of higher education—its impact on students, college student development, and international educational development. Previously she worked for the Study Abroad for Global Engagement project at the University of Minnesota, which investigated the long-term impact of study abroad with more than 6,000 study abroad alumni in the United States.

Eun-Young Kim is a researcher in Korean Educational Development Institute. She's currently involved in the OECD AHELO Project. She received her PhD from the University of Illinois at Urbana-Champaign. She has been interested in examining intersection of political economy, cultural systems and education policy. Her research interests include international higher education policy studies, globalization theories, institutionalism and organizational theory, higher education in East Asia, and comparative and international education.

John D. Palmer is an associate professor at Colgate University in the Department of Educational Studies. Palmer's research and teaching concentrates on the sociocultural aspects of education, with specific interests in racial and ethnic identity development, cross-cultural competency, and Asian American immigrants and Korean adoptees. He just completed a manuscript entitled, *The Dance of Identities: Korean Adult Adoptees' Identity Journeys* (2010). He is currently working on two major research endeavors. In the first project, he is exploring the types of resistance from both White students and students of color to anti-racist curriculum and pedagogy. And in the second project, he is investigating the development of multicultural education in South Korean elementary schools.

Amy Roberts is associate professor of Curriculum and Instruction and adjunct in the International Studies Program at the University of Wyoming in Laramie, Wyoming. Her research focus in international comparative education is aligned with ideologies that inform efforts to explore English as the language of contemporary globalization, contrasting paradigms of educational practices, technology training and delivery systems, curriculum reform, and program evaluation. Roberts has lived, taught, and conducted field research in Thailand, Taiwan, Spain, Guatemala, Costa Rica, and the United States.

Heejin Park is a research associate of the Institute of the International Studies in Education (IISE) at the University of Pittsburgh. Her research focuses on education issues related to cultural, linguistic, and ethnic minorities in Asia. Before joining IISE, she has served as a project specialist and a managing editor of an educational policy series in the Korean Educational Research Institution (KEDI). Her current research project is on intercultural issues in a context of South Korea focusing on foreign mothers and their bi-racial children's education.

Anthony R. Welch is professor of Education, University of Sydney. A policy specialist, he has consulted to state, national, and international agencies and governments, and U.S. institutions and foundations. His project experience includes East and Southeast Asia, particularly in higher education. His work has been translated into numerous languages, and he has been Visiting Professor in the United States, United Kingdom, Germany, France, Japan, and Hong Kong (China). A Fulbright New Century Scholar (2007-2008), his most recent books are *The Professoriate: Profile of a Profession* (2005), *Education, Change and Society* (2007), *Association of Southeast Asian Nation (ASEAN) Industries and the Challenge from China* (2011), and *Higher Education in Southeast Asia: Changing Balance, Blurring Borders* (2011). Welch also directs the national research project, The Chinese Knowledge Diaspora.

Mary Shepard Wong holds a doctorate in International and Intercultural Education (University of Southern California), a master's degrees in East Asian Languages and Cultures (University of California, Los Angeles) and Teaching English to Speakers of Other Languages (TESOL) (Azusa Pacific University). She is a full professor at Azusa Pacific University in southern California, where she directs both the field-based and online TESOL programs. She has taught English as a Second Language (ESL) for two decades and has been in teacher education for one decade teaching in the United States, China, and Thailand. She has conducted over 40 presentations and has a textbook with Cambridge University Press, an edited volume with Routledge coedited with Suresh Canagarajah and one under contract coedited with Zoltan Dornyei and Carolyn Kristjansson. She has served in leadership positions in TESOL, California TESOL (CATESOL), and Cambodian TESOL (CamTESOL). Her research interests include teacher identity, the role of Christianity in English language teaching, and internationalization and global competence.

Shuang Frances Wu is Global Learning Faculty at Azusa Pacific University's Center for Global Learning and Engagement. She holds a PhD in Higher Education Policy and Organization and a master's degree in Postsecondary Administration, both from the University of Southern California. She received her early education in China, having obtained a BA in English Language and Literature from Nankai University in Tianjin. Her research interests include curriculum internationalization, foreign language education, and the role of experiential learning in intercultural competency development.

Rui Yang is an associate professor and assistant dean (Research Projects and Centres), Faculty of Education, University of Hong Kong. He has worked in different higher education systems, with particular interest in crossculturalism in education policy, higher education, and sociology of education. After nearly a decade of teaching and research at Shantou University in Guangdong, he received a PhD from the University of Sydney in 2001. He has then taught and researched at universities of Western Australia, Monash and Hong Kong. He has written extensively in the field of comparative and international education. His current interest is focused on comparative and global studies in education policy and higher education internationalization.

Index

Page numbers in *italics* denote illustrations.

Academic Ranking of World Universities (ARWU), 7, 173, 174, 176–7, *177,* 179, 182, 184–93. *See also* international ranking systems
academics in East Asia. *See* faculty
ACE (American Council of Education), 203–4
AERA (American Education Research Association), 2
AHCI (Arts and Humanities Citation Index), 56
Altbach, Philip G., 41, 84, 148
American Council of Education (ACE), 203–4
American Education Research Association (AERA), 2
Americanization. *See* Western models of higher education
analytical frameworks for internationalization, 204–9
Anhui College, China, 72
Apple, Michael W., 91
Arts and Humanities Citation Index (AHCI), 56
ARWU (Academic Ranking of World Universities), 7, 173, 174, 176–7, *177,* 179, 182, 184–93. *See also* international ranking systems
Asia Pacific University of Ritsumeikan, Japan, 151
assessment of internationalization process, 206–7

Bao Erhan, 72
Barnett, Ron, 52
Bernasconi, Andres, 166
Bowden, Rachel, 178
brain drain
  of ethnic Koreans in China, 114
  of South Koreans studying abroad, 121
  at XU, China, 79–81
Burbules, Nicholas C., 91

C-EDB (Chinese Education Bureau), 22, 34n4
CASE (Consumer Association of Singapore), 28, 29
Central Asia Regional Economic Cooperation, 85
Chan, David Kinkeung, 3, 11, 199, 200–1, 209, 215
change, typology of, *207,* 207–9
Children of Sanchez (Lewis, 1961), 66
China
  cross-border education of students from: in Hong Kong, 20, 22, 30; in South Korea and Japan, 160, 167
  ethnic minorities in. *See* ethnic minorities in China

China—*Continued*
  future directions in studying, 211
  Hong Kong's Memoranda of
    Understanding with the
    Mainland, 18, 22
  international ranking systems and,
    178, 183
  internationalization studies in,
    63–4, 84
  marketization and globalization of
    economy in, 91, 106
  211 Project, 73
  XU. *See* Xinjiang University (XU),
    China
China National Petroleum
  Corporation (CNPC),
  81, 85n1
Chinese Education Bureau (C-EDB),
  22, 34n4
Chinese Service Center for Scholarly
  Exchange (CSCSE), 22
Ching, Gregory S., 3, 41, 47, 203,
  206, 215
Cho, Young Ha, 6, 119, 124, 125,
  202–3, 215–16
CIES (Comparative and International
  Education Society), 2
City University of Hong Kong,
  22, 34n2
CNPC (China National Petroleum
  Corporation), 81, 85n1
Coming of Age in Samoa
  (Mead, 1973), 66
Comparative and International
  Education Society (CIES), 2
Confucius and Confucianism, 63–4
Consumer Association of Singapore
  (CASE), 28, 29
cooperative arrangements. *See*
  partnerships between
  international universities
Cremomini, Leon, 180
Cronbach, Lee J., 50
cross-border education

of Chinese students: in Hong Kong,
  20, 22, 30; in South Korea, 160
immersion/segregation of
  international students, 52,
  128–9, 131, 158–60, 200
Japan and. *See under* Japan
mobility trends and patterns, 45–6,
  174
NCCU, Taiwan, 42, 50–3
scholarships. *See* scholarship
  programs
service-learning requirements, 53
  in Singapore and Hong Kong. *See
  under* Singapore and Hong Kong
South Korea and. *See under* South
  Korea
XU, China. *See under* Xinjiang
  University (XU), China
CSCSE (Chinese Service Center for
  Scholarly Exchange), 22
Cultural Revolution, 72
curriculum internationalization,
  importance of, 202–3

Davis, Jay, 46
de Wit, Hans, 13–14, 207
developing countries
  importance of internationalization
    of higher education to, 91–2
  South Korean universities,
    globalization studies at, 139–40
Du Chongyuan, 71–2
dual-degree programs, 138–9
Duke University, 138–9

East Asia, internationalization
  of higher education in. *See*
  internationalization and
  globalization of higher education
  in East Asia
EGM (emerging global model), 44–5
Ellingboe, Brenda, 206
emerging global model
  (EGM), 44–5

English, use of
  in East Asian context, 198–9
  ethnic Koreans in China,
    educational opportunities for,
    106–8
  in Japan, 150–1, 162–4, 165–6,
    198–9
  at NCCU, Taiwan, 42, 44, 53–5,
    198–9
  publication pressures on faculty
    and, 45, 55–7, 133, 137
  in Singapore and Hong Kong,
    30, 199
  at South Korean universities. *See
    under* South Korea
entrance examinations
  ethnic Koreans in China and, 101,
    102, 103, 104, 107, 108, 113
  South Korean universities, 119, 127,
    129–30, 155, 166
  XU, China, 81–4, *82, 83*
ethnic Koreans in China, educational
  opportunities for, 5, 91–118
  awareness of value of higher
    education, 101–2
  brain drain, 114
  cultural distinctness from both
    Chinese and South Korean
    societies, 109–10
  diaspora community, characteristics
    of, 98–101
  effects of globalization on
    marginalized peoples,
    91–3, 103–4
  English proficiency, 106–8
  entrance examinations, 101, 102,
    103, 104, 107, 108, 113
  heritage education, 96
  invisibility in Chinese society,
    110, 113
  language issues. *See under* language
    issues
  marketization and globalization of
    economy, effects of, 108–9, 113

  methodology of study, 93–5
  "model minority" discourse and,
    96–9
  preferential education policies,
    ethnic Koreans' use of, 104–5
  quota system for local students,
    effects of, 105–6
  underrepresentation of ethnic
    Koreans as students and
    faculty, 101
  Yanbian University, 96, 101, 105–6,
    109, 110–12, 113–14, 202
ethnic minorities generally, effects of
  globalization on,
  91–3, 103–4
ethnic minorities in China. *See
  also* ethnic Koreans in China,
  educational opportunities for;
  and under Xinjiang University
  (XU), China
  incidence of, 96, 112
  preferential education policies for,
    104–5, 113
evaluation of internationalization
  process, 206–7
Ewha Womans University, South
  Korea, 132

faculty
  EGM, negative reactions to, 45
  international ranking systems and.
    See under international ranking
    systems
  in Japan, 151, 163–5, 166
  at NCCU, Taiwan, 42, 45, 53–5, 203
  publication pressures on. *See*
    publication pressures
    on faculty
  at South Korean universities,
    131–6, 137–8, 157–8, 166, 200
  student-to-staff ratio, 176, *177,* 185,
    188–92
  support for internationalization,
    importance of, 203

faculty—*Continued*
  Western models of student instruction, cultural problems with, 199–200
  at XU, China. *See under* Xinjiang University (XU), China
Fantini, Alvino, 204
Fields medals, *177*, 179, 185, 188, 189, *189*, 190
Flippo, Rona, 53
foreign campuses of Hong Kong universities, 21
foreign students. *See* cross-border education
foreign universities, collaboration with. *See* partnerships between international universities
foreign universities with campuses in East Asia
  Hong Kong, 20, 21
  Singapore, 24–5, 26, 27, 30
Friedman, Thomas, 103–4

Garrod, Andrew, 46
General Agreement on Trade in Services (GATS), 1, 12, 14
Ghazarian, Peter Gregory, 7, 173, 216
global competency development as goal of internationalization, 203–4
global ranking systems. *See* international ranking systems
globalization. *See* internationalization and globalization of higher education in East Asia; marketization and globalization of economy
"Gold Triangle," 111
government involvement with educational system
  international ranking systems and, 175, 183, 193
  in Singapore and Hong Kong. *See under* Singapore and Hong Kong

Green, Madeleine F., 206
Guarino, Cassandra M., 180

Hanyru (Korean Wave), 108
Harari, Maurice, 202
Hazelkorn, Ellen, 182, 192–3
Healey, Mick, 180
heritage education of ethnic Koreans in China, 96
higher education in East Asia, internationalization of. *See* internationalization and globalization of higher education in East Asia
HKCAAVQ (Hong Kong Council for Accreditation of Academic and Vocational Qualifications), 23
HKTDC (Hong Kong Trade and Development Council), 21
Hong Kong. *See* Singapore and Hong Kong, *and specific universities*
Hong Kong Baptist University, 22, 34n2–3
Hong Kong Council for Accreditation of Academic and Vocational Qualifications (HKCAAVQ), 23
Hong Kong Government Task Force on Economic Challenges, 17
Hong Kong Institute of Education, 22, 34n2
Hong Kong Lingnan University, 34n2
Hong Kong Polytechnic University, 22, 34n2
Hong Kong Trade and Development Council (HKTDC), 21
Hong Kong University of Science and Technology, 18, 34n2–3

IIE (Institute of International Education), 148
immersion/segregation of international students, 52, 128–9, 131, 158–60, 200

INSEAD, 27
insider/outsider perspectives of researchers, 3, 47, 66, 125, 153, 186–7, 192, 212n1
Institute for Scientific Information (ISI) database, 45, 56–7
Institute of International Education (IIE), 148
International Christian University, Japan, 151
international ranking systems, 7, 173–96
  academic resistance to, 177–8
  ARWU, 7, 173, 174, 176–7, *177*, 179, 182, 184–93
  comparison of educational institutions using, 181
  conclusions regarding, 190–3
  as consumer information, 180–1
  criticism of, 178–82
  in East Asian context, 183–4, 201–2
  faculty and: academic resistance to rankings, 177–8; involvement with ranking systems, 182–3; Nobel Prize and Fields medal winners, *177*, 179, 185, 188, 189, *189*, 190; student-to-staff ratio, 190–3; unintended consequences for, 181–2
  foreign presence as element in, 132
  government relations with educational systems and, 175, 183, 193
  indicators: ARWU total score regressions and, 188–9, *189*; correlation, indicator-to-indicator, 187–8; methodology of study and, 184–5; recursive partitioning analysis, 189–90; relative importance, 184; *THE* and ARWU rankings, 176–7, *177*, 185
  Japanese universities and, 147, 177–8, 183–4
  methodology of study, 184–7
  publication pressures on faculty and, 181–2, *189*, 189–90, 190–2
  research, stress on, 176–7, 190–1
  role and importance of, 173–5, 192–3
  South Korean universities and, 132, 136, 147, 184
  Taiwan and, 184
  technological and methodological concerns, 179–80
  THE, 7, 34n3, 128, 132, 136, 173, 174, 176–8, *177*, 180, 182, 184–9, 191–3
  unintended consequences of, 181–2
  U.S. News & World Report, 173
  widespread adoption of, 92
  "world-class" university, concept of, 174
international students. *See* cross-border education
International Survey of the Academic Profession (Carnegie Foundation, 1996), 66
internationalization and globalization of higher education in East Asia, 1–9, 197–213
  analytical frameworks for, 204–9
  assessment of, 206–7
  curriculum internationalization, importance of, 202–3
  definitions of internationalization and globalization, 122–3, 206
  developing countries, importance to, 91–2
  distinct processes, globalization and internationalization as, 43
  East Asian contextualization versus Westernization, 2, 198–201
  ethnic Koreans in China, 5, 91–118. *See also* ethnic Koreans in China, educational opportunities for
  faculty and, 203. *See also* faculty

internationalization—*Continued*
  future directions in studying,
    209–11
  global competency development as
    goal of, 203–4
  in Japan, 6–7, 147–71. *See also*
    Japan
  NCCU, 3–4, 41–61. *See also*
    National Cheng- Chi University
    (NCCU), Taipei, Taiwan
  ranking systems, 7, 173–96. *See also*
    international ranking systems
  rationales for, 204–6
  researchers, insider/outsider
    perspectives of, 3, 47, 66, 125,
    153, 186–7, 192, 212n1
  in Singapore and Hong Kong, 3,
    11–39. *See also* Singapore and
    Hong Kong
  in South Korea, 5–7, 119–45,
    147–71. *See also* South Korea
  typology of change for, *207,* 207–9
  Westernization and. *See* Western
    models of higher education
  "world-class" university, concept
    of, 201–2. *See also* "world-class"
    university, concept of
  XU, 4–5, 63–89. *See also* Xinjiang
    University (XU), China
ISI (Institute for Scientific
  Information) database, 45, 56–7
Islam, influence of, at XU, China,
  65, 69–70

Jacob, W. James, 5, 91, 216
Japan, 6–7, 147–71. *See also specific
  universities*
  cross-border education: foreign
    students in Japan, 147, *150,* 162–5,
    167; recruitment of international
    students, 149; study abroad by
    Japanese students, 147, 148, *150*
  demographics of native students in,
    149, 165, 167

  English, use of, 150–1, 162–4,
    165–6, 198–9
  ethnic Koreans in, 97–8
  faculty in, 151, 163–5
  future directions in studying, 211
  international ranking systems and,
    147, 177–8, 183–4
  methodology of study, 152–3
  strategies of internationalization in,
    147–9, 165–9
  Western models of higher education
    and, 148, 151–2, 163–9
  XU, China, and, 78
Jay, Paul, 1
Johns Hopkins University Division
  of Biomedical Sciences in
  Singapore, 32
Jon, Jae-Eun, 6, 147, 153, 158,
  160, 216

KAIST (Korea Advanced Institute of
  Science and Technology), 151
KEDI (Korean Educational
  Development Institute), 126
Kim, Eun-Young, 6, 147, 153, 216
Kimura, Michael Tuan, 124
Knight, Jane, 13–14, 29
Korea. *See* ethnic Koreans in China,
  educational opportunities for;
  North Korea; South Korea
Korea Advanced Institute of Science
  and Technology (KAIST), 151
Korea University, 151
Korean Educational Development
  Institute (KEDI), 126
Kuwamura, Akira, 151

language issues. *See also* English,
  use of
  ethnic Koreans in China: educational
    access, language barriers to,
    102–5; heritage education for,
    96; Yanbian University, Korean
    language at, 111

Index

future directions in studying, 211
local language requirements for international students, lack of, 129–31, 200
at XU, China, 82, *82*
Lassegard, James, 163, 164, 167
Lee, Soo Chin, 124
Lee, Steven K., 96
Lee Myung-bak, 121
Levin, Henry M., 44
Lewis, Oscar, 66
Lin Jilu, 71

Mao Tse Tung, 4, 72
Marginson, Simon, 180
marketing of education in Singapore and Hong Kong. *See under* Singapore and Hong Kong
marketization and globalization of economy
 in China, 91, 106
 ethnic Koreans in China affected by, 108–9, 113
 in Singapore and Hong Kong, 11–13, 33
"marriage emigration" of South Koreans to China, 100
Massachusetts Institute of Technology (MIT), 26
Mazzarol, Tim, 46
McMahon, Mary, 46
Mead, Margaret, 66
MIT (Massachusetts Institute of Technology), 26
"model minority" discourse and ethnic Koreans in China, 96–9
Mok, Ka Ho, 92, 148, 168
mutual cooperation. *See* partnerships between international universities

Nanyang Technological University (NTU), Singapore, 24, 25, 26, 28
National Cheng-Chi University (NCCU), Taipei, Taiwan, 3–4, 41–61
 cross-border education of international students at, 42, 50–3
 English, use of, 42, 44, 53–5, 198–9
 faculty at, 42, 45, 53–5, 203
 history and statistics, 47
 methodology of study, 42–3, 47–50
 mobility trends and patterns for international students and, 45–6
 publication pressures, 42, 45, 55–7
 "world-class" university, concept of, 41–5
National Science Council, Taiwan, 42, 51
National University of Singapore (NUS), 24, 25, 26, 28
NCCU. *See* National Cheng-Chi University (NCCU), Taipei, Taiwan
neoliberalism, 2, 31, 32
Nobel Prize, 132, *177*, 179, 185, 188, 189, *189*, 190
North Korea, 100, 111
Novosibirsk State University (NSU), Siberia, 78
NTU (Nanyang Technological University), Singapore, 24, 25, 26, 28
NUS (National University of Singapore), 24, 25, 26, 28

OBU (Oklahoma Baptist University), 77
OECD (Organization for Economic Cooperation and Development) PISA Programme, 98, 173
offshore campuses of Hong Kong universities, 21
Oklahoma Baptist University (OBU), 77
Olson, Christa, 206
Open University of Hong Kong, 22
Organization for Economic Cooperation and Development (OECD), PISA Programme, 98, 173

outsider/insider perspectives of researchers, 3, 47, 66, 125, 153, 186–7, 192, 212n1

Pak, Yongsook, 97–8
Palmer, John D., 1, 6, 119, 124, 125, 202–3, 216–17
"parachute kids," 120
Park, Heejin, 5, 91, 94, 217
partnerships, public-private, 12
partnerships between international universities, 200–1
   dual-degree programs between South Korean and foreign universities, 138–9
   in Japan, 151
   NCCU, Taiwan, 42
   twinning partnerships, 14, 20, 26, 34n1
   XU, China, 75, 77–9
   Yanbian University, Korean autonomous prefecture, China, 112
People's Republic of China. *See* China
PISA (Programme for International Student Assessment), 98, 173
Polytechnic University of Hong Kong (PolyU), 20, 34n3
Potthoff, Maggie, 53
private sector in Singapore and Hong Kong. *See under* Singapore and Hong Kong
professorate. *See* faculty
Programme for International Student Assessment (PISA), 98, 173
Project 211, 73, 106, 111, 112
publication pressures on faculty
   English, use of, 45, 55–7, 133, 137
   international ranking systems and, 181–2, *189*, 189–90, 190–2
   at NCCU, Taiwan, 42, 45, 55–7
   in South Korea, 133, 137
   Western models of higher education and, 42, 56

public-private partnerships in education, 12
push-pull models of international student mobility, 45–6

Qianlong (Chinese emperor), 68
quality assurance system in Singapore and Hong Kong. *See under* Singapore and Hong Kong

ranking systems. *See* international ranking systems
regional Chinese university, development of. *See* Xinjiang University (XU), China
regional education hubs, Singapore and Hong Kong aspiring to become, 12–13, 14, 18, 24, 30
Republic of Korea. *See* South Korea
research
   international ranking systems stressing, 176–7, 190–1
   South Korean universities' emphasis on, 137
   super-research institutions, emergence of, 2
researchers, insider/outsider perspectives of, 3, 47, 66, 125, 153, 186–7, 192, 212n1
Ritzer, George, 123
Roberts, Amy, 1, 3, 41, 47, 203, 206, 217
Royal Veterinary College of the University of London, 20
R-squares, 187, 188–9, *189*
Rubbia, Carlo, 132

Sanderson, Gavin, 26
Sautman, Barry, 82
Savino, Massimo, 176, 179
scholarship programs
   at NCCU, Taiwan, 51–2
   at South Korean universities, 126, 130
   at XU, China, 78, 79

Schugurensky, Daniel, 114
Schutz, Alfred, 66
Science Citation Index (SCI), 42, 56, 137, 188, 190
SCO (Shanghai Cooperation Organisation), 70, 85
S-EDB (Singapore Economic Development Board), 24, 25, 27, 34n4
segregation/immersion of international students, 52, 128–9, 131, 158–60, 200
Seoul National University (SNU), South Korea, 137, 138–9, 169n3
service-learning requirements for international students, 53
Shanghai Cooperation Organisation (SCO), 70, 85
Shanghai Jiao Tong University, China, 147, 173
Sheng Shicai, 71
Shue Yan University, Hong Kong, 19
Singapore and Hong Kong, 3, 11–39. *See also specific universities*
  creative and critical thinking, Singaporese curricula emphasizing, 43
  cross-border education: concept of, and rise in, 14; in Hong Kong, 20–1, 22; importance of, 29, 30; in Singapore, 25–7
  different strategies adopted by, 15
  English, use of, 30, 199
  future directions in studying, 211
  government involvement: conclusions regarding, 30–3; in Hong Kong, 17–20; importance of, 28–9; marketization of educational services and funding, effects of, 11–13; in Singapore, 24–5
  marketing strategies: in Hong Kong, 21–2; importance of, 30; in Singapore, 27–8
  marketization of educational services and funding and, 11–13, 33
  methodological issues, 15–17
  private sector: in Hong Kong, 18–19; marketization of educational services and funding, effects of, 11–13; in Singapore, 26, 27, 28–9
  problem-based learning, Hong Kong curricula emphasizing, 43
  quality assurance system: in Hong Kong, 22–4; importance of, 30, 31; in Singapore, 28–9
  regional education hubs, aspiring to become, 12–13, 14, 18, 24, 30, 32–3
  three-tiered systems: in Hong Kong, 19–20; in Singapore, 24–5
  trend toward internationalization, 13–15
  Western models of education, comfort with, 30, 201
Singapore Economic Development Board (S-EDB), 24, 25, 27, 34n4
"Singapore Education" (agency), 27–8
Singapore Institute of Management, 26
Singapore Institute of Marketing, 26
Singapore Institute of Technology, 26
Singapore Management University (SMU), 24, 28
Singapore Nurses Association, 26
Singapore Quality Class for Private Education Organization (SQC-PEO), 28
Singapore Tourism Board (STB), 26, 28
Smoot, George, 132
SMU (Singapore Management University), 24, 28
SNU (Seoul National University), South Korea, 137, 138–9, 169n3
Social Science Citation Index (SSCI), 42, 56, 57, 133, 188, 190

Sophia University, Japan, 151
South Korea, 5–6, 119–45, 147–71.
    See also ethnic Koreans in China, educational opportunities for; and specific universities
    cross-border education: foreign students in Korea, 126–31, 147, 150, 167; recruitment of international students, 137–8, 149–50; segregation of international students, 128–9, 131, 158–60; study abroad by South Korean students, 120–1, 123–4, 147, 150
    demographics of native students in, 167
    dual-degree programs with foreign universities, 138–9
    English, use of, 151–2; faculty issues with, 131–2, 134, 157–8, 166; publication pressures, 133, 137; student issues with, 126, 127, 130–1, 154–7, 165–6, 167; Western models of higher education and, 119–20, 121, 125–6
    entrance examinations, 119, 127, 129–30, 155, 166
    faculty issues, 131–6, 137–8, 157–8, 166, 200
    future directions in studying, 211
    globalization studies for developing country students, 139–40
    international and non-Korean, equation of, 134–5
    international ranking systems and, 132, 136, 147, 184
    internationalization, student attitude toward, 160–2, 165, 167
    methodology of study, 124–5, 152–3
    opportunities for Chinese ethnic Koreans in, 109
    policies of internationalization in, 119–22, 123–6, 136, 140–2
    publication pressures, 133, 137
    recruitment of top-notch students and academics, 137–8
    research agenda, 137
    strategies of internationalization in, 147–9, 165–9
    summer programs, 137–8
    theoretical framework for studying, 122–3
    Western models of higher education and, 121–2, 125–6, 127, 136, 148, 151–2, 165–9, 200
    "world-class" university, concept of, 132–3, 158, 166
Soviet Union and XU, China, 69, 71–2, 75
SPRING Singapore, 28
SQC-PEO (Singapore Quality Class for Private Education Organization), 28
SSCI (Social Science Citation Index), 42, 56, 57, 133, 188, 190
staff. See faculty
Statistics Package for Social Science (SPSS), 50
STB (Singapore Tourism Board), 26, 28
Stenhouse, Lawrence, 49
Stewart, David, 48
Street Corner Society (Whyte, 1943), 66
students, international education of. See cross-border education
summer programs at South Korean universities, 137–8
Sungkyunkwan University, South Korea, 132
super-research institutions, emergence of, 2

Taiwan. See also National Cheng-Chi University (NCCU), Taipei, Taiwan

future directions in studying, 211
international ranking systems and, 184
XU, China, and, 78–9
Taiwan Institute for Economic Studies, 79
tenure positions for foreign professors at South Korean universities, 133–4
THE (Times Higher Education) university rankings, 7, 34n3, 128, 132, 136, 173, 174, 176–8, *177,* 180, 182, 184–9, 191–3
three-tiered educational systems
in Hong Kong, 19–20
in Singapore, 24–5
Times Higher Education (THE)
university rankings, 7, 34n3, 128, 132, 136, 173, 174, 176–8, *177,* 180, 182, 184–9, 191–3.
See also international ranking systems
TMC Academy, Singapore, 26
Torres, Carlos A., 91
Tsang, Donald, 17, 18
Tsuneyoshi, Ryoko, 162–4
twinning partnerships, 14, 20, 26, 34n1
211 Project, 73, 106, 111, 112
typology of change, *207,* 207–9

UGC (University Grants Committee), Hong Kong, 17, 19, 23, 32
United Kingdom
international ranking systems, reaction to, 178
Singapore and Hong Kong colonial history, advantages of, 30
United States
ethnic Koreans in, 97–8
international ranking systems, reaction to, 178
University Grants Committee (UGC), Hong Kong, 17, 19, 23, 32

University of Chicago Graduate School of Business, 27
University of Hong Kong, 18, 34n2–3
University of Iowa, 125
University of Minnesota, Twin Cities, 206
University of Pittsburgh, 94
Uruguay Round negotiations, 12
U.S. News & World Report university rankings, 173
Usher, Alex, 176, 179
USSR and XU, China, 69, 71–2, 75
Uyghur ethnic minority and XU, China. *See* Xinjiang University (XU), China

Wächter, Bernd, 168
Wang, Hongcai, 183
Wang, Shirley, 47
Welch, Anthony R., 4, 63, 200, 217
West-East Gas Pipeline project, 74
Western models of higher education
East Asian contextualization versus, 2, 198–201
ethnocentricity of internationalization literature, 63–4, 84
faculty problems with, 199–200
internationalization and globalization viewed as encapsulating, 42
Japanese universities and, 148, 151–2, 163–9
publication pressures and, 42, 56
Singapore and Hong Kong's comfort with, 30, 201
South Korean universities and, 121–2, 125–6, 127, 136, 148, 151–2, 165–9, 200
"world-class" universities equated with, 174
XU, China, and, 200
Whyte, William Foote, 66

Wong, Mary Shepard, 7, 197, 212n1, 217–18
World Bank, 74
"world-class" university, concept of, 201–2
   compromises entailed in, 202
   in developing countries, 92
   EGM (emerging global model) of, 44–5
   future directions in studying, 211
   international ranking systems and, 174
   problems associated with, 92
   in Singapore, 24–5, 27
   in South Korea, 132–3, 158, 166
   in Taiwan, 41–5
   Western models of higher education, equated with, 174
World Trade Organization (WTO), 1, 12
Wu, Shuang Frances, 7, 197, 212n1, 218

Xibu Da Kaifa Zhanlüe (Great Development in China's West) policy, 65, 68
Xinjiang Normal University, China, 72
Xinjiang University (XU), China, 4–5, 63–89
   brain drain and internationalization of, 79–81
   cross-border education: brain drain and, 80; foreign students at XU, 76, 76–7, 85; Japan and Taiwan, XU students studying in, 78–9
   cultural, political, and economic situation of, 65, 67–71, 74, 80–1
   entrance examinations, 81–4, *82, 83*
   ethnic minorities: brain drain and, 80; cross-border education, participation in, 78–9;
   demographics of, 68–9, *69,* 73;
   educational practice and entrance exam scores, 81–4, *82, 83*; Islam, influence of, 65, 69–70; as reason for studying XU, 65
   faculty: brain drain and, 79–81; ethnic minorities as, 73; interest in internationalization, 70–1, 73–4
   history and development of, 71–4
   interest in internationalization at, 70–1, 73–4
   methodology of study, 66–7
   mutual cooperation agreements with international universities, 75, 77–9
   process of internationalization at, 75–9
   reasons for studying, 63–5
   USSR and, 69, 71–2, 75
   Western models of higher education at, 200
Xinjiang Uyghur Autonomous Region (XUAR), China, 65, 68, 72, 81
XU. *See* Xinjiang University (XU), China
XUAR (Xinjiang Uyghur Autonomous Region), China, 65, 68, 72, 81
Xuexi Sulian Laodage (Learn from Big Brother, Soviet Union), 75

Yanbian University, Korean autonomous prefecture, China, 96, 101, 105–6, 109, 110–12, 113–14, 202
Yang, Rui, 4, 45, 63, 66, 200, 218
Yang Zhengxin, 71
Yonsei University, South Korea, 120, 125, 138
Yu Xiusong, 71

Zhao, Zhenzhou, 104
zhong ti xi yong, 64

GPSR Compliance

The European Union's (EU) General Product Safety Regulation (GPSR) is a set of rules that requires consumer products to be safe and our obligations to ensure this.

If you have any concerns about our products, you can contact us on

ProductSafety@springernature.com

In case Publisher is established outside the EU, the EU authorized representative is:

Springer Nature Customer Service Center GmbH
Europaplatz 3
69115 Heidelberg, Germany

www.ingramcontent.com/pod-product-compliance
Lightning Source LLC
LaVergne TN
LVHW051913060526
838200LV00004B/122